Lincolnshire's Archaeology from the Air

CW01090776

Occasional Papers in Lincolnshire
History and Archaeology, 11

Lincolnshire's Archaeology
from the Air

Edited by Robert H. Bewley

General Editor: Mark Bennet

The Society for Lincolnshire History and Archaeology,
Jews' Court, Steep Hill, Lincoln LN2 1LS

The Royal Commission on the Historical Monuments of England
National Monuments Record Centre, Great Western Village, Kemble Drive, Swindon SN2 2GZ

Published by the Society for Lincolnshire History and Archaeology
in partnership with the Royal Commission on the Historical Monuments of England

©The Society for Lincolnshire History and Archaeology

First published 1998

ISBN 0 903582 11 2

British Library Cataloguing in Publication Data
A CIP catalogue record for this book is available from the British Library

Printed in Great Britain by G. W. Belton Ltd,
Heaton Street, Gainsborough, Lincolnshire DN21 2ED
Telephone 01427 612291   Fax 01427 810520

Lincolnshire's Archaeology from the Air

Contents

ACKNOWLEDGEMENTS

For this edited volume, with seven authors, reporting on a project which has taken over six years to complete, there have been numerous colleagues who have helped in so many ways. The dedication of the team of air photo interpreters was notable and it is their skill and hard work which has made the increase in knowledge and understanding possible; they were Yvonne Boutwood, Ann Carter, Alison Deegan, Pamela Grace, Damian Grady, Dilwyn Jones, Antonia Kershaw, Dave MacLeod, Julia Millard and Helen Winton.

We are grateful to so many staff in the RCHME, past and present, for their help and support in all aspects of the project; they are too numerous to mention but assisted in loans of photographs, as well as material from the archive and advice on archaeological matters. Special thanks must go to Peter Horne under whose guidance the project was managed, who also undertook the more recent reconnaissance work with Dave MacLeod, and paved the way for the integration of reconnaissance and mapping in the future. We are also grateful to the pilot, Anthony Crawshaw, for his perseverance and safe returns. The advice, enthusiasm and support from Paul Everson deserves a special mention as he provided solutions to archaeological questions and helped expand the project through his deep knowledge of Lincolnshire. We are also grateful to Davina Turner for her proof reading.

Similarly the project would not have been successful without the support from colleagues in Lincolnshire (especially in the SMR) in particular Mark Bennet, but also Steve Catney, Sarah Grundy, Ian George and Julia Wise; also to Jon Watson, of the Highways and Planning Directorate of Lincolnshire County Council for the information he provided. Dave Start has been very supportive throughout the project, especially in assisting in the form and approach to publication. In addition there were those who attended the project progress meetings from other bodies, Tom Lane, Naomi Field, Hilary Healey and representatives from English Heritage.

David Wilson, the curator, and his staff at the Cambridge University Collection of Air Photographs were very helpful throughout the project, dealing with our numerous requests and in particular for permission to publish one of their aerial photographs (D. Jones, Fig.7).

We are all very grateful to Phil Newman (RCHME) who took on the task of producing the line drawings within a relatively short timescale. Many of the figures have been reproduced from the Ordnance Survey mapping with the permission of Her Majesty's Stationery Office © Crown Copyright. RCHME Licence No. GD03133G/3/98. We are grateful to the Ordnance Survey for their help in providing some of the maps prior to publication. We are also grateful to the British Geological Survey for the use of Sheets 91 and 115, 1990 (1:50,000) which have been reproduced with the permission of the Director, British Geological Survey © NERC (D. Grady Figs 1 and 4-7, and A. Carter Figs 3b and 4b). Similarly information from the Soils Survey of England and Wales, National Soil Map and Sheet 4 has been produced with the permission of Cranfield University, Soil Survey and Land Research Centre (A. Carter Figs 3a and 4a).

We are grateful to the MOD for permission to reproduce the aerial photograph (D. Jones Fig.10) and to the RCHME for permission to publish the other aerial photographs. Special thanks must go to Arthur and Dorothy Owen for their encouragement and provision of information on the Marshland. Thanks also to Hilary Healey, Betty Kirkham and David Robinson for advice and access to unpublished work: and Professor Jens Vellev, University of Aarhus, Denmark, and Professor Hugo Thoen, University of Ghent, Belgium, for information on the European salt industry. Special thanks also to James Rackham and Simon Colcutt for providing information on excavated sites. A debt of gratitude is owed to the external referees who volunteered their time and efforts to comment on the texts; all errors of fact or presentation remain the responsibility of the authors and editor.

Finally the hard work and professional approach to the task of copy editing, by Mark Bennet, has to be acknowledged as a major contribution to the production of this book. Without his invaluable advice, support and dedication to the task this volume would not have been possible.

Note on Imperial and metric measurements

Within these papers SI (Système International d'Unités) units of measurement have been used. One kilometre (km) is one thousand metres or 0.621 miles; one metre (m) is 1.094 yards; and one hectare (ha) is one hundred metres by one hundred metres or 2.471 acres.

FOREWORD

Much of the landscape of Lincolnshire can be compared to a vast open-air food factory. As a consequence of this intense agricultural regime, the field archaeology of the county has suffered gradual, and in some cases extremely serious erosion over the past fifty years. Previous RCHME projects have focused on the extant field monuments but the project which is the subject of this book has been firmly based on the aerial photographic evidence – often the only source of information for many of the sites. As in each of the other counties covered by the RCHME's National Mapping Programme the compilation of the maps and computerised records has provided a crucial starting point for understanding the spatial and chronological dimensions which have shaped Lincolnshire's diverse archaeological landscape.

These complex landscapes, so many of which are invisible to the observer on the ground, are revealed through the techniques of aerial survey. They are of all periods and extend across all the landscape zones in the county. However, the understanding that we have now achieved is still a partial one as the sites have to be visible, on aerial photographs, before they can be mapped and interpreted. Nevertheless, the breadth and depth of archaeological study which has taken place in Lincolnshire this century means that the picture which is laid before the reader here is a representative sample of past human activity.

This volume of collected papers, many of which were presented at the Society's Archaeology Day in October 1997, is a new departure for the National Mapping Programme. It is an attempt to provide the people of Lincolnshire with an appreciation of the archaeological resources that surround them to throw a little more light on the history of their county.

The full information for this project is available in the National Monuments Record in Swindon and the maps can be examined in the county's Sites and Monuments Record in Lincoln.

The RCHME would like to thank all those involved in the project, especially the dedication of its staff and the support from colleagues in Lincolnshire and welcomes the collaboration with the Society that the publication of this volume represents.

T. G. Hassall
Secretary and Chief Executive of RCHME
August 1998

England's National Mapping Programme: A Lincolnshire Perspective.

Robert H. Bewley

Introduction and background.

Aerial survey, which combines surveying and taking photographs from an aeroplane, as well as examining historic vertical and oblique photographs is exciting and intriguing to professionals and amateurs alike. The voyage of discovery (either literally in the air or vicariously by interpreting photographs) is what sustains archaeologists and those interested in archaeology. The new discoveries helped maintain the commitment of all those involved in this project, which took over five years to complete. Lincolnshire has had a long association with aerial photography (Philips 1932; Hallam 1970) and more recently the works of Everson and Hayes (1984), Jones (1988) and Start (1993) have shown how important the aerial perspective can be.

Aerial survey for archaeology has a ninety-year history and the majority of that time has been spent in obtaining photographs and surveying landscapes from the air (Bewley 1997a & b; Deuel 1969; Wilson 1995). O. G. S. Crawford, who is often called the father of aerial survey, attempted to bring together information from aerial photographs in mapped form but his efforts were thwarted by the Second World War (Crawford 1955, p.275). Since then the RCHME has taken a keen interest in the use and potential of aerial photography and its mapping. The publication in 1960 of *A Matter of Time* (RCHME 1960) was a seminal step, whose message is as relevant today as it was then – that river valleys contain a wealth of archaeological sites, which can be recorded most effectively and efficiently by aerial photography and that these sites are under great threat. Since the 1950s it has become very clear that river valleys do not have a monopoly on concentrations of sites, and nearly all the landscape zones of England contain important archaeological information and nearly all are under threat from one source or another. Lincolnshire, with its variety of landscape types is no exception and threats from agriculture (nationally) are finally being recognised as significant (Darvill & Fulton 1998).

From the late 1970s the mapping and analysis of the results of aerial surveys has been given a high priority and an increase in resources, in conjunction with continued aerial reconnaissance, attests to the importance of this general approach (Bewley 1984 & 1994b; Palmer 1984 & 1996; Stoertz 1997; Whimster 1989).

Within the RCHME, aerial survey has been seen as a *process,* and the approach of taking photographs for mapping purposes was a fundamental principle established in 1965 by John Hampton as the first head of the Air Photography Unit, within the National Monuments Record (NMR) (Hampton 1989). In the late 1980s one of the major stimuli for mapping and analysis from aerial photographs was English Heritage's Monuments Protection Programme (MPP) (English Heritage 1996). Although by that date most county-based Sites and Monuments Records had done some mapping from aerial photographs this had tended to concentrate on sketch plotting of selected specialist archaeological photography. None had undertaken systematic examination of all the available photographs for mapping and interpretation purposes, nor had a standard approach and methodology been developed, as it has now (RCHME 1995).

In 1988 four pilot projects, designed to map, interpret and record archaeological information from aerial photographs, were begun for Kent, Hertfordshire and the Thames Valley, each of them jointly funded by English Heritage and the RCHME (Bewley 1995). These projects were aimed at assessing the methodology and resource requirement for mapping and recording sites visible as cropmarks and soilmarks to standard specifications at a scale of 1:10,000 (Fenner & Dyer 1994; Bewley 1993). In 1989 a fourth pilot project was initiated to examine the same questions but in an upland environment, the Yorkshire Dales (Horne & MacLeod 1994). The results and success of these projects led to the creation of a National Mapping Programme (NMP) for England and the Lincolnshire project became the first and largest NMP project in 1992 (Bewley 1995).

There were many reasons why Lincolnshire was chosen and the work of Paul Everson (1983; Everson *et al.* 1991) and Dilwyn Jones (1988) had shown the potential for an integrated approach of aerial survey and fieldwork. So far NMP has had to focus on the aerial survey aspect of interpretation and recording and can provide the maps and records for fieldwork, but integration at the outset for future projects is still a goal to aim for.

At the time of writing 22% of England has been mapped (Fig.1) and the Lincolnshire project covered 3.6% of England. The aim of this short introduction is to place this project in a national context and to provide a brief summary of the potential of the information which awaits further research and evaluation. The volume was not conceived as a total review of Lincolnshire's archaeology from prehistory to the twentieth century, but as selective highlights of a large body of information which is available for anyone to use. The topics for the papers which follow were chosen by the authors, individually and by group discussions, as members of the Lincolnshire NMP team: their years spent working on the project and current interests and experience provided the basis for the choice of topic. Recommendations about future research are made in each paper so need not be summarised here.

Lincolnshire and the NMP results.

The acquisition of new information is an important factor in continuing the NMP for England. The project area did not encompass the whole of Lincolnshire (see below, Kershaw (1997) and this volume) but covered 191 maps (4,775 sq. km) at 1:10,000 scale and 14,043 records[1] were created, of which 67.7% are 'new'; that is the sites they describe had not been recorded in either the NMR or the SMR prior to the project.

A primary function of the papers and their selected topics is simply to raise awareness of and to illustrate the wealth and variety of information, now readily available for the first time. It will also provide a first, rather than final definitive synthesis which will hopefully stimulate research in these and other areas. The overlay maps, on which the air photo interpretations are plotted, are in daily use in the county's SMR, by English Heritage for MPP use, and the RCHME continues to undertake aerial reconnaissance in Lincolnshire so that the new information can build on the foundation laid by this project.

Research agendas are now fashionable again (Olivier 1996). The project has information which can be used to help formulate these research strategies and the Lincolnshire Archaeology Forum has 'research' as a priority for discussion. Figures 2-6 are examples of the different approaches to the NMP data, taking the whole project area and examining the distribution of particular categories of site, either by date or by site type. A good example is the work by D. Jones (1998),

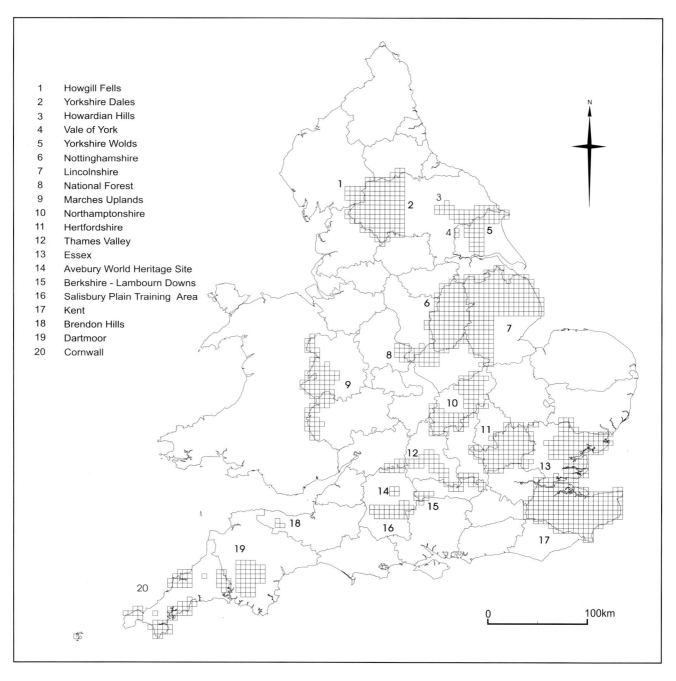

1   Howgill Fells
2   Yorkshire Dales
3   Howardian Hills
4   Vale of York
5   Yorkshire Wolds
6   Nottinghamshire
7   Lincolnshire
8   National Forest
9   Marches Uplands
10 Northamptonshire
11 Hertfordshire
12 Thames Valley
13 Essex
14 Avebury World Heritage Site
15 Berkshire - Lambourn Downs
16 Salisbury Plain Training Area
17 Kent
18 Brendon Hills
19 Dartmoor
20 Cornwall

0   100km

Fig.1. Progress of the National Mapping Programme to 30 June 1998.

where the information has been used to analyse the form, location and distribution of long barrows and mortuary enclosures. Research projects should be encouraged to develop from this approach as there are hundreds of site types, from all periods, which are amenable to further study.

There are a number of research questions which the NMP data could help to resolve. The adjacent county of Nottinghamshire has been the subject of another NMP project (Deegan, forthcoming) and an examination of the information in the Trent valley would shed light on the extent to which the river was a cultural divide through the prehistoric, Roman and medieval periods. The information from both the Nottinghamshire and Lincolnshire projects can be combined to enable research into such an important landscape zone.

There were 4,173 prehistoric sites recorded for the project and analyses on the prehistoric settlement of the whole county is now possible, using a landscape approach examining the juxtaposition of settlements, burials, and land division boundaries against the cultural and environmental background

of Lincolnshire and in comparison with other regions. The majority of the prehistoric sites (3,479 records) cannot be closely dated from the aerial evidence alone (Fig.2) and only a small percentage have been given a date: 57 Neolithic; 555 Bronze Age, because of confidence in identifying the majority of ring ditches as plough-levelled Bronze Age round barrows; and 82 Iron Age sites.

A number of research questions are immediately apparent when further scrutiny of the maps and records is undertaken. The quantity of sites and their distribution forces us to reassess previous estimates of population size and density, both up and down, at different times since the Neolithic period. The new information contains its bias, not least the dependence on aerial survey data, and yet the current (NMP) picture is likely to be a representative sample of Lincolnshire's archaeology (see Carter, this volume).

Analysis of morphological characteristics of certain site types, or by analogy or association, leads to questions such as – why are there no cursus monuments in the county? Why are

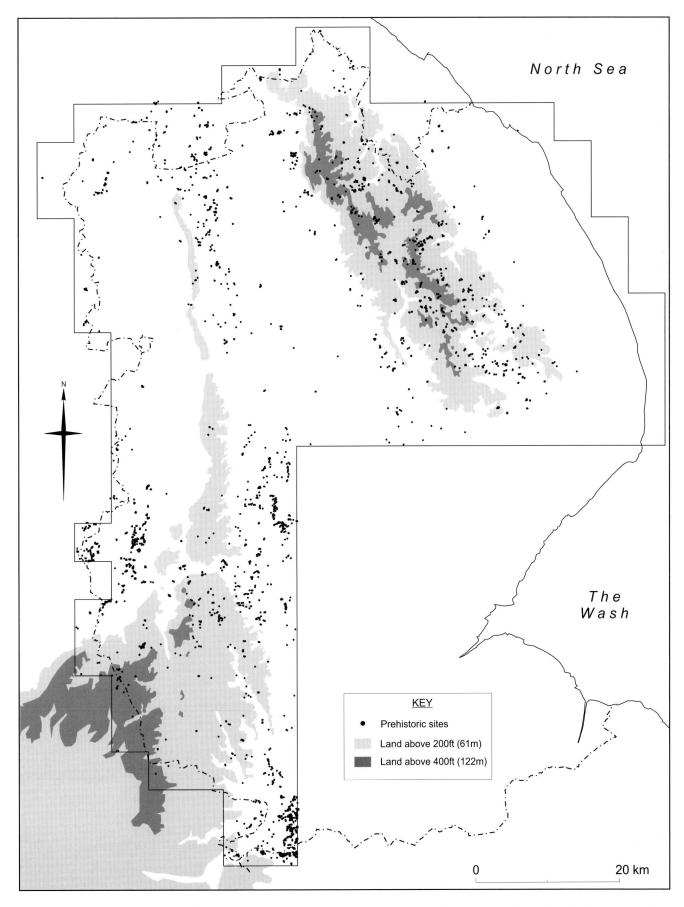

Fig.2. Distribution of sites recorded as 'prehistoric in date' but without closer definition to a specific period (© Crown copyright. RCHME 1998).

there so few henges? As with so much of England, where are the early prehistoric settlements (see Bewley 1994a)? The paucity of square barrows in Lincolnshire requires an explanation; is it a taphonomic phenomenon or a survey recovery question or a function of Iron Age society in Britain? There are a few Iron Age square barrows in Lincolnshire, a few isolated ones in west Lincolnshire and one good example of a group is situated between Dembleby and Scott Willoughby, twelve kilometres east of Grantham, on the limestone dipslope. This paucity is in direct contrast to the Yorkshire Wolds, further north (Stoertz 1997, Fig.31 and Maps 2 & 3), and in areas to the south in the Welland valley.

For the Roman period the nature and reasons for particular land use still require an explanation in the light of the NMP data, despite its addition of so much new material. The lack of Roman military installations in the east of the county is probably a true representation of the Roman military campaigns. Even so there are only 620 records from the Roman period, though many more possible Roman rural settlements will have been recorded as having an unspecified date or function in the prehistoric period. The distribution and nature of Roman rural settlement is being addressed at a national level as part of English Heritage's Monuments Protection Programme: the NMP data can therefore be used to help place Lincolnshire in a national context.

For the medieval period the work of Brian Roberts and Stuart Wrathmell (Roberts & Wrathmell 1995; Wrathmell 1992) on medieval settlement in England provides a good basis on which to assess Lincolnshire, in a national context. The work of the RCHME in north Lincolnshire (Everson 1983) and in particular West Lindsey (Everson et al. 1991) showed the potential for medieval settlement studies in the area as well as highlighting the need for a combination of field and aerial survey as the earthwork sites have been under such pressure from agriculture. This project mapped and recorded 331 medieval settlements, and the density of medieval activity is clearly visible in figure 5. The majority of Lincolnshire lies firmly within the central province of nucleated settlement (Roberts & Wrathmell 1995, p.86) and future research (including documentary research, field and aerial survey) could focus on dispersed settlements of medieval date as Taylor has already proposed (Taylor 1995, p.28).

Future potential.

There are a number of topics which have not been covered in this volume but which were noted during the project which might be of special interest to Lincolnshire, either a particular site type (for example monasteries and granges, moated sites and duck decoys) or the wider issues of how Lincolnshire fits into a national context at any one time. The National Mapping Programme is now reaching a stage where the data are available for regional rather than sub-regional or county-based analyses. The different landscape zones throughout the county (and across England) did not exist in isolation but interacted in different ways depending on the varying conditions of both the natural and human environments.

The significance and understanding of the data will be greater when linked to adjacent areas and the Trent valley has already been mentioned as a landscape zone worthy of further investigation. The ability to examine the whole length of a river system (as was attempted for the River Thames west of London) (Fenner & Dyer 1994) was a fruitful exercise but highlighted the need to encompass the catchment areas of the river; the land above the river formed part of the way in which the river was used just as much as the water itself or the flood plain. The information is available now for the River Trent to allow such an archaeological analysis to start.

The original intention had been to map the fens but financial constraints prevented this (Palmer 1996) and it is hoped that the incomplete NMP Fen project can be resurrected, as it will provide a wider context for the Fenland Survey project (Hall & Coles 1994). Understanding the changing interaction of the fen edge with the fens proper is one of the most interesting and challenging research topics for the future.

The coastline also requires a dedicated survey at an appropriate scale, combining the expertise of those experienced in field survey, survey in the inter-tidal zone, aerial as well as underwater archaeology (Fulford et al. 1997). Recent aerial reconnaissance over the coast of north Lincolnshire has found a fish trap, of a sort which is more familiar in Essex (Strachan 1998) and surveys similar to those in the Severn Estuary (Godbold & Turner 1994) combined with aerial survey will pay dividends.

The remains of the Second World War have been within the NMP's sphere of interest since 1992 and where possible were recorded by this project. There is no doubt that the next twenty years will see an increase in surveys of the archaeological remains of the twentieth century, especially with current projects, such as the Defence of Britain project (which is a data collection exercise initially) and other projects (Dobinson 1996) which are analysing the survival of certain site types. These projects, concentrating on decoys for airfields and towns, anti-aircraft installations, coastal batteries and radar sites, build on the information derived from aerial photographs (Dobinson et al. 1997). Lincolnshire's role in the Second World War and the Cold War should mean that the NMP project will be seen as a beginning in terms of providing a back-drop for developing an understanding of the county's archaeology as a whole.

This short introduction has meant to provide a guide to the type of information which is available for study and the ways in which it can be used. There has been a deliberate policy within the project not to allow time for an in-depth analysis of every possible aspect of Lincolnshire's archaeology. The RCHME has to provide a balance between access to information and the synthesis and analysis of the information it has generated and holds; this volume has been prepared with this balance very much in mind. One reason for this is that aerial survey is but one strand of evidence and needs to be integrated with other forms of field survey and excavation. This integrated approach will allow for a fuller and greater understanding of the archaeological landscapes to be achieved.

Note.

1. The number of records quoted in this paper refer to the records created using the MORPH2 database (Edis et al. 1989). Records also were created in MONARCH, the RCHME's national database for each site. The MORPH2 database is available for analysis and was designed as a systematic recording tool to allow for rapid retrieval and analysis. Although approaches to computerised recording and database management have changed dramatically since 1988, which mean there have been and will continue to be changes to the NMP's recording practice, the fundamental principles remain: to record those archaeological sites which have recordable size and shape characteristics in a consistent and systematic way so that sites and groups of sites can be analysed. One of the idiosyncrasies of recording using the MORPH2 system is that the sites which were thought to have a prehistoric and Roman date have been lumped together and could not be distinguished for analysis. New recording systems will overcome this and records in MONARCH can have a late prehistoric/Roman date. All the sites for which the interpreters have assigned dates by the nature of the aerial evidence alone, are to be used with caution; the studies and analyses are based on aerial photographic interpretation, which is only one strand of evidence and therefore the dating of sites has to be tentative.

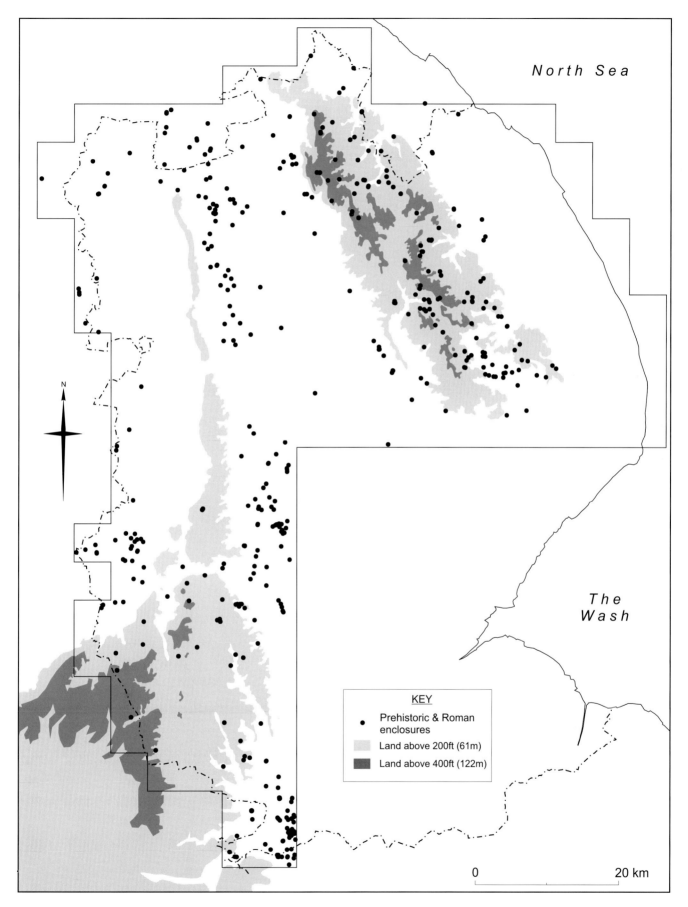

Fig.3. Distribution of all prehistoric and Roman enclosures with a length of 40-90m and a breadth of 30-80m (area range of 1200 – 7200 sq. m). These enclosures (373 in total) can be analysed further into size and shape categories to look for possible new site types for field evaluation (© Crown copyright. RCHME 1998).

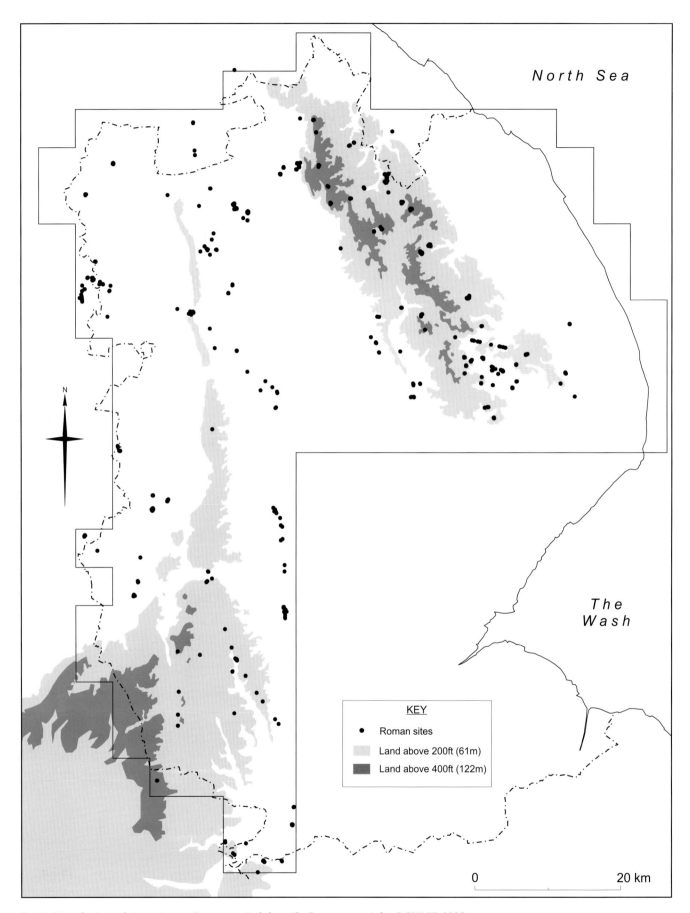

Fig.4. Distribution of sites given a Roman period date (© Crown copyright. RCHME 1998).

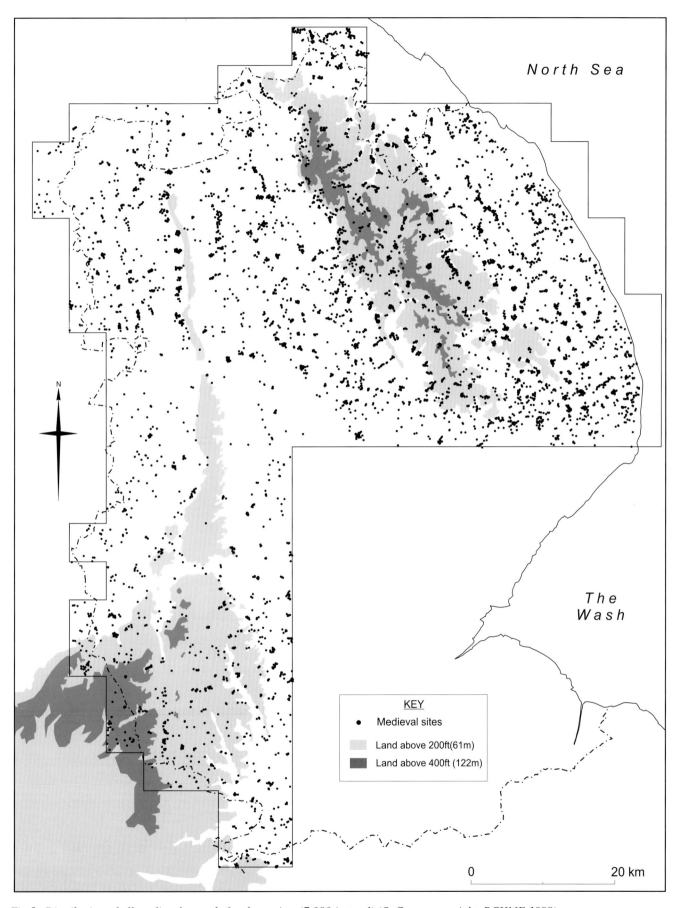

Fig.5. Distribution of all medieval records for the project (7,080 in total) (© Crown copyright. RCHME 1998).

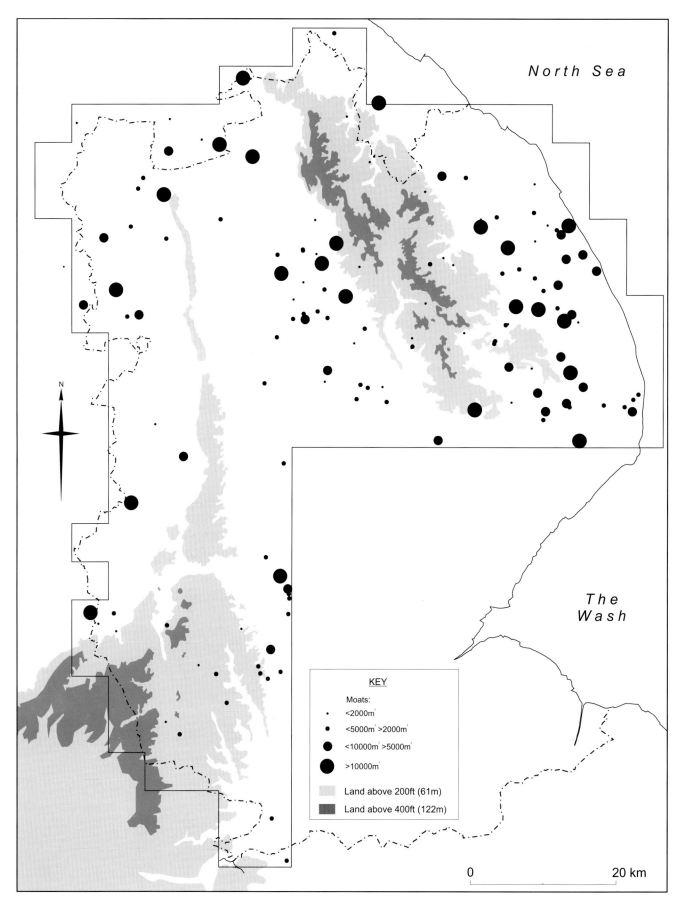

Fig.6. Distribution of moats in the project area (© Crown copyright. RCHME 1998).

Bibliography.

Bewley, R. H. 1984. *Prehistoric and Romano-British Settlement in the Solway Plain, Cumbria.* Ph.D. dissertation, University of Cambridge.

Bewley, R. H. 1993. Aerial photography for Archaeology. In Hunter and Ralston, eds 1993, pp.197-204.

Bewley, R. H. 1994a. *Prehistoric Settlements.*

Bewley, R. H. 1994b. *Prehistoric Romano-British Settlement in the Solway Plain, Cumbria.* Oxbow monograph 36. Oxford.

Bewley, R. H. 1995. A National Mapping Programme for England. In *Luftbildarchäologie in Ost- und Mitteleuropa. Forschungen zur Archäologie im Land Brandenburg*, 3, pp.83-92. Potsdam.

Bewley, R. H. 1997a. From military to civilian: a brief history of the early development of aerial photography for archaeology. In *Aus der Luft – Bilder unserer Geschichte: Luftbildarchäologie in Zentral europa.* Dresden.

Bewley, R. H. 1997b. Aerial Photography for Archaeology (Short Guide 41). *In Short Guides to Records Second Series: Guides 25-48*, edited by K. M. Thompson.

Crawford, O. G. S. 1955. *Said and Done. An autobiography of an archaeologist.*

Darvill, T. C. and Fulton, A. K. 1998. *MARS: The Monuments at Risk Survey of England. Main Report.* Bournemouth University and English Heritage. Bournemouth and London.

Deegan, A., forthcoming. *Nottinghamshire NMP project.* Internal RCHME report.

Deuel, L. 1969. *Flights into Yesterday.*

Dobinson, C. S. 1996. *Twentieth-century fortifications in England.* Council for British Archaeology and English Heritage.Unpublished reports.

Dobinson, C. S., Lake J. and Schofield, A. J. 1997. Monuments of War: defining England's 20th-century heritage. *Antiquity*, vol.71, pp 288-99.

Edis, J., Macleod, D. and Bewley, R. H. 1989. An archaeological guide to the classification of cropmarks and soilmarks. *Antiquity*, vol.63, pp.112-26.

English Heritage. 1996. *The Monuments Protection Programme 1986-1996 in Retrospect.*

Everson, P. 1983. Aerial photography and fieldwork in north Lincolnshire. In Maxwell, ed. 1983, pp.14-26.

Everson, P. and Hayes, T. 1984. Lincolnshire from the air. In *A Prospect of Lincolnshire*, edited by F. N. Field and A. J. White, pp.33-41. Lincoln.

Everson, P. L., Taylor, C. C. and Dunn, C. J. 1991. *Change and Continuity: Rural Settlement in North-West Lincolnshire.*

Fenner, V. E. P. and Dyer, C. 1994. *The Thames Valley Project. A Report for the National Mapping Programme.* RCHME internal report.

Fulford, M., Champion, T. and Long, A. 1997. *England's Coastal Heritage.* English Heritage Archaeological Report No.15.

Godbold, S. and Turner, R. C. 1994. Medieval fishtraps in the Severn Estuary. *Medieval Archaeology*, vol.38, pp.17-36.

Hall, D. and Coles, J. M. 1994. *Fenland Survey. An essay in landscape and persistence.* English Heritage Archaeological Report No.1.

Hallam, S. J. 1970. Settlement round the Wash. In *The Fenland in Roman Times*, edited by C. W. Philips. Royal Geographical Society Research Series: No.5. pp.22-113.

Hampton, J. N. 1989. The Air Photography Unit of the Royal Commission on the Historical Monuments of England 1965-85. In Kennedy 1989, pp.13-28.

Horne, P. and MacLeod, D. 1994. *The Yorkshire Dales Mapping Project. A Report for the National Mapping Programme.* RCHME internal report.

Hunter, I. and Ralston, I., eds. 1993. *Archaeological Resource Management in the UK: An Introduction.* Bradford.

Jones, D. 1988. Aerial reconnaissance and prehistoric and Romano-British archaeology in northern Lincolnshire - A sample survey. *Lincolnshire History and Archaeology*, vol.23, pp.5-30.

Jones, D. 1998. Long barrows and Neolithic elongated enclosures in Lincolnshire: An analysis of the air photographic evidence. *Proceedings of the Prehistoric Society*, vol.64.

Kennedy, D. 1989. *Into the Sun. Essays in Air Photography in Archaeology in Honour of Derrick Riley.* Sheffield.

Kershaw, A. 1997. *Lincolnshire Mapping Project Review.* RCHME internal document.

Maxwell, G. S., ed. 1983. *The Impact of Aerial Reconnaissance on Archaeology.* Council for British Archaeology, Research Report 49.

Olivier, A. 1996. *Frameworks For Our Past. A Review of Research Frameworks, strategies, and perceptions.* English Heritage.

Palmer, R. 1984. *Danebury An Iron Age Hillfort in Hampshire, An Aerial Photographic Interpretation of its Environs.* RCHME Supplementary Series No.6.

Palmer, R. 1996. Air photo interpretation and the Lincolnshire Fenland. *Landscape History*, vol.18, pp.5-16.

Phillips, C. W. 1932. The long barrows of Lincolnshire. *Archaeological Journal*, vol.89, pp.174-202.

Roberts, B. K. and Wrathmell, S. 1995. *Terrain and Rural Settlement Mapping. The Methodology and Preliminary Results.* English Heritage. Unpublished report.

RCHME. 1960. *A Matter of Time.*

RCHME. 1995. *Guidelines and specification Manual for the National Mapping Programme.* NMP. Internal RCHME document. June 1995.

Start, D. 1993. *Lincolnshire from the Air.* Sleaford.

Stoertz, C. 1997. *Ancient Landscapes of the Yorkshire Wolds: Aerial Photographic Transcription and Analysis.* Swindon.

Strachan, D. 1998. *Essex from the Air. Archaeology and History from Aerial Photographs.* Essex County Council.

Taylor, C. 1995. Dispersed settlement in nucleated areas. *Landscape History*, vol.17, pp.27-34.

Whimster, R. P. 1989. *The Emerging Past, Air Photography and the Buried Landscape.*

Wilson, D. R. 1995. History of Aerial Archaeology – success and failure. In *Luftbildarchäologie in Ost- und Mitteleuropa. Forschungen zur Archäologie im Land Brandenburg*, 3, pp.13-22. Potsdam.

Wrathmell, S. 1992. Medieval rural settlements in the Monuments Protection Programme. *Medieval Settlement Research Group Annual Report*, pp.13-14.

The Lincolnshire National Mapping Programme Project.

Antonia Kershaw

The mapping of the archaeological sites of the major part of Lincolnshire from aerial photographs was carried out by the Aerial Survey section of the RCHME as part of the National Mapping Programme (NMP). This programme aims to map, interpret and record all archaeological cropmarks, soilmarks and earthworks visible on aerial photographs from prehistory through to more recent industrial and military remains. A stimulus for the development of the National Mapping Programme was the need to identify sites which would be worthy of preservation and protection as part of English Heritage's Monuments Protection Programme (Bewley 1995). However, as well as providing information for this programme, NMP is also able to provide the National Monuments Record (NMR) and Sites and Monuments Records (SMRs) locally with a comprehensive database of archaeological information, recorded from aerial photographs. This information can be used for planning purposes by local authorities. It can also be used to build upon and consolidate work previously undertaken in a county, establishing the archaeological potential of the area and

identifying areas for further reconnaissance and research. The Lincolnshire Mapping Project was funded entirely by the RCHME as part of England's National Mapping Programme.

Lincolnshire covers an area of 5,915 square kilometres (Fig.1a), covering 279 Ordnance Survey (OS), 1:10,000 quarter sheets, and includes in its south-east quarter, a large area of fenland that was the subject of an external, RCHME-funded project which has not yet been completed (see below and Palmer 1996). It must be noted that the Lincolnshire Mapping Project did not cover the whole of historic Lincolnshire. Local government reorganization means that the County of Humberside no longer exists and the historic County of Lincolnshire now has two unitary authorities and the County Council which cover an area from the Wash in the south to the Humber in the north. However, when the project area for the Lincolnshire Mapping Project was defined, south Humberside was excluded. The project area was split into seven blocks (Fig.1b), on the basis of the county's landscape zones (Boutwood on Physical Landscape this volume Fig.3). This was partly a practical consideration for the purposes of mapping (for example organising loans of air photographs), but also it was hoped that each block might exhibit recognisable patterns of archaeological evidence related to these landscape zones.

The features observed on the aerial photographs were manually transcribed onto overlays (at a scale of 1:10,000) placed over an Ordnance Survey base map. The sites were then described on a database in terms of archaeological interpretation, possible function and date, location, size and morphology (Edis et al. 1989). This information was transferred to the RCHME's National Monuments Record database, 'MONARCH'. These records, both graphical and written, formed the basis of information from which the studies

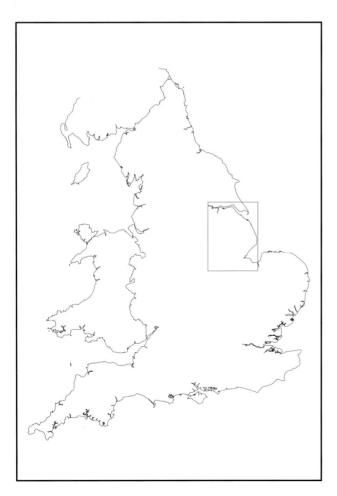

Fig.1a. Location of Lincolnshire Mapping Project area.

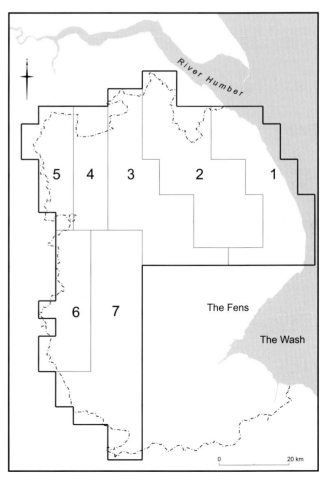

Fig.1b. The project area split into blocks on the basis of landscape zones.

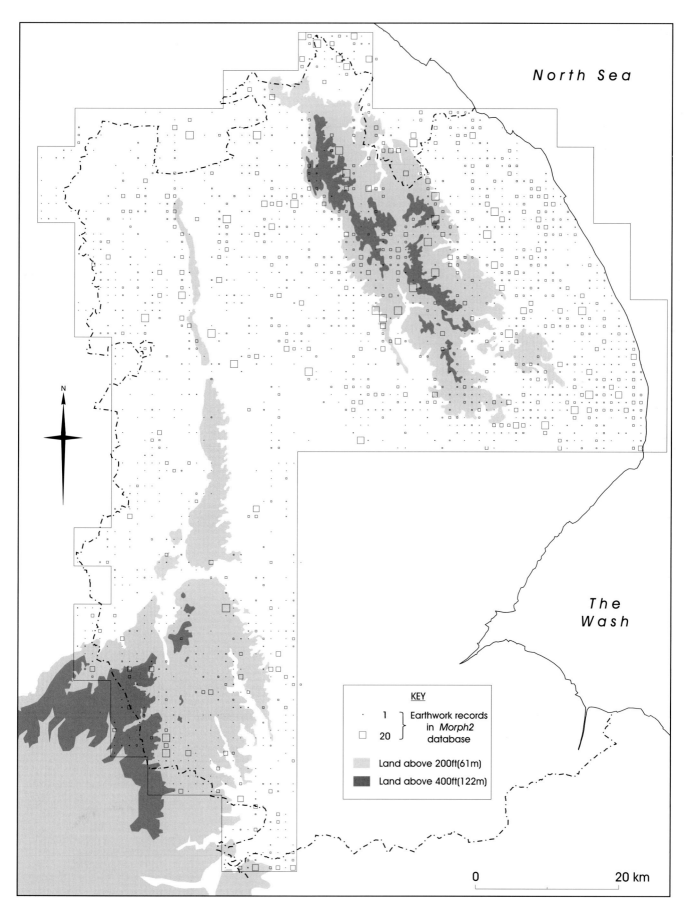

North Sea

The
Wash

KEY

- 1 ⎤ Earthwork records
- 20 ⎦ in *Morph2* database

Land above 200ft(61m)

Land above 400ft(122m)

0   20 km

Fig.2. Density distribution of earthworks in the project area (© Crown copyright. RCHME 1998).

in this volume were taken. Copies of the overlays and accompanying MONARCH records are available from the National Monuments Record Centre in Swindon (see address on p.22).

The main source of photography used for the mapping was the RCHME's own aerial photograph collection, which covers the whole of England and contains several million prints. For the Lincolnshire Mapping Project over 20,000 oblique photographs and nearly 31,000 vertical prints from this collection were consulted. Another major collection used for the mapping is held by the Cambridge University Committee for Aerial Photography. The project team consulted over 3,000 prints from this collection. Also, nearly 1,800 vertical prints taken by Hunting Surveys Limited were borrowed from the Lincolnshire County Council Highways and Planning Directorate.

Other sources of photography which were used were those from local fliers including T. Hayes, B. Simmons, P. Everson, J. Pickering, F. Hartley and D. Riley. The earliest specialist photographs used were those from 1928 in the RCHME's Crawford Collection and the most recent were 1994 prints from recent RCHME reconnaissance. The earliest vertical photographs used were from 1940 taken by the Royal Air Force, and the most recent were from 1987 taken by Aerofilms Limited. The RCHME uses the data from NMP to inform its flying programme and in the past few years many new sites have been photographed in Lincolnshire, including (in the 1995 flying season alone) six previously unknown long barrows (Jones 1998).

Prior to the NMP no project had attempted to map systematically the information from the vast number of aerial photographs covering Lincolnshire. Parts of Lincolnshire have been the subject of intensive archaeological study in terms of excavation, and geophysical and field survey, for example by English Heritage's Fenland Project (Hall & Coles 1994) and the RCHME field survey of the medieval and post-medieval settlement in West Lindsey (Everson *et al.* 1991). However, other areas were relatively untouched by survey, for example the Marshland, and this was an opportunity to redress this balance and to demonstrate the ability of aerial survey to record entire archaeological landscapes at a relatively low cost.

Since the early 1950s aerial photographic transcription of archaeological remains has been carried out intermittently and to varying standards and levels in different parts of the county. In the north of the county, there were four main programmes of plotting. From 1975 to early 1983, Paul Everson carried out a programme of rapid sketch plotting in the West and East Lindsey Districts for the purposes of record enhancement. Dilwyn Jones carried out the three other plotting programmes. From 1982 to 1985 transcriptions were produced of selected upstanding and levelled earthwork sites in West Lindsey District as a contribution to a volume on medieval and post-medieval settlement (Everson *et al.* 1991). From 1985 to 1987 a pilot survey was undertaken to examine the aerial photographic record and evidence of early settlement in northern Lincolnshire under the auspices of Nottingham University (Jones 1988). From mid 1988 to late 1989 a programme of systematic plotting of cropmark sites in the county was initiated. The survey excluded medieval and later earthwork sites, the existence of which was merely outlined. Transcription was completed for the area of the chalk Wolds, and extended to cover the whole of south Humberside.

Outside the Fens, in southern Lincolnshire, no systematic plotting of information derived from aerial photographs had taken place. Individual sites had been sketch plotted by staff of the South Lincolnshire Archaeological Unit for planning purposes as required. From 1950 to 1952 the archaeological sites and natural ancient features in the Fenland Basin were recorded by S. J. Hallam (1970). In 1980 a pilot survey using computer-aided transcription was carried out by the RCHME of an area of Fenland between Sleaford and Boston. From 1991 to 1992 a sample survey was undertaken by Air Photo Services, on behalf of the RCHME, of an area along the western edge of the Fens in advance of a projected programme of systematic plotting of that landscape.

The original intention was to have the Lincolnshire Fenland NMP project running alongside Lincolnshire NMP so that the two would finish simultaneously, completing the mapping for the county as it then was. However, the RCHME was unable to continue funding for the Lincolnshire Fenland NMP project with the result that many of the maps in that area remain unrecorded. Some results of this project have been published (Palmer 1996).

The proposed specifications, as laid out in the project design (RCHME 1993), for mapping Lincolnshire were changed little. The project included all earthwork sites visible on aerial photographs (whether previously surveyed or not), to enable a more comprehensive picture of the development of the landscape of the county to be compiled (Figs 2 & 3). Where earthwork sites had been the subject of ground survey the existing survey diagram was used as a basis for transcription. The latest photographs (both oblique and vertical) were examined so that a record of the extent of surviving (upstanding) ridge-and-furrow, could be depicted in broad outline only (using a standardized convention).

The survey did not include buildings in its brief, other than where these were recorded as earthworks, as masonry foundations (for example ecclesiastical monuments), as cropmarks or as soilmarks. However, an exception was made in the case of some twentieth-century military architecture, for example searchlight batteries, pill-box sites, gun emplacements, slit trenches and anti-aircraft obstructions. The survey recorded evidence of the major historic industries of the county (ironstone mining, salt extraction) but generally excluded evidence of more marginal significance (chalk pits, gravel pits), unless the marks of these features could be misconstrued as archaeological features.

Under its Royal Warrant the RCHME has a responsibility to record sites and monuments on, or under the sea bed within the territorial sea adjacent to England. The presence of archaeological remains along Lincolnshire's extensive coastline is well attested by ground survey. The inter-tidal zone was examined on available aerial photographs (although photography held by the National Rivers Authority was not seen), and a variety of features were identified including clay extraction/salt-working sites, military structures and sea defences. The archaeology of the coastal zone has seen an increase in its priority as a research area (Fulford *et al.* 1997)

It is important to emphasise that although aerial survey is a very important technique, information from aerial photography is only one method of revealing archaeological sites. Some sites are less well represented in the aerial photographic record than others. This is partly due to the difficulty of distinguishing particular site types without complementary dating evidence from excavation or field survey. Mesolithic sites in Lincolnshire have not been identified from aerial photographs, and those sites of Neolithic and Bronze Age date that are seen on aerial photographs are often only those that show evidence of burial practice. Also the Anglo-Saxon period is not well represented in terms of either settlement or burial sites, which, for this period especially, may be a problem of site recognition. A cropmark site of sub-rectangular enclosures, assumed to be prehistoric, was excavated at Riby Cross Roads, Lincolnshire, and found to be Anglo-Saxon in date (Steedman 1994). Thus if sites of different periods have a similar cropmark form, the dates and interpretations provided by aerial photographic information alone have to be treated with caution. One of the fundamental reasons for recording the size and shape of enclosures is to be able to analyse groups of sites to test the assumption that they are of a similar date or function (Edis *et al.* 1989). It is important therefore, to use the NMP data as a basis from which to conduct research which uses information from other sources.

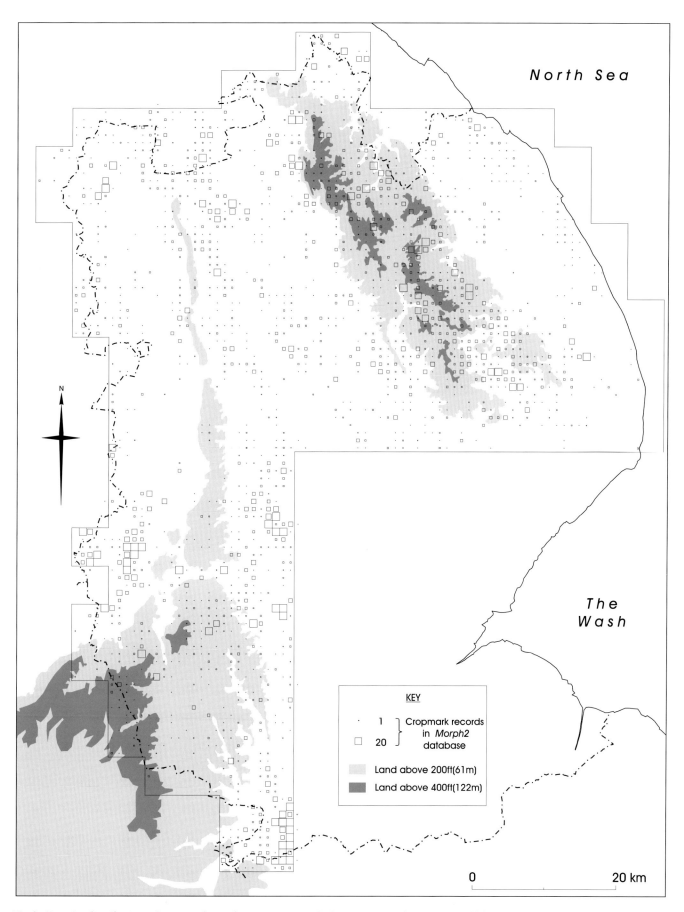

Fig.3. Density distribution of cropmarks in the project area (© Crown copyright. RCHME 1998).

The results of a project of this size can most easily be illustrated by the number of new records created. In general terms the percentage of sites recorded which are new (that is they had no NMR or SMR reference) is 67.7%. The number of newly recorded prehistoric and Roman sites is 3,736, for the medieval period it is 3,894 and for the post-medieval and modern periods it is 999. It is encouraging that although prehistoric and Roman sites have been the focus of intensive survey and study in the past, a significant number of new sites were recorded for these periods. In the Lincolnshire project the percentage of new records for these periods is 26.6% of the total number of records. In Lincolnshire there has been a great deal of research into rural medieval settlement in the north of the county, particularly in the north-west. The RCHME carried out detailed field survey work and documentary research in West Lindsey in the late 1970s and early 1980s (Everson *et al.* 1991). Therefore, one would not expect there to be a significant number of new records for the medieval period in this area of the county. However, 34% of all the medieval sites recorded in the district of West Lindsey are new. The majority of these new sites are extensive field systems of ridge-and-furrow which would not have been within the scope of the RCHME's field survey. This illustrates how the two forms of survey can reveal complementary evidence.

One of the values of NMP is that it can serve to highlight areas which would benefit from further research. On occasion the RCHME is in a position to pursue these research topics. This was the case with a study of the long barrow tradition in Lincolnshire carried out by Dilwyn Jones (project co-ordinator for the Lincolnshire Mapping Project). The basis of this work was derived from NMP information as well as his extensive fieldwork in the county. With an analytical approach a new understanding of the regional significance of the Neolithic remains in Lincolnshire is emerging (Jones 1998). The NMP data can be used as a guide to areas requiring more detailed survey and can help to put such surveys in their proper context. For example, the Owmby Cliff Project was carried out in response to a request from English Heritage to aid their evaluation of the site of a Roman settlement (RCHME 1995). An area of about forty hectares was re-mapped at 1:2500 scale and covers a group of possible Romano-British or Iron Age enclosures which lie mainly to the east of Ermine Street. The NMP mapping, which was done before the more detailed 1:2500 plot, puts the site in context with more features being seen to the north and east.

A rapid assessment of the use of NMP data at the Lincolnshire SMR and from queries to the NMR Public Services section shows similar trends, with archaeological consultants, English Heritage, and students involved in research, being the main users. The SMR uses the NMP data on a daily basis.

The Lincolnshire Mapping Project was started in June 1992 and finished in March 1997. There were ten people working on the project at various times but the main mapping team comprised just six people, including Dilwyn Jones (the project co-ordinator). These members of the team are the contributors to this volume. The articles are just small windows into Lincolnshire's archaeological heritage and the varied archaeological data recorded in summary form by the NMP project. The aim is to show the potential of this data for future research.

For further information about this project or to obtain copies of the overlays or accompanying records please contact:

Public Services, National Monuments Record
National Monuments Record Centre
Great Western Village
Kemble Drive
Swindon
Wiltshire
SN2 2GZ

Tel: 01793 414600
Fax: 01793 414606
E-mail   info@rchme.gov.uk

Bibliography.

Bewley, R. H. 1995. A National Mapping Programme for England. In *Luftbildarchäologie in Ost- und Mitteleuropa. Forschungen zur Archäologie im Land Brandenburg*, 3, pp.83-92. Potsdam.

Edis, J., Macleod, D. and Bewley, R. H. 1989. An archaeological guide to the classification of cropmarks and soilmarks. *Antiquity*, vol.63, pp.112-26

Everson, P. L., Taylor, C. C. and Dunn, C. J. 1991. *Change and Continuity: Rural Settlement in North-West Lincolnshire*.

Fulford, M., Champion, T. and Long, A. 1997. *England's Coastal Heritage*. English Heritage Archaeological Report No.15.

Hall, D. and Coles, J. M. 1994. *Fenland Survey. An essay in landscape and persistence.* English Heritage Archaeological Report No.1.

Hallam, S. J. 1970. Settlement round the Wash. In *The Fenland in Roman Times*, edited by C. W. Philips. Royal Geographical Society Research Series: No.5. pp.22-113.

Jones, D. 1988. Aerial reconnaissance and prehistoric and Romano-British archaeology in northern Lincolnshire – A sample survey. *Lincolnshire History and Archaeology*, vol.23, pp.5-30.

Jones, D. 1998. Long barrows and Neolithic elongated enclosures in Lincolnshire: An analysis of the air photographic evidence. *Proceedings of the Prehistoric Society*, vol.64.

Palmer, R 1996. Air photo interpretation and the Lincolnshire Fenland. *Landscape History*, vol.18, pp.5-16.

RCHME 1993. *National Mapping Programme Lincolnshire Mapping Project: Project Design.* RCHME internal document.

RCHME 1995. *Owmby Cliff, Lincolnshire: Air Photograph Interpretation.* RCHME internal document.

Steedman, K. 1994. Excavation of a Saxon site at Riby Cross Roads, Lincolnshire. *Archaeological Journal*, vol.151, pp.212-306.

The Physical Landscape of Lincolnshire.

Yvonne Boutwood

Introduction.

The purpose of this article is to place the archaeological papers presented in this volume in a landscape context, by providing a background to the physical landscape of Lincolnshire. It briefly outlines the geology, topography and soils of Lincolnshire, and describes the landscape zones. The information is derived from four main sources: *The Geology of Lincolnshire from the Humber to the Wash* (Swinnerton & Kent 1981), *British Regional Geology: Eastern England from the Tees to the Wash* (Kent *et al.* 1980), *The Character of England: Landscape, Wildlife and Natural Features* (Countryside Commission & English Nature [1997]) and *An Historical Atlas of Lincolnshire*, (Bennett & Bennett 1993). Individual authors in the latter and other references are noted in the text where they provide more detailed information.

Geology, topography and soils.

Lincolnshire is the second largest county in England and although part of the East Midlands, it is to some extent isolated by natural boundaries. To the north lies the River Humber, to the west the River Trent and to the east the North Sea and the Wash, whilst in the south there is no physical boundary as it crosses limestone upland and fenland (Fig.1a).

The solid geology of Lincolnshire comprises rocks of Mesozoic ages, but several formations are concealed and only those of the Triassic, Jurassic and Cretaceous periods outcrop at the surface (Fig.2; Aram 1993b, p.4). The eastward dipping strata of these formations alternate between the harder limestone and chalk rocks, and the more easily eroded clays, producing a 'scarp and vale' topography (Linton 1954, p.67). This gives rise to distinctive landscape zones, which were used as a basis for mapping within the project area (Fig.3, see below).

The topography of Lincolnshire is influenced not only by its solid geology but also by its complex glacial and post-glacial history. Climatic changes during the Quaternary period resulted in eustatic and isostatic effects on sea level, giving rise to changes in drainage patterns, erosion and deposition of sediments. These drift deposits of till, silt, clay, sand, gravel, peat and aeolian cover sands (blown sands), occur mainly within the valleys and along the coast, whilst the uplands areas remain largely drift free (Aram 1993a, p.2, 1993c, p.6; Kent *et al.* 1980, pp.118-20).

Lincolnshire's landscape is characterised by relatively low relief (Figs 1a & 1b). Three-quarters of its area is below thirty metres Ordnance Datum (OD) and much of this lies close to sea level. The highest relief occurs along the Wolds rising to 168 metres OD. The main rivers draining the county are the Trent, Ancholme, Witham and Welland (Fig.1a). The Rivers Trent and Ancholme flow northward into the Humber, the Ancholme draining the northern Lincoln Clay Vale. The upper Witham flows northward, then through the Lincoln Gap and continues as the lower Witham flowing eastward and south-east to the Wash. Several streams drain eastward from the Lincolnshire Wolds and Marsh to the North Sea coast. The River Welland and its tributary the Glen, drain north-eastward to the Wash. This network of rivers and navigation canals has been important for local transport and trade (Wright 1993a, p.80). River fords and road intersections, for example at the Lincoln and Ancaster Gaps, also became important foci for settlement.

The soils of Lincolnshire are varied, dependent on parent rock, slope, aspect, climate, vegetation, past and present agricultural practice and land utilisation. They fall into seven main soil groups: lithomorphic, pelosols, podzolic, surface-water gley, ground-water gley and peaty soils (Fig.4, Hodge *et al.* 1984, pp.58-63). The superior quality of the county's soils, together with the favourable topography and climate has resulted in predominantly agricultural land use (Lincolnshire County Council 1995, p.48, Table 2.4). The extent of agricultural land has been increased by extensive reclamation, drainage and land improvement, particularly along the north-east coast, the Wash, the Fens, the Isle of Axholme and the Trent Valley (Robinson 1993b, p.72). Some areas retain heathland vegetation and woodland, but the latter only comprises 4.6% of the county area (Carter, this volume, Fig.1; Gibbons 1975, pp.36-41; Nature Conservancy Council 1985-89). The nature of the geology, soils and agricultural regimes affect cropmark formation and the subsequent identification of archaeological sites through aerial reconnaissance, which is discussed more fully by Carter (this volume).

The landscape of Lincolnshire is scarred by open pits and quarries, but many more disused workings, evident on aerial photographs, are water-filled or have been infilled. The practice of claying and marling land for agricultural improvement, during the medieval and post-medieval periods, also produced numerous pits (Beastall 1978, pp.116, 238). The economic geological resources of Lincolnshire (Kent *et al.* 1980, pp.128-36; Swinnerton & Kent 1981, pp.106-10) are primarily sand, gravel, limestone, chalk and ironstone (Wright 1993b, p.114), utilised for building and road stone, and cement and iron manufacture. Clay extraction was important on a local scale for brick and tile manufacture, but is now in decline, with few sites remaining (Robinson 1993c, p.116). Sandstone, limestone and chalk deposits are also important aquifers used for water supply.

The landscape zones.

The solid and drift geology, topography and soils of Lincolnshire have produced distinctive landscape zones, which in turn have influenced land use and settlement (Fig.3; Kent *et al.* 1980, pp.2-6; Robinson 1975, pp.8-15, 1993a, p.8; Countryside Commission & English Nature [1997]). In northern and central Lincolnshire these zones comprise, west to east, the Trent Valley, Lincoln Edge (or Heath), Lincoln Clay Vale (or Mid Clay Vale), Lincolnshire Wolds and Lincolnshire Marsh. In southern Lincolnshire the Vale of Belvoir fringes the western border, opening into the upper Witham and Brant valleys. The dissected limestone plateau of the Kesteven Uplands gives way to the Lincolnshire Fens in the east.

The Trent Valley.

The River Trent flows north to the Humber within a broad vale. The description here concentrates on those areas within the project area (Fig.3), the Isle of Axholme and east of the Trent. The river is cut into Mercia Mudstone and Liassic clays, which are overlain by alluvium and Quaternary deposits. In the lower Trent valley the Isle of Axholme lies to the west, originally an isolated tract of land cut off by the Rivers Trent, Idle and the former course of the Don, with carr lands to the east. South of Gainsborough are low hills with a bluff of Mercia Mudstone close to the east bank of the Trent. River terraces are overlain by gravels and in places cover sands. Bordering the east Trent

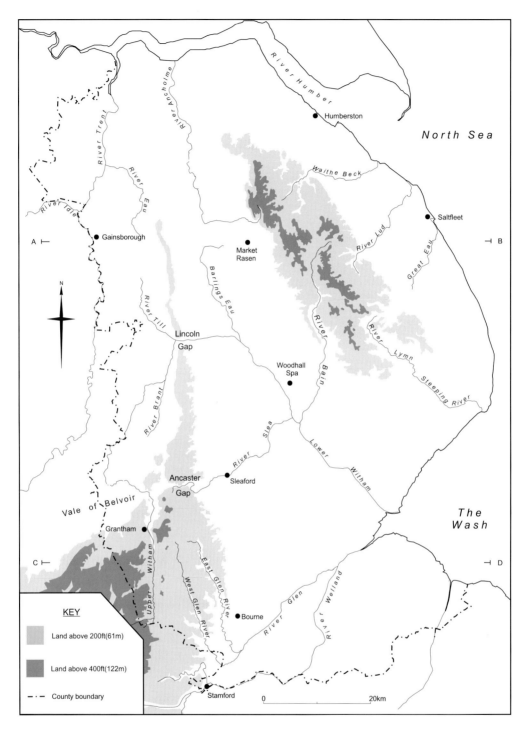

Fig.1a. The physical landscape of Lincolnshire.

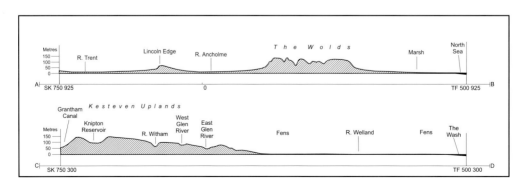

Fig.1b. Transects across north and south Lincolnshire showing the relief (A-B after Jones 1988).

Period	Formation
Quaternary	Drift: till, sand, gravel, silt, clay, peat, alluvium, blown sand.
Cretaceous, Upper	Burnham Chalk
	Welton Chalk Formation
	Ferriby Chalk Formation
Cretaceous, Lower	Red Chalk
	Carstone
	Sutterby Marl
	Skegness Clay
	Fulletby Beds (includes Roach Stone)
	Tealby Formation
	Claxby Ironstone
	Spilsby Sandstone (in part)
Jurassic, Upper	Spilsby Sandstone (in part)
	Kimmeridge Clay
	Ampthill Clay
	Oxford Clay
	Kellaways Beds
	Upper Cornbrash
Jurassic, Middle	Lower Cornbrash
	Blisworth Clay
	Snitterby Limestone (formerly Great Oolite Limestone)
	Upper Estuarine Beds
	Lincolnshire Limestone
	Grantham Formation
	Northampton Sand
Jurassic, Lower	Upper Lias
	Middle Lias (includes Marlstone Rock)
	Lower Lias (includes *Pecten* and Frodingham Ironstone)
Triassic	Penarth Group (formerly Rhaetic)
	Mercia Mudstone Group (formerly Keuper Marl)

Fig.2. Geological formations of Lincolnshire (after Kent et al. 1980, Table 1).

floodplain is a broad undulating vale, mostly below thirty metres OD and drained by the Rivers Eau, Till and their tributaries. These small incised valleys have left upstanding areas of drift free Lias, on which villages are sited, whilst further east the area is primarily covered by till with pockets of cover sands. In the south, to the east of the River Trent lie the Witham and Brant valleys.

Historically the lower Trent Valley was a poorly drained wetland environment, of limited use for arable farming. However, land use over the past three centuries has been transformed by warping and artificial drainage to produce high quality agricultural land (Everson 1979, p.41; Van de Noort & Ellis 1998, p.14). Land use within the Trent Valley once favoured pasture for livestock, but cereal production is now more predominant. Large areas of cover sands, south-east and north-east of Gainsborough and between Lincoln and Newark-on-Trent, have tracts of woodland, particularly coniferous plantations (Gibbons 1975, p.27, Fig.7). Sands and gravels are quarried, particularly west of Lincoln. The Marlstone Rock forms a scarp to the west of Grantham and this ironstone has been extensively quarried.

The Lincoln Edge (or Heath) and Kesteven Uplands.

At the eastern edge of the Trent valley the steep west facing escarpment of the Lincoln Edge dominates the landscape.

These north-south uplands extend from the Humber to Stamford and are cut by the Lincoln and Ancaster Gaps. The uplands are also known as the 'Cliff' north of Lincoln and the 'Heath' between Lincoln and Ancaster. South of the Ancaster Gap they broaden to form a plateau, the Kesteven Uplands.

These uplands vary in width from five kilometres in the north to twenty-five kilometres in the south. Their height also varies, attaining only 77 metres OD north of Lincoln and 154 metres OD on the Kesteven Uplands, south of Grantham. The western scarp slope comprises the Upper Lias with the Northampton Sand and Grantham Formation capped by the Lincolnshire Limestone. Spring lines, which have been a focus for settlement, occur at the junction of the Lias and associated permeable rocks. In contrast water resources are scarce along the rolling crest and dip slope, which are largely drift free areas. However, in places the limestone is thin and gives rise to inliers of sand and clay where springs issue. In the north, the east-facing dip slope falls gently to twenty metres OD and is cut by several small streams that drain eastward to the River Ancholme in the Lincoln Clay Vale. Between Lincoln and Ancaster there are numerous dry valleys on the dip slope. In the south, the Kesteven Uplands plateau is deeply incised by the Rivers Witham and Glen, and extensive till cover has remnants of ancient woodland. The landscape, once dominated by open heath and rabbit warrens, was transformed by eighteenth- and nineteenth-century enclosure. Land use today on the Lincoln

Edge is largely arable with emphasis on cereal and root crops grown in large fields. Limestone is extensively quarried. The dry open landscape provided ideal locations for numerous wartime airfields. The Jurassic Way, a presumed prehistoric trackway, and Roman roads have particularly influenced the modern road network (May 1976, p.7, Fig 4).

The Lincoln Clay Vale (or Mid Clay Vale).

Between the Lincoln Edge and the Lincolnshire Wolds is the Lincoln Clay Vale or Mid Clay Vale. This broad, twelve kilometres wide lowland area, is formed by the erosion of Jurassic clays. It is drained by the River Ancholme in the north and the lower Witham and its tributaries in the south. The vale has extensive deposits of till, gravels, alluvium and cover sands, hence some soils are heavy clay and loam, which become seasonally waterlogged. Land use is mixed agriculture with forestry on the sandy drift from Market Rasen to Woodhall Spa, with some gravel extraction in the south of the vale. Settlement is sparse and villages line the western edge of the vale.

The Lincolnshire Wolds.

The eastern edge of the Clay Vale is marked by the steep scarp of the Lincolnshire Wolds. The north-west to south-east belt of upland is fifteen kilometres wide and seventy kilometres long. The rivers Lud, Great Eau and Waithe Beck flow east and north-east into the Marshland. The River Bain flows south-west to join the lower Witham. The River Lymn, flows south-east, forming the Steeping river as it reaches the Wash. The upland summit is capped with Cretaceous chalk, overlying Tealby Limestone, Claxby Ironstone and Spilsby Sandstone. The character of the chalk plateau changes from north to south. In the north there is a simple west facing escarpment and dip slope with dry valleys. The central Wolds attain a height of 168 metres OD and form a wide plateau, dissected by streams. The dip slope has been truncated by sea-cliffs, which are partially overlain by glacial deposits. The southern Wolds is divided by a secondary scarp running north-west to south-east, exposing the Spilsby Sandstone to the west and the chalk to the east. Some of the steep river valleys have cut into and exposed the Kimmeridge Clay. Cover sands have accumulated along the foot of the scarp, and settlement, as elsewhere on the Wolds, makes use of spring lines. Land use, which once favoured sheep rearing, is largely arable now, but some areas of chalk grassland survive. The landscape of large, hedge-lined fields, is crossed by drove roads and trackways of possible medieval and prehistoric date: the Bluestone Heath Road, Barton Street and the High Street (May 1976, p.9, Fig.4). Woodland cover is sparse on the plateau, with only a few areas in the south-east. Chalk and other stone resources are extensively quarried. As with the Lincoln Edge, the Wolds provided a location for wartime airfields.

The Lincolnshire Marsh.

To the east of the Wolds lies the Lincolnshire Marsh, a coastal plain, fifteen kilometres wide, extending from the Fenland Basin in the south to the Humber in the north. Several streams drain off the Wolds in an easterly and north-easterly direction across the Marshland. The chalk platform is overlain by Quaternary clays, giving rise to the undulating topography of the Middle Marsh. Small pockets of woodland occur along the lower slopes of the Wolds and edge of the Marsh. To the east of this, the Outmarsh, has deposits of marine and estuarine alluvium with storm beach deposits fringing the coast. The complicated history of sea level changes, submergence and re-emergence of the coastline and related episodes of erosion and accretion has produced a complex series of deposits of peat, clay, silt, gravel, shingle and blown sand (Robinson 1970).

Post-medieval and modern reclamation and drainage has increased the area of agricultural land, now used for pasture and arable. But areas of sand dune, saltmarsh and intertidal mudflats still dominate parts of the coast. A long history of sea defence construction is evident both inland and along the coast. Sea salt was an important resource, exploited from prehistoric to post-medieval times and the later phases of its extraction are most evident from Humberston to Saltfleet where numerous saltern mounds, accumulations of de-salted silt, have been recorded (Grady, this volume).

The Lincolnshire Fens.

The project area excludes much of the Lincolnshire Fens, except for the western and northern fringes and the Witham fens. The Fenland Basin is formed by a shallow depression in Cretaceous and Jurassic rocks, which are overlain by glacial deposits, recent marine and fluvial deposits. The basin is on average four and a half metres above OD and is limited by the fifteen metre contour, which includes part of the lower Witham. The Fens are drained by the Rivers Witham and its tributaries, the Slea and Bain, flowing south-eastward, and the Welland, Glen and Nene flowing north-eastward to the Wash. Along the inner edge of the Fenland Basin, particularly between Sleaford and Bourne, are river and beach gravel deposits. Extensive peat fen also occurs along this edge and into the Witham fens. The open terrain of the fens landscape is characterised by large fields with drains, dykes and canalised rivers, bounded by embankments. Land drainage and reclamation has transformed the extensive areas of saltmarsh into one of the richest agricultural areas of Lincolnshire (Robinson 1993b, p.72). The Car Dyke, constructed in Roman times, was used as a catchwater drain at the inner edge of the Fenland Basin. The saltmarsh environment was exploited during Iron Age and Roman times for salt production (Lane 1993, p.26), but it is the medieval saltern mounds that are most evident on the coast (Healey 1993, p.28; Grady, this volume).

Bibliography.

Aram, S. 1993a. The making of the landscape. In Bennett & Bennett 1993, pp.2-3.

Aram, S. 1993b. Solid geology. In Bennett & Bennett 1993, pp.4-5.

Aram, S. 1993c. Drift geology. In Bennett & Bennett 1993, pp.6-7.

Beastall, T. W. 1978. *The Agricultural Revolution in Lincolnshire*. History of Lincolnshire VIII. Lincoln.

Bennett, S. and Bennett, N., eds 1993. *An Historical Atlas of Lincolnshire*. Hull.

Countryside Commission and English Nature, [1997]. *The Character of England: Landscape, Wildlife and Natural Features*. (loose leaf binder), Cheltenham.

Everson, P. 1979. Cropmark evidence and the reclamation of Blyton and Laughton Commons. *Lincolnshire History and Archaeology*, vol.14, pp.40-43.

Gibbons, E. J. 1975. *The Flora of Lincolnshire*, Lincolnshire Natural History Brochure, No.6. Lincolnshire Naturalists' Union, Lincoln.

Healey, H. 1993. Salt-making II: Saxon and medieval. In Bennett & Bennett 1993, pp.28-29.

Hodge, C. A. H., Burton, R. G. O., Corbett, W. M., Evans, R. and Seale, R. S. 1984. *Soils and Their Use in Eastern England*. Soil Survey of England and Wales Bulletin No.13.

Jones, D. 1988. Aerial reconnaissance and prehistoric and Romano-British archaeology in northern Lincolnshire - A sample survey. *Lincolnshire History and Archaeology*, vol.23, pp.5-30.

Kent, P., Gaunt, G. D. and Wood, C. J. 1980. *British Regional Geology: Eastern England from the Tees to the Wash*. 2nd edition.

Lane, T. 1993. Salt-making I: Iron Age and Roman. In Bennett & Bennett 1993, pp.26-27.

Lincolnshire County Council & Cobham Resources Associates 1995. *Lincolnshire State of the Environment Report*.

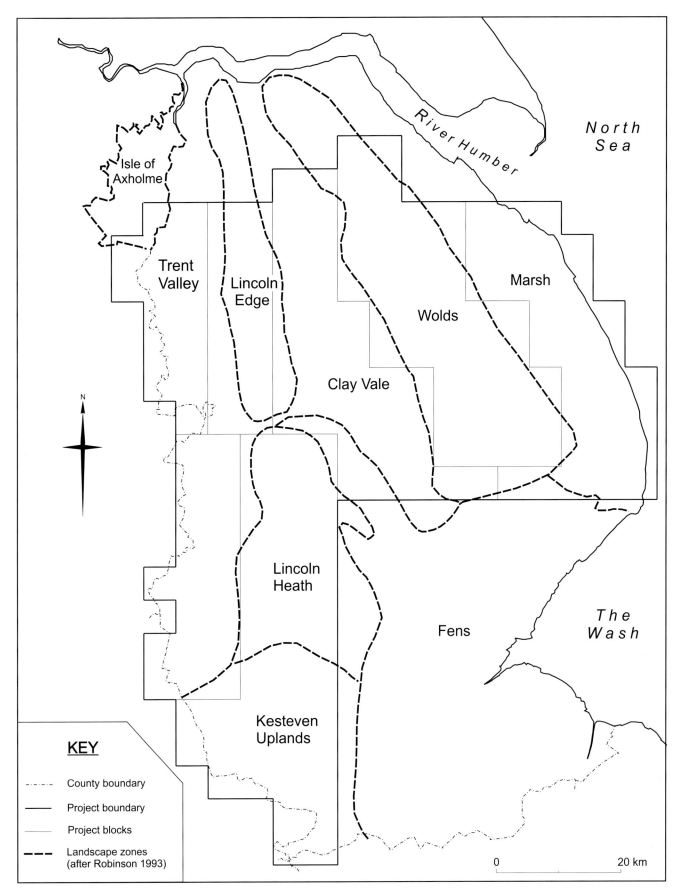

Fig.3. The landscape zones of Lincolnshire and project area.

Linton, D. 1954. The landforms of Lincolnshire. *Geography*, vol.39, pp.67-78.

May, J. 1976. *Prehistoric Lincolnshire*. History of Lincolnshire I. Lincoln.

Nature Conservancy Council 1985-89. *Inventories of Ancient Woodland*.

Robinson, D. N. 1970. Coastal evolution in north-east Lincolnshire. *East Midland Geographer* vol.5, pp.62-70.

Robinson, D. N. 1975. Geology and scenery. In Gibbons 1975, pp.8-15.

Robinson, D. N. 1993a. Natural regions. In Bennett & Bennett 1993, pp.8-9.

Robinson, D. N. 1993b. Drainage and reclamation. In Bennett & Bennett 1993, pp.72-73.

Robinson, D. N. 1993c. Brick and tile making. In Bennett & Bennett 1993, pp.116-17.

Swinnerton, H. H. and Kent, P. E. 1981. *The Geology of Lincolnshire from the Humber to the Wash*. 2nd edition. Lincolnshire Naturalists' Union, Lincoln.

Van de Noort, R. and Ellis, S. 1998. *Wetland Heritage of the Ancholme and Lower Trent Valleys: An Archaeological Survey*. Hull.

Wright, N. 1993a. Navigable waterways and canals. In Bennett & Bennett 1993, pp.80-81.

Wright, N. 1993b. Ironstone mining. In Bennett & Bennett 1993, pp.114-15.

Fig.4. Soils of Lincolnshire (within the project area).

Major Soil Group/ parent rock	Soil Group	Soil No.[1]
Lithomorphic soils: mostly shallow, well-drained, loamy calcareous soils, over Jurassic limestone and Cretaceous chalk.	Rendzinas: grey	342
	brown	343
	Sand pararendzinas	361
	Gleyic rendzina-like alluvial soils	372
Pelosols: calcareous or non-calcareous, clayey, slowly permeable, seasonally waterlogged soils, over Jurassic and Cretaceous clay, Triassic mudstone.	Calcareous pelosols	411
	Argillic pelosols	431
Brown soils: may be shallow but mostly deep, well-drained, either loamy, calcareous and/or clayey soils, develop below 300 metres OD, with various parent materials.	Brown calcareous earths	511
		512
		513
	Brown calcareous sands	521
	Brown earths	541
		543
		544
	Brown sands	551
	Argillic brown earths	571
	Stagnogleyic argillic brown earths	572
	Paleo-argillic brown earths	581
Podzolic soils: humic, well-drained, sandy soils, over glaciofluvial drift or aeolian cover sand.	Podzols	631
	Gley-podzols	641
Surface-water gley soils: loamy/clayey, seasonally waterlogged, affected by groundwater, slowly permeable over glaciofluvial drift, till, alluvium, Jurassic and Cretaceous clay.	Stagnogley soils	711
		712
Ground-water gley soils: deep sandy, coarse loamy, seasonally waterlogged, affected by groundwater, over marine and river alluvium.	Alluvial gley soils	811
		812
		813
		814
	Sandy gley soils	821
	Cambic-gley soils	831
		832
	Argillic gley soils	841
	Humic alluvial gley soils	851
	Humic sandy gley soils	861
Peaty soils: deep peat soils, over glaciofluvial drift and Cretaceous sand.	Earthy peat soils	1024

1. Refers to soil classification numbers used in the Soil Survey of England and Wales (source: Hodge *et al.* 1984, Table 7).

Prehistoric Linear Boundaries in Lincolnshire and its Fringes.

Yvonne Boutwood

Introduction.

Aerial reconnaissance in the 1970s revealed cropmarks of several sections of multiple-ditched boundary in Lincolnshire (Everson 1978, 1979, 1980), which were considered in the wider context of prehistoric boundary systems in the East Midlands (Pickering 1978). The Lincolnshire Mapping Project and continued reconnaissance by the RCHME have provided a sizeable data set of thirty-five monument records[1] of multiple-ditched boundaries, primarily distributed in western Lincolnshire (Figs 1, 2). This study analyses the form and distribution of these prehistoric multiple-ditched boundaries and assesses their archaeological context and associated features, placing them within their wider context of other linear boundaries, including pit alignments; it also reviews the dating evidence from excavations and their possible function within the Lincolnshire landscape.

Research into linear boundary systems elsewhere in Britain (Bowen 1978; Bradley *et al.* 1994; Bradley & Richards 1978; Dyer 1961; Spratt 1982, 1987, 1993), has highlighted some of the problems in interpreting such features. The fragmentary nature of the earthwork and cropmark evidence, distributed over large landscape zones, makes synthesis difficult, as the dispersed features may not be contemporary. Secondly, features in close proximity, apparently associated with the boundaries, may not be contemporary either. Dating evidence is scarce and similar boundary forms have been attributed a wide range of dates from the Neolithic to medieval periods. Prehistoric boundaries may also have continued in use, or have been subsequently re-used, as some coincide with present day parish boundary alignments. This suggests they potentially have a multi-period and multi-functional nature, as either large scale territorial or political boundary systems, or small scale economic or 'estate' boundaries (Spratt 1987, p.15).

Form of multiple-ditched boundaries.

Almost all the multiple-ditched boundaries recorded as being of prehistoric, Iron Age or Roman date were visible as cropmarks on aerial photographs. Two boundaries were visible as earthworks and survived as part of medieval parish boundaries. The first earthwork example lies between Habrough and Brocklesby parishes (Fig.1, No.19)[2], but the earthwork has since been ploughed level. The second, King Lud's Entrenchments (No.13), is still extant and forms a 750 metre section of boundary between Croxton Kerrial and Sproxton parishes in Leicestershire. It has been surveyed and partially excavated and consists of three banks and two ditches (Liddle 1982, p.16, Fig.7).

The cropmark form of multiple-ditched boundaries is quite distinctive, in that the ditches, broadly aligned parallel to each other, are individually quite sinuous, commonly with three ditches, but they may have up to five. Excavations at Brauncewell (Tipper 1994, p.3) indicate that a single ditch, visible on aerial photographs, had been recut several times. At Rectory Farm, West Deeping a triple-ditched boundary, visible on aerial photographs, had additional parallel ditches revealed

during excavation (Hunn & Rackham, forthcoming). The width and depth of the ditches and spacing between them in any one alignment may vary. Excavated examples were between 0.3 and 1.6 metres deep and 0.9 and 4.5 metres wide, with distances of 1.1 to 10 metres between ditches (Tipper 1994, Table 1). Narrower ditches are relatively shallower than broader ones and profiles vary between 'U' or 'V' shape, the latter often being the deeper and cut into bedrock. The overall width of the boundaries can change erratically over short distances and the width of triple ditches ranges from 8.6 to 18 metres, but sections with five ditches may be up to fifty metres wide. Only three cropmark examples have evidence of plough-levelled banks between the ditches, but excavations at Riseholme Lane, Nettleham, have also revealed traces of levelled banks, 0.25 metres high, which were estimated from the ditch fill to have stood to 1.5 metres (Palmer-Brown 1994). The term 'multiple-ditched boundary' describes the cropmark form, but this belies the scale and complexity of these bank and ditch boundaries, which would have been impressive earthworks in their contemporary landscape.

Although pit alignments are often found in the vicinity of multiple-ditched boundaries (see below), the inclusion of pit alignments within the boundary is not common and only three examples are recorded. At Long Bennington (No.23), a single pit alignment closely aligns with two ditches. At Barkston (No.3) a single ditch is flanked by pit alignments and is the only example of this configuration within a linear boundary, recorded in Lincolnshire. Combinations of ditches with adjacent pit alignments raises the question of chronology. Excavations at St Ives, Cambridgeshire, indicated that pit alignments pre-date ditches adjacent to them, and re-cutting of the ditches possibly served to emphasise the pit alignment boundary (Pollard 1996, p.105). Studies of the Cleave Dyke system in Yorkshire revealed it had developed from a pit alignment boundary system into a series of ditches and banks (Spratt & White 1986).

In many cases multiple-ditched boundaries are discontinuous, which probably reflects the discontinuity of the cropmark, not necessarily the original feature. This is demonstrated north-east of Lincoln, where several sections of boundary extend for 5.7 kilometres, from Grange de Lings (No.16) to Greetwell (No.18), producing the longest recorded discontinuous section of multiple-ditched boundary in Lincolnshire. Recent reconnaissance has revealed more ditches visible as cropmarks, infilling some of the gaps between sections, when compared with the first photographs taken between 1971 and 1979 (Everson 1979). Excavations at Brauncewell (TF 032 521), Greetwell (TF 007 724) and Nettleham Glebe (TF 003 733) have revealed ditch termini within boundary alignments, forming gaps. At both Nettleham Glebe and Brauncewell, the termini were in the central ditch, and associated post and pit structures at the latter site, have been interpreted as some form of entrance (Tipper 1994, p.6). At Greetwell all three ditches terminated against a watercourse (Armour-Chelu 1998, p.10). Some cropmark forms exhibit ditches which curve sharply and terminate against an adjacent ditch. At Hemswell (No.20) a triple-ditched section has an incurved outer ditch which terminates; the middle ditch also terminates, whilst the third ditch continues the boundary alignment. In this instance the form may be a definitive ditch terminus, perhaps of some significance, as the boundary marks a prominent topographical position in the landscape, from which other boundaries radiate.

The course of multiple-ditched boundaries is variable, from very straight sections at Allington (No.1) to a more arcuate route at Brauncewell (No.7) and some sections at Stubton (No.10) have right-angled 'dog-legs'. Junctions occur between sections of multiple-ditched boundary and other linear boundaries, of which ten examples are recorded. At Long Bennington (Figs 3, 4), the longest continuous section of multiple-ditched boundary, two kilometres in length, forms a right angled junction with a kilometre-long section, which

Fig 1. Multiple-ditched boundaries recorded in Lincolnshire and its fringes.

No.	Parish	NMR No.[1]	Grid Ref.	Topographical location
1	Allington	SK83NW14	SK 849 397	valley slope of beck
2	Barkston	SK94SW26	SK 906 421	flat valley, S of upper Witham
3	Barkston	SK94SW31	SK 932 423	flat valley, E of upper Witham
4	Blyborough	SK99NW34	SK 915 954	flat valley, E of River Eau
5	Blyborough	SK99SE36	SK 960 941	aligns with beck, on limestone dip slope
6	Brant Broughton and Stragglethorpe	SK95NW24	SK 931 553	flat valley, W of River Brant
7	Brauncewell	TF05SW16	TF 030 527	above spring line, on limestone dip slope
8	Carlton Scroop	SK94NW75	SK 947 452	west of beck
9	Caythorpe	SK94NW65	SK 944 475	east of beck
10	Caythorpe/Stubton/Hough-on-the-Hill	SK84NE6	SK 894 497	flat valley, W of River Brant
11	Coleby	SK96SE40	SK 980 606	limestone scarp
12	Cranwell and Byard's Leap	TF04NW29	TF 022 491	limestone dip slope
13	Croxton Kerrial/Sproxton	SK82NE1	SK 862 280	dry valley bottom, on limestone plateau
14	Folkingham	TF03SE19	TF 060 317	valley slope
15	Fulbeck	SK95SW35	SK 907 517	valley terrace, W of River Brant
16	Grange de Lings	SK97NE26	SK 988 771	limestone dip slope, beck nearby
17	Grayingham	SK99NW18	SK 944 964	limestone scarp
18	Greetwell/Nettleham	TF07SW61	TF 003 734	limestone dip slope
19	Habrough/Brocklesby	TA11SW46	TA 139 132	aligns with beck, on flat carr land
20	Hemswell/Willoughton	SK99SW41	SK 937 917	limestone scarp
21	Hibaldstow	SE90SE45	SE 970 020	crosses small valley, W of River Ancholme
22	Hough-on-the-Hill	SK84NE10	SK 897 490	flat valley, west of River Brant
23	Long Bennington	SK84NW17	SK 823 450	flat valley, W of upper Witham
24	Long Bennington	SK84NW63	SK 824 469	flat valley, W of upper Witham
25	Metheringham	TF06SW12	TF 038 613	limestone dip slope
26	Nettleham	SK97NE25	SK 998 755	limestone dip slope, beck nearby
27	Newton-on-Trent	SK87SW	SK 839 740	flat valley, E of River Trent
28	North Rauceby	TF04NW28	TF 024 480	limestone dip slope
29	Scawby	SE90SE38	SE 968 049	valley slope, W of River Ancholme
30	Scawby	SE90SE39	SE 969 042	valley slope, W of River Ancholme
31	Scotter	SE80SE35	SE 871 007	flat valley, between Rivers Eau and Trent
32	Scotton	SK89NE28	SK 881 998	valley slope of beck
33	Skillington	SK82NE51	SK 887 256	valley slope of beck, on limestone plateau
34	Welby	SK93NE34	SK 969 366	dry valley slope, on limestone dip slope
35	Willoughton	SK99SW36	SK 942 935	dry valley bottom, on limestone scarp

1. A monument record may include more than one section of boundary.

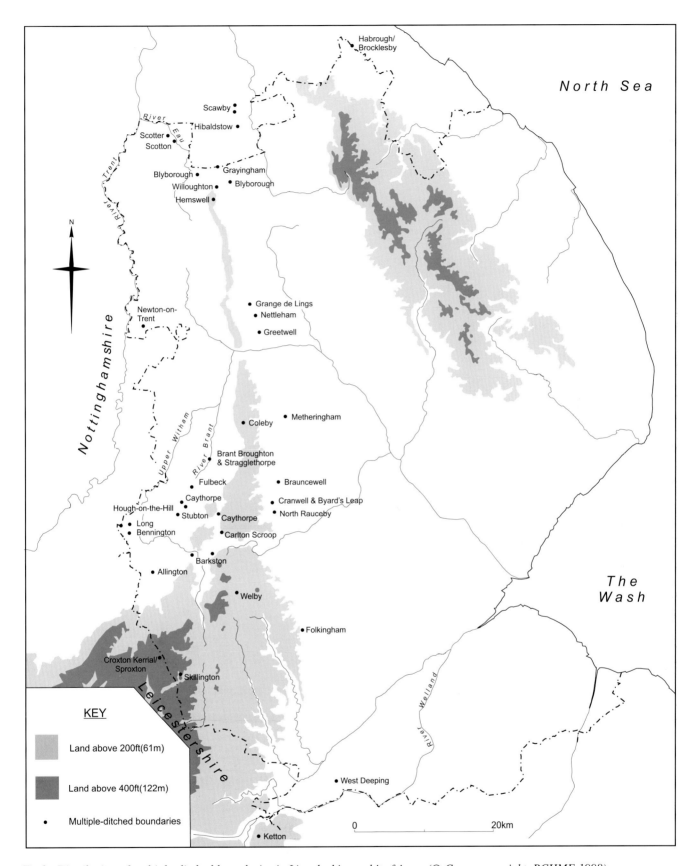

Fig.2. Distribution of multiple-ditched boundaries in Lincolnshire and its fringes (© Crown copyright. RCHME 1998).

comprises two ditches and a pit alignment. The only other example of a junction of multiple-ditched sections is at Caythorpe (No.10, Fig.5). The most common form of junction is between multiple ditches and a single ditch, of which seven examples are recorded. Apart from Long Bennington, there is only one other example of a pit alignment forming a junction with a multiple-ditched section, recorded at Blyborough (No.4).

Distribution of multiple-ditched boundaries.

The multiple-ditched boundaries recorded in the project are primarily distributed in western Lincolnshire on, or flanking, the Jurassic limestone of the Lincoln Edge or Heath, but also in the valleys of the upper Witham, Brant and Eau and eastern bank of the Trent (Fig.2). One section at Habrough (No.19) lies east of the chalk Wolds. The distribution of the multiple-ditched boundaries mainly in western Lincolnshire may correlate with specific soil types and underlying geology, as some soils are more responsive to cropmark formation than others (Carter, this volume); or the distribution may be more archaeologically significant and relate to the function and period of use of the multiple-ditched boundaries. Cropmark evidence indicates that prehistoric features and settlement are more widely dispersed than the boundaries (Fig.6). The absence of multiple-ditched boundaries from some areas of prehistoric settlement, such as the chalk Wolds, suggests their distribution in western Lincolnshire is archaeologically significant. The cropmark

evidence indicates the boundaries are distributed in an area extending ninety-three kilometres north to south and thirty kilometres west to east. The Nottinghamshire Mapping Project has recorded a possible section of multiple-ditched boundary, comprising five ditches, just east of the River Trent, at Newton-on-Trent (No.27). Aerial reconnaissance has revealed cropmarks of multiple-ditched and other boundaries on the Fen edge (Pickering 1988). Excavations of multiple-ditched boundaries lie just beyond the limits of the project area in Ketton, Rutland (Mackie 1993) and, West Deeping, Lincolnshire (King Street: Colcutt & Field 1990; Rectory Farm: Hunn & Rackham, forthcoming). In Lincolnshire this potentially extends the distribution of multiple-ditched boundaries westward to the River Trent, southwards into the Welland valley and eastward to the Fen edge. Although the area south of the Humber, formerly south Humberside, was not included in the Lincolnshire project area, an aerial photographic survey in 1988-89 (Kershaw, this volume) revealed there were no cropmark multiple-ditched boundaries.

Pickering (1978) suggested the multiple-ditched boundaries in Lincolnshire were part of a larger network, extending from Northampton to the Humber. Observations accrued from many years of aerial reconnaissance in the East Midlands and the work of St Joseph in East Anglia, particularly Cambridgeshire, led Pickering (personal communication) to observe linear boundaries and rectilinear field systems either parallel, or at ninety degrees, to the Icknield Way, a long distance prehistoric

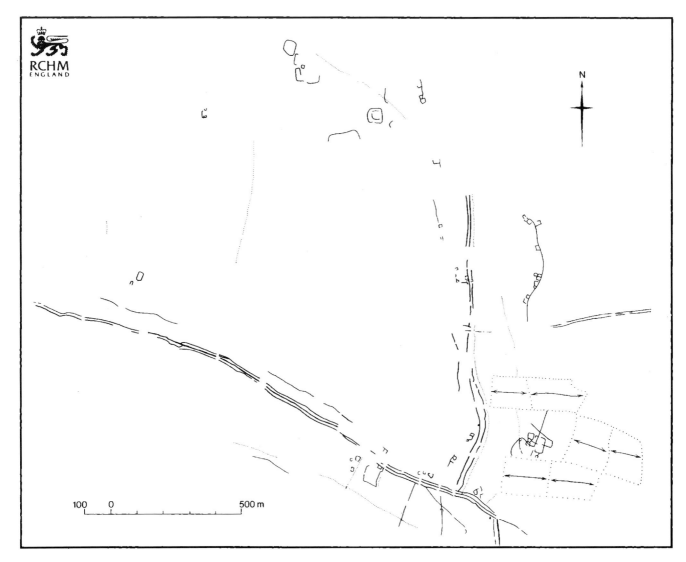

Fig.3. Cropmark sites at Long Bennington showing the junction between two boundaries, pit alignments, 'washing line' enclosures and other archaeological features (© Crown copyright. RCHME 1998).

Fig.4. Cropmark sites at Long Bennington (NMR SK8245/104, 12838/35, 15 July 1996, © Crown copyright. RCHME 1998).

trackway, running through Hertfordshire, Bedfordshire and Cambridgeshire. This model, in which boundaries follow a pattern, associated with a trackway and laid out irrespective of the terrain, was also postulated for Lincolnshire. In contrast, within Yorkshire contexts (Spratt 1982, 1987, 1993) the layout of boundaries were more topographically sensitive, enclosing areas of 'ranch size' and providing an alternative model. Pickering (1978) used the analogy of a 'Jurassic Spine', with the main north-south alignment coinciding with the Jurassic Way, a prehistoric corridor or routeway following the western edge of the limestone scarp (Grimes 1951), with other west to east alignments at right angles to this. Although the broad distribution of these boundaries does coincide with and flank the limestone scarp of the Lincoln Edge, their alignments do not conform to Pickering's suggested pattern, as a north-west to south-east and south-west to north-east orientation predominates over a west to east and north to south orientation.

There are three contexts where the concentration of multiple-ditched and other linear boundary forms gives some suggestion of spatial relationships and dimensions of areas of land division. The first is in northern Lincolnshire at Hemswell, Willoughton,

Blyborough and Grayingham, secondly at North Rauceby and thirdly in the upper Witham valley at Long Bennington. In the latter two contexts a broadly parallel and perpendicular arrangement of boundaries defines areas of 1.8 to 2.2 kilometres between multiple-ditched boundaries, with intervening single ditches and pit alignments giving smaller divisions of between 500 and 600 metres. At North Rauceby the same pattern of parallel and perpendicular boundaries occurs, but the parallel multiple-ditched boundaries lie within 650 metres of each other. If all are contemporary this suggests a system of land division based on fairly small-scale areas.

Contexts.

Examination of contexts in which multiple-ditched linear boundaries occur may give some indication as to their function within the landscape. Two approaches can be applied, firstly to examine their setting within the physical landscape and secondly to look at archaeological features, in both their immediate and wider contexts. In studying a landscape using

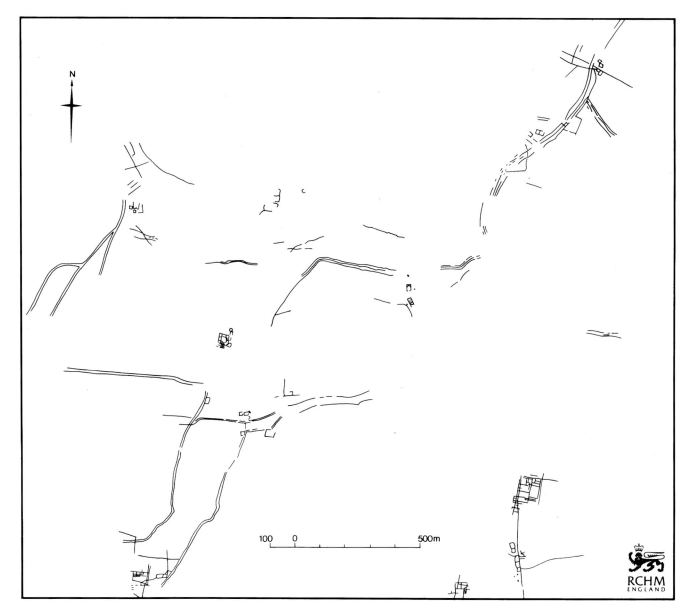

Fig.5. Cropmark sites at Caythorpe and Stubton showing boundaries with 'dog-legs' and junctions and other archaeological features (© Crown copyright. RCHME 1998).

only evidence from aerial photographs it may be possible to comment on the spatial relationship of other cropmark features to the boundaries, but it is not possible to establish the contemporaneity or phasing of such features from aerial photographs, this can only be confirmed through excavation.

Reviewing the landscape contexts in which multiple-ditched boundaries occur, of the thirty-five records listed in figure 1, fifteen contexts are on the Lincoln Edge or Heath and the remainder are associated with major river valleys or small becks. These form two very diverse landscape areas, contrasting between the low-lying river valleys and the limestone uplands. On the limestone they occur on both the scarp and dip slope, above and below the spring lines, attaining heights of up to 145 metres above Ordnance Datum. They occur on soils which are primarily shallow, well-drained, calcareous rendzinas over limestone, but occasionally on deeper brown earths over ironstone bedrock. Their alignment across the limestone varies, but a north-west to south-east orientation predominates and their relationship with the topography varies. For example the boundaries may traverse valleys and cross the spurs between them, or align with watercourses along the bottom of the valleys, or lie upslope along the crest. In the cropmark examples a correlation with watercourses is noted and excavations at Riseholme Lane, Nettleham (SK 997 756), indicated that the

boundary followed a glacial channel, in fact in places the eastern ditch was cut into the channel (Palmer-Brown 1994).

By contrast, the river valleys of the upper Witham, Brant, Eau and the east bank of the Trent are low-lying areas, with becks draining small subsidiary valleys and some areas are flat carr land. Soils vary from deep, well-drained brown earths to seasonally waterlogged, gley soils. Again the correlation with watercourses is noted, as some boundaries run parallel to rivers, or in the case of small becks may lie directly adjacent to them, closely following their course. At Long Bennington one section of boundary aligns with the junction of two soil types, which may be coincidental, or a deliberate division between areas of potential different land use. Prehistoric boundaries were presumably constructed in an open landscape, where remaining pockets of woodland may have been significant in both the flat river valleys and open limestone terrains. In the absence of other natural topographical features, the trees could be used as markers between which the boundaries ran.

Examining the archaeological contexts shows that apart from the junctions with single ditches and pit alignments discussed previously, the only other feature which directly adjoin the multiple-ditched boundaries, are ditched enclosures, of which seven examples are recorded from cropmark evidence. In two cases at Caythorpe (No.9) and Long Bennington (No.23) the complete enclosures (60m x 30m and 70m x 50m respectively) contain smaller enclosures (15m x 10m and 11m x 8m). The other adjoining enclosures broadly fall within the same range of dimensions, between forty metres and sixty metres, except at Long Bennington where a cluster of small (10m x 10m) enclosures also abut the boundaries. Excavations at Brauncewell revealed enclosures, both overlying the boundary ditches and lying parallel to them, respecting the position of the boundary (Tipper 1994; Taylor 1998). One of the enclosures contained a structure, interpreted as a post-built livestock enclosure of possible late Iron Age date (Taylor 1998).

Some features have a close spatial relationship with the boundaries, notably other linear features, particularly pit alignments and 'washing line' enclosures, which are parallel or perpendicular to the multiple-ditched boundaries. At Long Bennington the pattern of pit alignments suggests a system of land division aligned on the two boundary sections. The 'washing line' enclosures consist of single sinuous ditches, but occasionally pit alignments, along which are strung, small attached enclosures, often grouped in clusters (Fig.3). This association of both pit alignments and 'washing line' enclosures with multiple-ditched boundaries occurs at a further three locations, at Caythorpe (No.10), Fulbeck (No.15) and Allington (No.1, Fig.7). Other clusters of small enclosures adjacent to the boundaries also occur at these locations. The cropmark evidence shows that these 'washing line' enclosures are fairly uncommon within the project area, with a restricted distribution primarily in the upper Witham valley, which lies within the zone of multiple-ditched boundary distribution. Cropmark evidence from outside the project area, along the Fen edge at Billingborough (TF 126 334), indicate similar 'washing line' enclosures in close proximity to excavated Bronze Age settlement features (Chowne 1978, p.17, Fig.2). The coincidence of multiple-ditched boundaries and pit alignments occurs at several other contexts, besides those mentioned above. Single ditches also lie parallel to the boundaries, but maintaining distances of approximately fifty metres, as occurs at Long Bennington and Brauncewell. Excavations at the latter site concluded that they were probably contemporary or at least closely phased with the boundaries (Tipper 1994, p.7). The relationship of double ditches and multiple-ditched boundaries is uncertain, as there are only a few coincidences. At Long Bennington one double-ditch linear lies perpendicular to a multiple-ditched section and others lie to the north in the same alignment as the latter boundary. At Stubton (Fig.5) an extensive network of double ditches lies directly south of the multiple-ditched boundary, but the relationship is unclear.

Research elsewhere (Bonney 1978, p.50; Bradley & Richards 1978, p.55; Spratt 1993, p.90) has shown that boundaries have a close association with Bronze Age round barrows, often directly aligning or sometimes circumventing them. In such contexts the boundaries may be using the barrows as markers for their alignment. Within the project area, at King Lud's Entrenchments, Leicestershire, a Bronze Age barrow cemetery lies adjacent to the eastern end of the boundary (Clay 1981). In Lincolnshire there are no examples of multiple-ditched boundaries and round barrows having such a close spatial relationship, but four examples have barrows within ten to two hundred metres of them. At Brauncewell, a Bronze Age barrow cemetery lies 750 metres from the curving arc of a multiple-ditched boundary. In these contexts the Bronze Age barrows may pre-date the boundaries, but the siting of the two monument-forms within the landscape may be significant. Elsewhere in the project area, for example in the upper Witham and Brant valleys where barrows are scarce, there does not seem to be any association of the two types of feature. In Wessex (Bradley et al. 1994, p.150) and Berkshire (Bradley & Richards 1978, p.56) the association of Iron Age hillforts with linear boundaries has also been noted. In Lincolnshire only six 'defended' enclosures have been recorded as potential Iron Age hillforts and are distributed mainly in the area south of the Ancaster Gap (May 1993, p.13). Few of these sites have

boundaries in close proximity to them, and those that do, have very narrow double ditches, which are possible trackways.

The cropmark evidence for prehistoric or Roman settlement, represented by enclosures, indicates several multiple-ditched boundaries have some form of settlement within their close or wider context. The range and form of these enclosures varies considerably and no significant correlation of site types is noted, except for the 'washing line' enclosures, discussed previously.

Other linear boundaries in the wider context.

It already has been noted that, in some contexts, pit alignments, and single and double ditches have a close spatial relationship with the multiple-ditched boundaries. Examining the wider landscape context shows there are numerous linear boundaries, which may potentially relate to the multiple-ditched forms. The distribution of pit alignments coincides with that of the multiple-ditched boundaries in western Lincolnshire (Fig.8). Their apparent absence on the limestone uplands, north and south of the Lincoln Gap, may reflect a bias in the aerial photographic record, as the Military Air Traffic Zones (MATZ) have restricted aerial reconnaissance in this area (Carter, this volume). Pit alignment boundaries are notably absent from the chalk Wolds, with only one record at the northern end, at Great Limber (TA 158 064). 'Pit alignments' at Stenigot and Bag Enderby on the Wolds, have a distinctive form, comprising a short alignment of paired opposed pits and are not considered to be boundaries, but some form of ceremonial monument (Jones 1998). Single and double ditches occur more widely, but the discussion of these will be confined to the broad zone of multiple-ditched boundaries distribution in western Lincolnshire. One drawback to this approach is the lack of excavation and dating evidence for these other linear boundaries. From an aerial survey perspective, the features have been attributed a broad date of 'prehistoric or Roman', or sometimes 'uncertain' and any discussion of them presumes a broad contemporaneity with the multiple-ditched boundaries.

Analysis of pit alignments recorded in Lincolnshire shows single alignments are the commonest form, and rarer combinations include double rows, pits parallel to a ditch, or lengths of ditch alternating with pits. They occur both in river valleys and on the limestone uplands in four main contexts; settlements, rectilinear field systems, dispersed boundaries and pit defined structures. In settlement contexts they sometimes overlap with other ditched enclosures, indicating a multi-phase site, but in general probably functioned as boundaries, perhaps as part of field systems. Several pit alignment field systems are recorded, mainly located in river valley contexts, particularly the Welland valley. On the limestone uplands they are more dispersed when compared with the closely parallel field systems of the river valleys. However, their consistent alignment, predominantly south-west to north-east and north-west to south-east, and their association with single, double and multiple-ditched boundaries, suggests they are part of an integrated system of land division. The longest section of pit alignment, measuring 1,090 metres, occurs on the limestone dip slope, orientated north to south, at Brauncewell (TF 033 550). Two shorter sections occur to the south-west, which may form part of the same alignment, which would extend the length to 2,070 metres. A substantial section of boundary lies 950 metres to the south of these pit alignments, which reiterates the coincidence of the two types of feature within the landscape. The form of this curvilinear multiple-ditched boundary with associated linear boundaries and pit alignments, has a potential parallel at Barton-le-Street, North Yorkshire, where an extensive boundary system was recorded by the RCHME Howardian Hills Mapping Project (Figs 9a, 9b).

In some cases pit alignments occur in close proximity to Neolithic mortuary enclosures and Bronze Age barrows and in these contexts they may be contemporary with them. Two

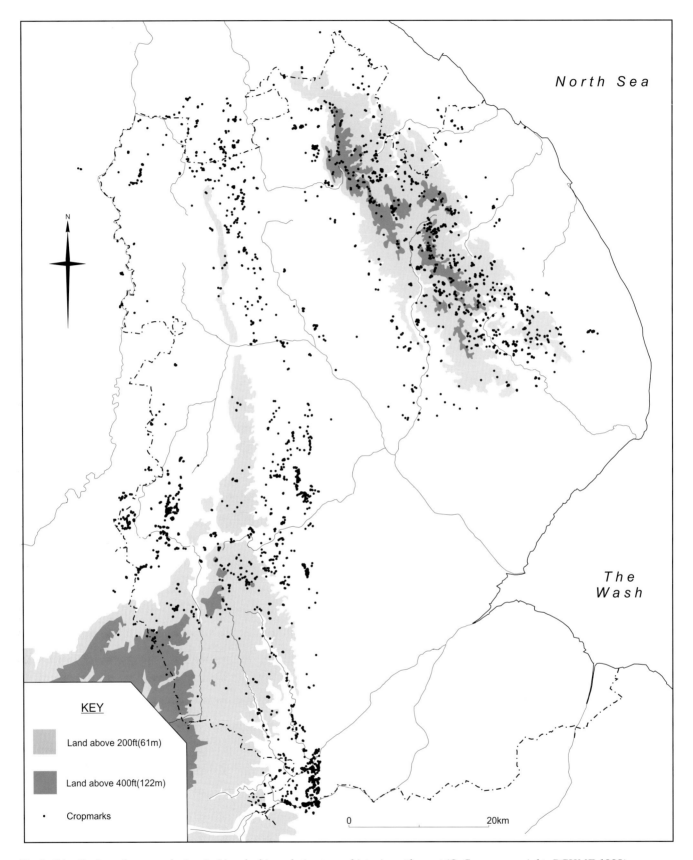

North Sea

The
Wash

KEY

Land above 200ft(61m)

Land above 400ft(122m)

• Cropmarks

0   20km

Fig.6. Distribution of cropmark sites in Lincolnshire relating to prehistoric settlement (© Crown copyright. RCHME 1998).

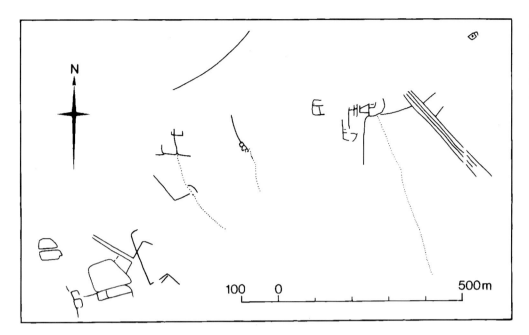

Fig.7. Cropmarks at Allington of boundaries, pit alignments, 'washing line' enclosures and other archaeological features (© Crown copyright. RCHME 1998).

similar contexts occur at South Rauceby (TF 036 448) and Wyville-cum-Hungerton (SK 860 296), where long lengths of pit alignment, or combinations of pit alignment and ditch, flank burial structures and converge (Figs 10a, 10b). In both cases other pit alignments or single and double-ditched boundaries lie close by, which suggests they are part of an integrated system of land division. The pit alignments flanking the burial structures appear to be separating them from the surrounding area, but whether they are contemporary with the burial structures or constructed later is uncertain. At Harlaxton (SK 893 340) an unusual example of four parallel pit alignments and a ditch occurs, which Pickering (1978) considered was part of the prehistoric boundary network. However, in this context with other pit defined monuments and burial structures, the 200 metre length of multiple pit alignment may be part of a 'ritual' landscape. This is distinct from contexts where pit alignments are functioning as a form of land division, either delineating small field units or larger scale boundaries.

Single and double-ditched linear features of prehistoric or uncertain date occur within the broad zone of multiple-ditched boundary distribution and are interpreted as boundaries or trackways. Their form is broadly sinuous, though some of the double-ditched sections may be quite straight, and they are occasionally embanked. Their alignment is variable and their relationship with topographical features varies, occurring in similar topographical locations as noted for the multiple-ditched boundaries. Their alignment along junctions of different soil types is also noted. At North Rauceby (No.28), two, parallel, multiple-ditched boundaries, 650 metres apart, with single ditches and pit alignments, form a fairly coherent network of land division. Within this group of boundaries a single ditch, four kilometres long, cuts across the heads of small valleys, with other boundaries perpendicular to it. If projected south-west, these other boundaries would descend the valley slopes to Honnington Beck and intersect with Pottergate, a prehistoric trackway identified as the potential route of the Jurassic Way. The four kilometre ditch crosses Ermine Street and, therefore, probably pre-dates the Roman road.

In some contexts the distance between boundaries ranges between 250 and 500 metres, sometimes with definite entrance gaps in the boundary ditches. It is debatable whether the term 'field systems' could be applied to these fairly sinuous and irregular land divisions. Certainly regular rectilinear field systems, like the 'brickwork' field pattern recorded in Nottinghamshire (Riley 1980, Fig.3) or 'Celtic' fields of Wessex (Bradley *et al.* 1994, Fig.22), were not visible on the

aerial photographs for Lincolnshire. There are a few contexts, at Tallington, Stubton and Osbournby, where settlements incorporate limited field systems and trackways. In contrast, extensive field systems and trackways have been recorded in the Lincolnshire Fens (Palmer 1996, Fig.2).

Single and double-ditched boundaries show a more positive correlation with Bronze Age round barrows, than was noted for the multiple-ditched boundaries. This coincidence suggests some single and double-ditched boundaries may have been constructed at a time when the barrows were extant and significant landscape features and so may have influenced their siting in the landscape. As with the multiple-ditched boundaries, enclosures abut the single and double-ditched boundaries or lie in close proximity to them. Their size is similar to those occurring in multiple-ditched boundary contexts, with one exception at Silk Willoughby (SK 038 427), where an extensive curvilinear boundary system, cutting off a spur between two becks, has a large (150m x 100m) enclosure attached to it as well as smaller ones (Fig.11). Linear boundaries are incorporated in other structures, which occur primarily on the limestone uplands. Some of these structures have converging ditches that form funnels; others have broad, parallel ditches with entrances; and there are also enclosures with attached double-ditched trackways. All of these sites are possible indications of pastoral activity (Fig.12).

Dating evidence for linear boundaries.

Within Lincolnshire there have been a number of excavations of multiple-ditched boundaries, at Brauncewell (Taylor 1998; Tipper 1994), Greetwell (Armour-Chelu 1998), Long Bennington (Fearn 1993), Nettleham Glebe (Field 1980), Riseholme Lane, Nettleham (Palmer-Brown 1994) and King Street and Rectory Farm, West Deeping (Colcutt & Field 1990; Hunn & Rackham, forthcoming), but many have been inconclusive in producing dating evidence for the construction of the multiple-ditched boundaries. Iron Age and Roman pottery sherds from ditch fills, especially the upper layers, are either intrusive, or associated with silting and possibly reuse of the ditches. At Riseholme Lane, Nettleham, the predominance of Iron Age domestic pottery, dating to the first and second century BC, was interpreted as evidence for an Iron Age farmstead nearby. The ditches also produced third-century AD Roman pottery, which suggests the process of ditch silting occurred over a long period (Palmer-Brown 1994). At Brauncewell (Tipper 1994) post holes flanking the ditches were

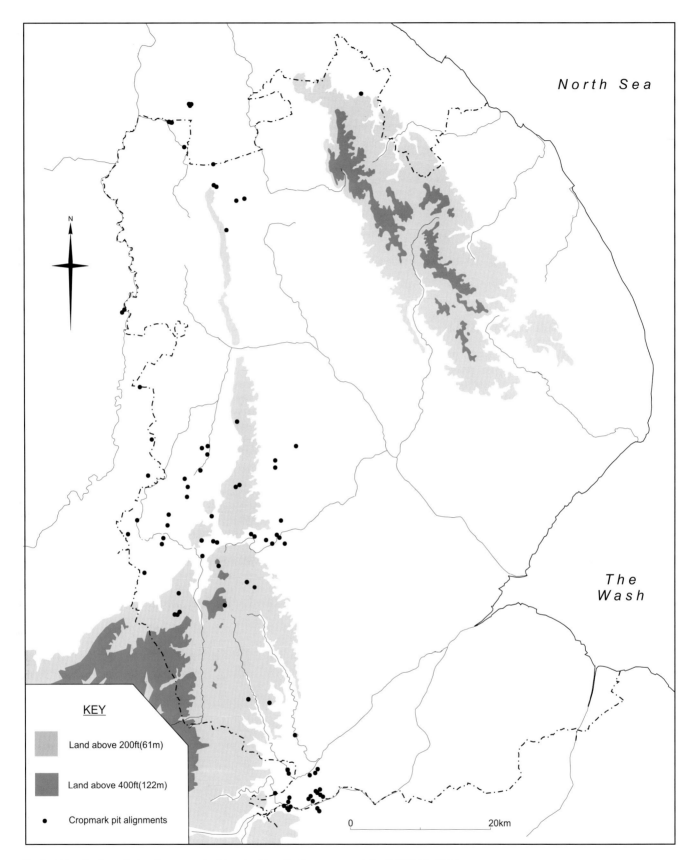

Fig.8. Distribution of pit alignments in Lincolnshire (© Crown copyright. RCHME 1998).

interpreted as a palisade and some contained Roman pottery, but there was no stratigraphical relationship with the boundaries. At Greetwell pottery finds from one ditch were middle Iron Age and another contained late Iron Age/early Roman pottery. The latter, which was the largest of the two, was cleaned and maintained up to, and possibly beyond the start of the Roman period (Armour-Chelu 1998, p.9). In close proximity to the boundaries at Greetwell substantial Roman remains, including buildings and industrial activity, dated to the third and fourth century were recorded (Johnson 1994; Armour-Chelu 1998). Similarly at Brauncewell (Tipper 1994; Taylor 1998) there is evidence of Roman structures and activity adjacent to, and overlying, the boundary. A single sherd of late Bronze Age pottery from one of the ditches at King Street, West Deeping, gave an indication that the multiple-ditched boundaries may have been of earlier construction than suggested by the Iron Age and Roman pottery (Colcutt & Field 1990). This was confirmed at Ketton, Rutland, where pottery dating from the late Bronze Age to the middle Iron Age was recovered from a multiple-ditched boundary. Late Iron Age metal work from the upper ditch fill was considered to derive from later reuse of the ditches (Mackie 1993). Radiocarbon dates from primary fills of two boundary ditches at Rectory Farm, West Deeping indicate a date range from the late Bronze Age to the middle/late Iron Age (Hunn & Rackham, forthcoming).[3]

There is little explicit dating evidence for the other forms of linear boundaries in Lincolnshire. Excavation of pit alignments at Messingham (Laskey 1979, p.73) and Long Bennington (Fearn 1993, p.5) did not produce any dating evidence. A review of dating evidence elsewhere in Britain (Fearn 1993) indicates pit alignments have a wide range of dates from the Neolithic to Roman periods. It has been suggested that the shape of the pits in alignments, whether round, oval, elongated or sub-square, may be indicative of the date (Hingley 1989, p.3), alternatively it could reflect underlying geology (Cardwell 1989, p.26). This explicit morphological detail was not recorded for the project. Single and double-ditched boundaries similarly have little dating evidence derived from excavation in Lincolnshire, but radiocarbon dates from Rectory Farm, West Deeping (Hunn & Rackham, forthcoming) indicates a co-axial system of double ditches which pre-dates multiple-ditched boundaries. Cropmark evidence in Lincolnshire does indicate several single and double boundaries crossed by Roman roads, and which thus potentially pre-date the roads. Studies elsewhere in England, either by excavation or fieldwork studying linear boundaries and their related monuments, suggest a date of late Bronze Age to late Iron Age (Spratt 1993, pp.85-86; Bradley et al. 1994, p.137).

There is some uncertainty of the date of King Lud's Entrenchments, which survive as earthworks and align with the parish boundary between Croxton Kerrial and Sproxton in Leicestershire (Phillips 1934, p.136). They are recorded in medieval documents, which led to an attribution of an early medieval date, but Whitwell (1982, p.62) suggests they are more likely to be prehistoric. In Lincolnshire only one other multiple-ditched boundary aligns with a parish boundary, between Hemswell and Willoughton, but single and double-ditched boundaries do so as well. Research in Yorkshire and Wessex revealed that Saxon and medieval documents noted the use of prehistoric boundaries, which then frequently continued in use through to modern times (Spratt 1987, p.19).

The function of linear boundaries.

Within Lincolnshire there is a wide range of linear boundary forms, including multiple-ditched boundaries, pit alignments, single and double-ditched linear boundaries. The simplicity or complexity of linear boundary construction may reflect their intended function, relationship to topography, symbolic and prestige value, or it may also embody a chronological

dimension. Studies in Wessex (Bradley et al. 1994, p.148) indicate simple boundary forms constructed in the Bronze Age were often modified and became more elaborate in the Iron Age. This model of an evolving system, constructed over a long period of time may well apply to Lincolnshire. Studies of Yorkshire boundary (dyke) contexts (Spratt 1987, p.15), concluded that there is no simple explanation for multiple-ditched boundaries; they were multi-period and multi-functional, which may be pertinent to Lincolnshire contexts.

Pickering (1978) viewed the multiple-ditched boundaries as part of an extensive tribal and territorial system, and something of immense magnitude. In contrast Spratt viewed the boundaries of the Tabular Hills, Yorkshire, as locally significant, primarily relating to farm or 'estate' boundaries akin to medieval townships or parishes. However, the topographical position of some boundaries and their complex multiple form, led Spratt (1987, p.15) to suggest they may be marking out more important territories of tribal or political significance. Although the distribution of multiple-ditched boundaries is widespread and new sections are continually being recorded via aerial reconnaissance and survey work, it is debatable whether they were ever a continuous boundary system, running the entire length of Lincolnshire; rather they seem to be part of a mosaic of different boundary forms. In some Lincolnshire contexts multiple-ditched boundaries have a close spatial relationship, delineating relatively small areas of approximately two kilometres square at Long Bennington, or only 650 metres apart at North Rauceby. Areas are further subdivided by other forms of linear boundaries, particularly pit alignments. Therefore, these groups of boundaries are preferably explained within a local context of land division, rather than delineating large territorial areas.

Territorial models for the Iron Age often derive from geographical models of 'central place theory' (Clarke 1972, pp.50-52). Large scale territorial or political boundaries defining an area of land would be located at the periphery of a zone containing important or significant settlement at its core and other settlement dispersed within the territory. Whereas, smaller scale land division may be viewed as demarcating specific areas of land use, associated with farming regimes, amongst which settlement is scattered. It has not been possible to identify which settlements are contemporary with the boundaries in Lincolnshire and ascertain the spatial relationship. In some contexts, such as Long Bennington and Stubton, the multi-ditched boundaries and 'washing line' enclosures do seem to play a significant role as a focus for prehistoric settlement and activity, including movement, as many features are aligned on them or lie in very close proximity to them. It would seem this focus persisted through to the Roman period.

None of the boundaries discussed here are thought to be defensive, and even though the multiple-ditched boundaries attain considerable dimensions, they are not on the scale of more traditional defensive and prestigious structures, for example those associated with Iron Age hillforts. They are perhaps best interpreted within the context of sedentary populations, in a mixed or pastoral economy, constructed to maintain some spatial and social organisation within kinship groups, which does not necessarily need a climate of population pressure or conflict (Bradley et al. 1994, p.151).

Interpretations of linear boundaries have in the past emphasised their role in a pastoral economy, where their prime function is to contain livestock and deter cattle raiding (Crawford 1953, p.107). There has been some debate as to how effective such earthworks would have been for containing livestock, without additional structures, such as fencing or hedges (Huntingford 1934). Excavation evidence in Lincolnshire (Tipper 1994, p.4) has revealed palisades between the multiple-ditched boundaries, which would provide an additional barrier. Excavations of pit alignments at St Ives, Cambridgeshire (Pollard 1996, p.107), have shown hedges and

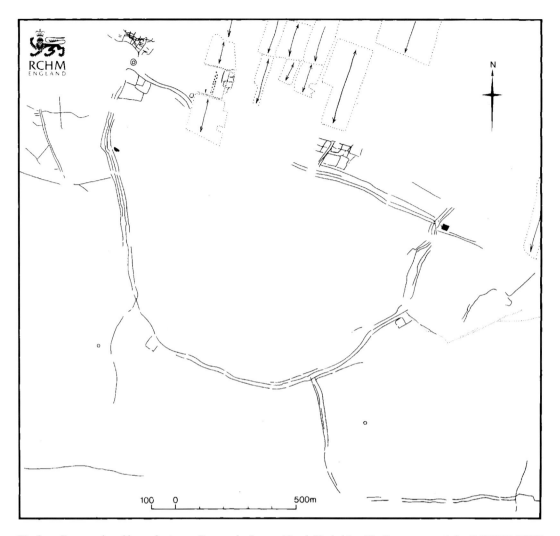

Fig.9a. Cropmarks of boundaries at Barton-le-Street, North Yorkshire (© Crown copyright. RCHME 1998).

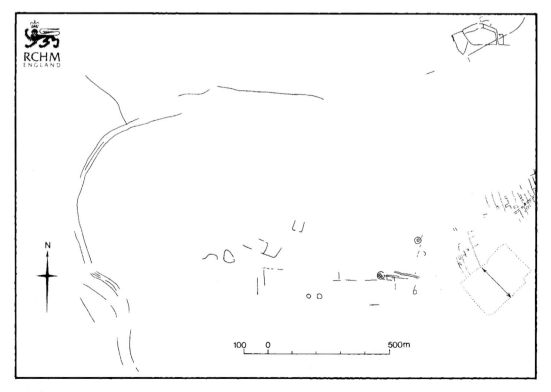

Fig.9b. Cropmarks of boundaries at Brauncewell, Lincolnshire (© Crown copyright. RCHME 1998).

fence lines were constructed parallel to them, although their relative chronology is uncertain. It has been suggested that in an open landscape pit alignments may have been used to nurture trees and saplings (Pickering 1992, p.418). In a mixed economy, arable areas would require some protection from cattle and the boundaries may thus serve to demarcate areas of differentiating land use, also to control resources. Angled bends are characteristic of both prehistoric and later boundaries, possibly reflecting differentiation of land use, zig-zagging between arable fields or pastoral areas, either within a community or between adjacent communities (Crawford 1953, pp.113-14). At Long Bennington the upper Witham forms a substantial natural boundary, yet one boundary broadly aligns with it, delineating a fairly broad band, one to one and a half kilometres wide, on the west bank of the river, potentially demarcating high quality agricultural land and possibly controlling access to water resources.

Some boundaries may also have been effective in controlling movement, by also functioning as trackways or droveways. This dual function is more commonly applied to double-ditched forms, but may also apply to the multiple-ditched boundaries. The suggestion that linear boundaries were used for controlling movement of people and for collecting tolls, had been proposed for contexts in Bedfordshire, where the Icknield Way cuts through causeways in the boundaries (Dyer 1961, p.40). The Jurassic Way lies within the zone of boundary distribution, and several multiple-ditched boundaries lie adjacent to the proposed route, with one even intersecting it at Grayingham (No.17). However, at this point the Jurassic Way route is now succeeded by a modern road, and identifying the relationship between the two and the existence of a possible causeway would be difficult. The complex entrance gap in the central ditch revealed by excavation at Brauncewell, may have controlled the movement of livestock or people (Tipper 1994, p.6). If this boundary is part of a large enclosure, as paralleled at Barton-le-Street, North Yorkshire, then it could have the dual function of a boundary and trackway, controlling movement of livestock, giving access to its interior and exterior, or to the small abutting enclosures (Figs 9a, 9b). Recurring contexts with enclosures abutting or lying in close proximity to single, double and multiple-ditched boundaries, suggests all these forms of linear boundary may have had a dual function as boundaries and trackways, associated with control and movement of livestock, utilising the enclosures as pounds. At Brauncewell evidence for a post-built structure, contained within a ditched enclosure was interpreted as a livestock enclosure (Taylor 1998, p.20). This dual function of linear ditches is possibly demonstrated by the variable form associated with 'washing line' enclosures, as the linear may be a pit alignment or a single ditch. At Foston and Marston (Fig.13) there are definitive entrances through the ditches, the latter being quite complex, which implies a boundary function. Other examples of 'washing line' enclosures at Long Bennington (Fig.3), with continuous sinuous ditches, suggests they are functioning as trackways and/or boundaries.

Although discussions here have focused on the practical function of linear boundaries, their symbolic context should not be overlooked. It has been suggested that the scale of a boundary form may be directly related to the importance and status of the boundary: multiple-ditched forms representing major territorial boundaries, whilst minor ones were of less importance (Jones 1988, p.19). However, the cropmark form of either single, double or multiple-ditched boundaries masks their complexity as revealed by excavation, where phasing in boundary construction, use and disuse, and associated activities, have been recorded (Armour-Chelu 1998; Taylor 1988; Tipper 1994). The recurrence of boundaries and water courses in close association has been noted for Lincolnshire. In such contexts the natural watercourse boundary is possibly being reinforced by a constructed boundary, and the symbolic importance of the latter should not be overlooked. Pit alignments at St Ives, Cambridgeshire, located parallel to a river, revealed wood and bone within the pits, which were possibly intentional deposits. The social and landscape context for this relatively 'simple' boundary form is therefore important in trying to explain its function (Pollard 1996, pp.93, 100, 111).

Future research.

Within Lincolnshire and its fringes aerial survey and mapping has provided an effective means of recording prehistoric linear boundaries, which have been ploughed level and are visible as cropmarks. Reconnaissance by the RCHME continues to reveal more linear boundary features, and these are incorporated in the National Monuments Record (NMR) database. This paper has focused on the multiple-ditched boundaries and their contexts. The data summarised in figure 1, together with the 1:10,000 transcriptions archived in the RCHME, National Monuments Record Centre in Swindon, thus provides the basis for future research. A number of approaches can be applied to studying prehistoric boundaries within the landscape. It would be useful to target landscape areas for future research where there is a concentration of multiple-ditched boundaries and other boundary forms, and three areas are notable. Firstly the upper Witham valley (Caythorpe, Stubton, Westborough and Dry Doddington, and Long Bennington), secondly north Lincolnshire flanking the River Eau (Hemswell, Willoughton, Blyborough and Grayingham, Fig.14), and lastly the eastern edge of the limestone from Brauncewell to North and South Rauceby.

Despite Lincolnshire's linear boundaries being predominantly levelled earthworks only visible as cropmarks, fieldwork does still have a role to play. Aerial survey techniques cannot reveal features masked by woodland and hedgerows. Areas of modern afforestation may still contain surviving earthworks preserved within them. Prehistoric boundaries were presumably not constructed within contemporary woodland, but may have skirted around it, therefore areas of ancient woodland may also be productive. Hedgerows may mask substantial earthwork boundaries, that although seemingly part of the medieval landscape, could have earlier prehistoric origins. In some contexts documentary research may prove useful, as medieval or earlier documents may identify boundaries of prehistoric date, utilised as Saxon or medieval boundaries (Everson & Knowles 1993).

In the past, excavations, primarily carried out as evaluations, have been variable in producing explicit dating evidence. In a research framework any further excavation should be carefully targeted. Surface finds collection was used in Wessex as a means of locating artefact concentrations and targeting potential excavation sites adjacent to linear boundaries (Entwistle 1994, p.27). However, the general paucity of pottery finds in some areas of Lincolnshire, particularly on the limestone uplands may not be conducive to such a strategy. Chronological issues are of particular interest, in areas such as Long Bennington, where structures abut and align with the multiple-ditched boundaries, and largely undated forms like the 'washing line' enclosures have been highlighted. Excavation and test pits should aim to achieve the maximum amount of data and specifically target waterlogged areas, where retrieval of environmental samples would be a priority. Environmental sampling undertaken as part of the Humber Wetlands Project (Van de Noort & Ellis 1998, p.4) provides data for the Ancholme and lower Trent valleys. An evaluation of data including Bronze Age, Iron Age and Roman contexts indicates a marked bias towards sample recovery in Fenland sites (Murphy 1998). Potential for environmental sampling of sites on the limestone uplands may be limited, compared to the more productive river valley contexts. Sampling from excavations of linear boundary contexts, like that undertaken at Rectory Farm, West Deeping (Hunn & Rackham, forthcoming) provides invaluable data. The establishment of a database as part of the English Heritage Midland Regional Review, including

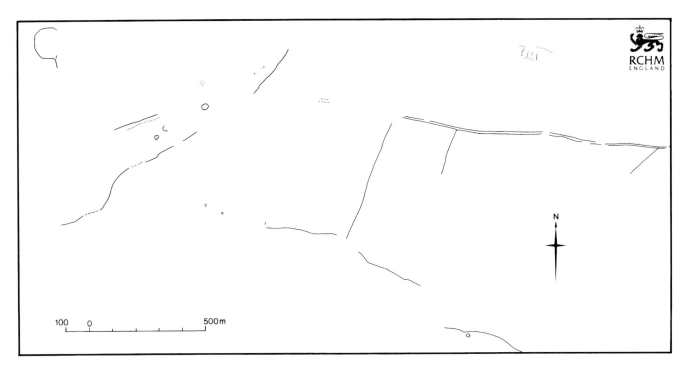

Fig.10a. Cropmarks of boundaries, pit alignments and round barrows at Wyville-cum-Hungerton (© Crown copyright. RCHME 1998).

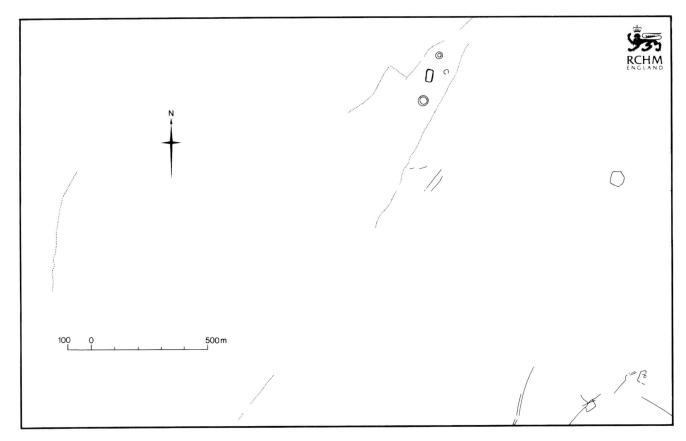

Fig.10b. Cropmarks of pit alignments, round barrows and a mortuary enclosure at South Rauceby (© Crown copyright. RCHME 1998).

Lincolnshire sites (Murphy 1998), will facilitate an integration of the archaeological record and environmental data, enabling a better understanding of the prehistoric landscape environment in which the linear boundaries occur.

The Lincolnshire project provides data on multiple-ditched boundaries and other boundaries in its regional landscape context of prehistoric settlement. Other projects of the RCHME National Mapping Programme in adjacent areas, of Nottinghamshire, Yorkshire and Northamptonshire, will facilitate research to compare these regions and develop national research strategies. Preliminary work on the Nottinghamshire project data has revealed there are few multiple-ditched boundaries. The archaeology of the west bank of the River Trent contrasts with that recorded in Lincolnshire. The River Trent appears to have been acting not only as a natural boundary, but also as a cultural boundary.

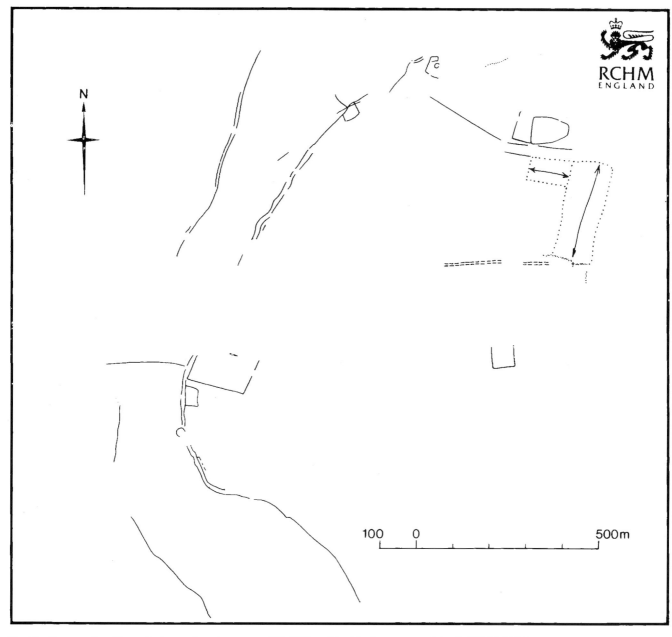

Fig.11. Cropmarks of boundaries and enclosures at Silk Willoughby (© Crown copyright. RCHME 1998).

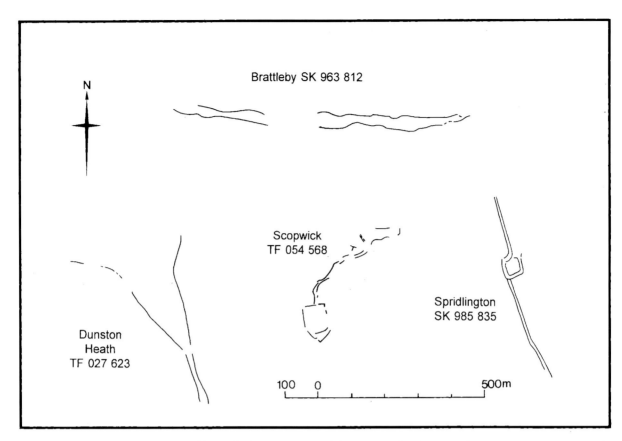

Fig.12. Cropmarks of single and double-ditched structures possibly associated with pastoral activity (© Crown copyright. RCHME 1998).

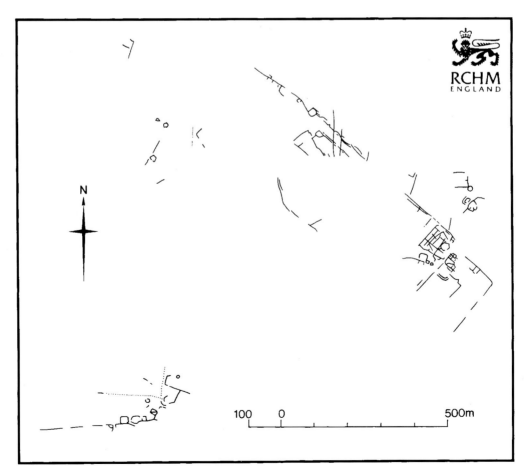

Fig.13. Cropmarks at Foston and Marston showing entrance structures within linear boundaries and associated settlement (© Crown copyright. RCHME 1998).

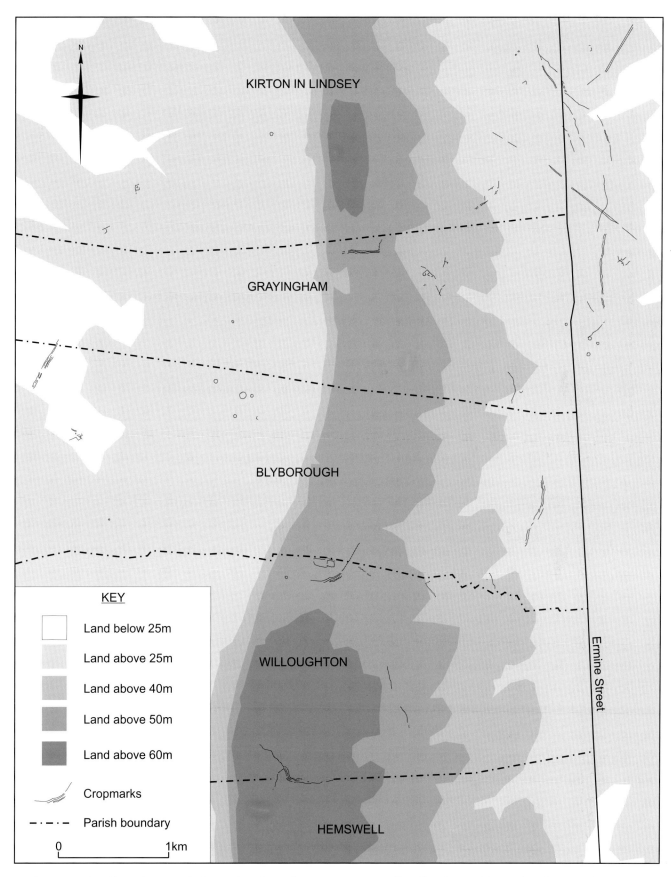

Fig.14. Cropmarks of boundaries and other archaeological features at Hemswell, Willoughton, Blyborough and Grayingham (© Crown copyright. RCHME 1998).

Notes.

1.	A monument record may include more than one section of multiple-ditched boundary.

2.	Numbers in brackets refer to those assigned to multiple-ditched boundary records listed in figure 1.

3	These radiocarbon dates are calibrated 760-670 BC and 550-345 BC and 310-210 BC (2350 ± 70) and calibrated 790-390 BC (2450 ± 60). Calibrated radiocarbon dates are at 2 sigma.

Bibliography.

Armour-Chelu, R. J. 1998. *Land at Greetwell, Lincoln, Proposal for Quarry Extension*. Lindsey Archaeological Services. Unpublished report.

Bennett, S. and Bennett, N., eds. 1993. *An Historical Atlas of Lincolnshire*. Hull.

Bowen, H. C. 1978. 'Celtic' fields and 'ranch' boundaries in Wessex. In *The Effect of Man on the Landscape in the Lowland Zone*, edited by S. Limbrey and J. G. Evans. Council for British Archaeology, Research Report 21, pp.115-23.

Bonney, D. 1978. Early fields and land allotments in Wessex. In *Early Land Allotment in the British Isles: A Survey of Recent Work*, edited by H. C. Bowen and P. J. Fowler. British Archaeological Reports, British Series 48, pp.49-51. Oxford.

Bradley, R., Entwistle, R. and Raymond, F. 1994. *Prehistoric Land Division on Salisbury Plain*, English Heritage. Archaeological Report No.2.

Bradley, R. and Richards, J. 1978. Prehistoric fields and boundaries on the Berkshire Downs. In *Early Land Allotment in the British Isles: A Survey of Recent Work*, edited by H. C. Bowen and P. J. Fowler. British Archaeological Reports, British Series 48, pp.53-60. Oxford.

Cardwell, P. 1989. Excavations at Cat Babbleton farm, Ganton, North Yorkshire. *Yorkshire Archaeological Journal*, vol.61, pp.15-27.

Chowne, P. 1978. Billingborough Bronze Age settlement: an interim note. *Lincolnshire History and Archaeology*, vol.13, pp.15-21.

Clarke, D. L. 1972. *Models in Archaeology*. London.

Clay, P. N. 1981. *Two Multi-phase Barrow Sites at Sproxton and Eaton, Leicestershire*. Leicestershire Museums Archaeological Report 2, pp.1-26.

Colcutt, S. N. and Field, N. 1990. *Land at West Deeping*. Oxford Archaeological Associates and Lindsey Archaeological Services. Unpublished report.

Crawford, O. G. S. 1953. *Archaeology in the Field*. pp.107-22.

Dyer, J. F. 1961. Dray's ditches, Bedfordshire, and early Iron Age territorial boundaries in the eastern Chilterns. *Antiquaries Journal*, vol.41, pp.32-43.

Entwistle, R. 1994. The development and application of the field methodology. In Bradley *et al.* 1994, pp.26-68.

Everson, P. 1978. Aerial reconnaissance in north Lincolnshire. *Lincolnshire History and Archaeology*, vol.13, pp.82-83.

Everson, P. 1979. Pre-Roman linear boundaries north of Lincoln. *Lincolnshire History and Archaeology*, vol.14, pp.74-75.

Everson, P. 1980. North Lincolnshire, aerial reconnaissance. *Lincolnshire History and Archaeology*, vol.15, p.80.

Everson, P. and Knowles, G. C. 1993. The Anglo-Saxon bounds of Æt Bearuwe. *The English Place-Name Society*, vol.25, pp.19-37.

Fearn, K. 1993. Excavations of two pits of an alignment at Moor Lane, Long Bennington. *Lincolnshire History and Archaeology*, vol.28, pp.5-8.

Field, N. 1980. Lincoln, Nettleham Glebe. *Lincolnshire History and Archaeology*, vol.15, pp.77-78.

Grimes, W. F. 1951. The Jurassic Way. In *Aspects of Archaeology in Britain and Beyond, Essays Presented to O. G. S. Crawford* edited by W. F. Grimes, pp.144-71.

Hingley, R. 1989. *Pit Alignment Boundaries*. Monuments Protection Programme Class Description. English Heritage Unpublished document.

Hunn, J. and Rackham, D. J., forthcoming. *Excavations on a Multi-Period Landscape at Rectory Farm, West Deeping, Lincolnshire*. British Archaeological Reports, British Series.

Huntingford, G. W. B. 1934. Defences against cattle-raiding. *Antiquity* vol.8, pp.429-36.

Jones, D. 1988. Aerial reconnaissance and prehistoric and Romano-British archaeology in northern Lincolnshire – A sample survey. *Lincolnshire History and Archaeology*, vol.23, pp.5-30.

Jones, D. 1998. Long barrows and Neolithic elongated enclosures in Lincolnshire: An analysis of the air photographic evidence. *Proceedings of the Prehistoric Society*, vol.64.

Johnson, A. E. 1994. *Land at Greetwell, Lincolnshire*. Oxford Archaeotechnics Ltd. Unpublished report.

Laskey, J. 1979. Messingham pit alignments. *Lincolnshire History and Archaeology*, vol.14, pp.73-74.

Liddle, P. 1982. *Leicestershire Archaeology: The Present State of Knowledge, vol.1 to the end of the Roman Period*. Leicestershire Museums Archaeological Report 4.

Mackie, D. 1993. Prehistoric ditch systems at Ketton and Tixover, Rutland. *Transactions of the Leicestershire Archaeological and Historical Society*, vol.67, pp.1-14.

May, J. 1993. The later Iron Age. In Bennett & Bennett, eds 1993, pp.12-13.

Murphy, P. forthcoming. Lincolnshire: Data from plant macrofossils on plant food foraging, arable farming and palaeoenvironments. Paper presented at The Archaeology of Lincolnshire: A Research Framework conference on 28 May 1998.

Palmer, R. 1996. Air photo interpretation and the Lincolnshire Fenland. *Landscape History*, vol.18, pp.5-16.

Palmer-Brown, C. 1994. *Welton-Lincoln Trunkmain: Excavations Along the Pipeline Route*. Pre-Construct Archaeology. Unpublished report.

Phillips, C. W. 1934. The present state of archaeology in Lincolnshire, part II. *Archaeological Journal*, vol.91, pp.97-187.

Pickering, J. 1978. The Jurassic spine. *Current Archaeology*. No.64, vol.6:5, pp.140-43.

Pickering, J. 1988. Aerial archaeology on the Fen edge in south Lincolnshire. *Fenland Research*, vol.5, pp.39-46.

Pickering, J. 1992. Pit alignments. *Current Archaeology*. No.130, vol.11:10, pp.417-19.

Pollard, J. 1996. Iron Age riverside pit alignments at St. Ives, Cambridgeshire. *Proceedings of the Prehistoric Society*, vol.62, pp.93-115.

Raymond, F. 1990. (revised Overy, C. G. D.) *Linear Boundaries (Prehistoric)*. Monuments Protection Programme Class Description. English Heritage Unpublished document.

Riley, D. N. 1980. *Early Landscape from the Air: Studies of Cropmarks in South Yorkshire and north Nottinghamshire*. Sheffield.

Spratt, D. A. 1982. The Cleave Dyke system. *Yorkshire Archaeological Journal*, vol.54, pp.33-52.

Spratt, D. A. 1987. *Linear Earthworks of the Tabular Hills, Northeast Yorkshire*. Sheffield.

Spratt, D. A. 1993. Prehistoric and medieval boundaries on the North York Moors. In *Yorkshire Boundaries*, edited by H. E. Jean Le Patourel, M. H. Long and M. F. Pickles, pp.85-94.

Spratt, D. A. and White, R. F. 1986. Further information on the Cleave Dyke. *Yorkshire Archaeological Journal*, vol.58, pp.195-97.

Taylor, C. 1998. *Brauncewell Limestone Quarry Extension Excavation 1997*. Lindsey Archaeological Services and Network Archaeology. Unpublished report.

Tipper, J. B. 1994. *Archaeological Excavations at Brauncewell Limestone Quarry*. Lindsey Archaeological Services. Unpublished report.

Whitwell, J. B. 1982. *The Coritani: Some Aspects of the Iron Age Tribe and the Roman Civitas*. British Archaeological Reports, British Series 99. Oxford.

Van de Noort, R. and Ellis, S. 1998. *Wetland Heritage of the Ancholme and Lower Trent Valleys: An Archaeological Survey*. Hull.

The Cropmark Evidence for Prehistoric and Roman Settlement in West Lincolnshire.

Helen Winton

Introduction.

The aim of this paper is to present the new information, provided by the National Mapping Programme (NMP) survey of Lincolnshire, on the prehistoric and Roman settlement of west Lincolnshire. The area of west Lincolnshire defined for the purposes of this article is illustrated in figure 1 and encompasses the distinctive landscape zones of the Lincoln Edge (Heath) and part of the Trent Valley (Boutwood, this volume).

Previous archaeological investigations have been largely based on finds and excavations. May (1976a, 1976b, 1984) and Whitwell (1970, 1982, 1995) provide general accounts of the region in the prehistoric and Roman periods respectively. Todd (1973) also places the county in the wider context of the 'territory' of the *Corieltauvi*[1], in the late Iron Age and Roman periods, and uses aerial photographs to illustrate some of the settlements. Since the 1970s Everson (1977, 1978, 1980, 1982), Everson and Hayes (1984) and Pickering (1979, 1989, 1995) have published aerial photographs and analyses of certain aspects of prehistoric activity in the region. Jones (1988) details the recovery, distribution, dating and classification of archaeological sites in a transect across the north of the county. The mapping of the rest of west Lincolnshire, undertaken as part of the NMP survey, provides a context within which to consider existing archaeological knowledge, and a chance to analyse certain settlement types and patterns in the wider context of the East Midlands (Bewley & Jones 1992).

Identification and dating of settlement visible as cropmarks.

The purpose of this section is to discuss definitions of settlement in the late prehistoric, Roman and early post-Roman periods, and to provide a framework for dating cropmarks of settlements and associated features.

It is unclear how representative the cropmark sites are of prehistoric or Roman settlement in west Lincolnshire. The cropmark sites illustrated are distinguishable from supposed Neolithic and Bronze Age monuments recorded in the course of the survey. For example Neolithic long barrows (Jones 1998), numerous Bronze Age round barrows, possible Neolithic 'causewayed enclosures' near Uffington and Barholm, a possible Neolithic/Bronze Age cursus in the Welland valley, pit defined avenues near Ryhall and multiple pit alignments near Harlaxton, are presumed to be Neolithic or Bronze Age ritual monuments. Similarly what appear to be major boundaries are considered elsewhere (Boutwood, this volume).

The cropmark sites under discussion are thought to be the remains of settlement, or indicators of agricultural activity, for example field systems, and generally take the form of enclosures, or systems of boundaries forming enclosures. For ease of use these have been divided into a number of categories based on their form. The simple forms are defined as enclosures with little or no attached or apparently associated features (Fig.2). The complex forms are defined as a number of enclosures conjoined and/or overlapping, sometimes linked by systems of boundaries and trackways. This group divides into a number of sub-groups: those apparently focused on a single enclosure with possibly subsidiary enclosures attached (Figs 3.1-10); those comprising a number of conjoined enclosures, sometimes in a linear pattern (Figs 3.11-16); those incorporating a rectilinear and/or double ditched element (Figs 4.1-3); and those attached to roads, tracks and boundaries (Figs 5, 6). It is hoped to show how these sites fit into an understandable pattern of settlement in the prehistoric and Roman periods and to provide a basic dating framework for use, and revision, in future research.

Archaeological evidence of occupation is usually represented by the remains of domestic structures, rubbish pits or domestic debris spreads. These types of features are often too insubstantial to form cropmarks and are difficult to identify from the air especially when not enclosed by a substantial ditch. Cropmarks of pits have been found apparently associated with some of the enclosures in the survey area but it is not possible to say if they relate to domestic use of the sites (Figs 2.1.1, 2.1.10, 2.1.17, 2.2.13, 2.2.16, 2.2.18). The round-house is usually an indication of pre-Roman settlement but use of this form of house did continue in the Roman period (Wilson 1974, p.255), for example the settlement at Staunton, Nottinghamshire (Todd 1975) consisted of circular timber huts, and pottery evidence suggested the main occupation was late third and early fourth century AD. The Iron Age round house is not well represented in the excavated archaeological record in Lincolnshire (Willis 1997, pp.208-09) but in west Lincolnshire (Fig.1) this survey has recorded the cropmarks of at least 120 circular features which may be the remains of the foundations, or the drip gully formed by water running off the roof, of Iron Age or Roman round-houses (Figs 2.1.10, 2.2.22, 2.3.10, 2.3.12, 3.6-8, 3.10). Cropmarks of a number of square enclosures of similar dimensions to the hut circles, measuring in the range ten to fifteen metres, have been interpreted, depending on their context, either as possible buildings, if found near enclosures thought to indicate settlements, (Figs 3.2, 3.15, 5a.3), or as Iron Age square barrows[2] if they seem apparently isolated from settlement features (for example the possible square barrow cemetery near Dembleby).

The majority of the cropmark sites recorded in this survey did not have features which suggested domestic occupation. Lack of evidence of occupation in some cases may be due to the poor quality of the aerial photographic cover or the relatively slight nature of the domestic structures: hut circles or post-built buildings, which need very good conditions to show as cropmarks. In some cases the enclosures may only have had seasonal or temporary occupation which left little tangible occupation evidence. Some of the enclosures with no evidence of internal occupation may still be closely associated with a settlement. Excavated examples of this have been found at the second phase of the Iron Age and Roman settlement at Wakerley, Northamptonshire (Jackson & Ambrose 1978, p.172) where the occupation area was thought to be adjacent to a contemporary and apparently unoccupied enclosure, and at Twywell, Northamptonshire (Jackson 1975, Fig.3) where the occupation extended well beyond the enclosed area. Caution is therefore required when classifying sites simply as open or enclosed settlement.

Cropmarks of enclosures may represent the remains of a field system or of some other land use but are still an indication of human activity and, by implication, settlement, in the vicinity. At excavations at Welland Bank Pit, a possible field system, which showed as a cropmark, was adjacent to the occupation areas which were not visible on aerial photographs (T. Lane personal communication; Taylor 1996). At Willington, Derbyshire (Wheeler 1979, pp.103-04) a system of ditches was laid out in the early Iron Age which was maintained through the Iron Age. Many phases of huts were associated with this field system in contrast to many other Iron Age settlements which are situated within a substantial homestead enclosure. It is

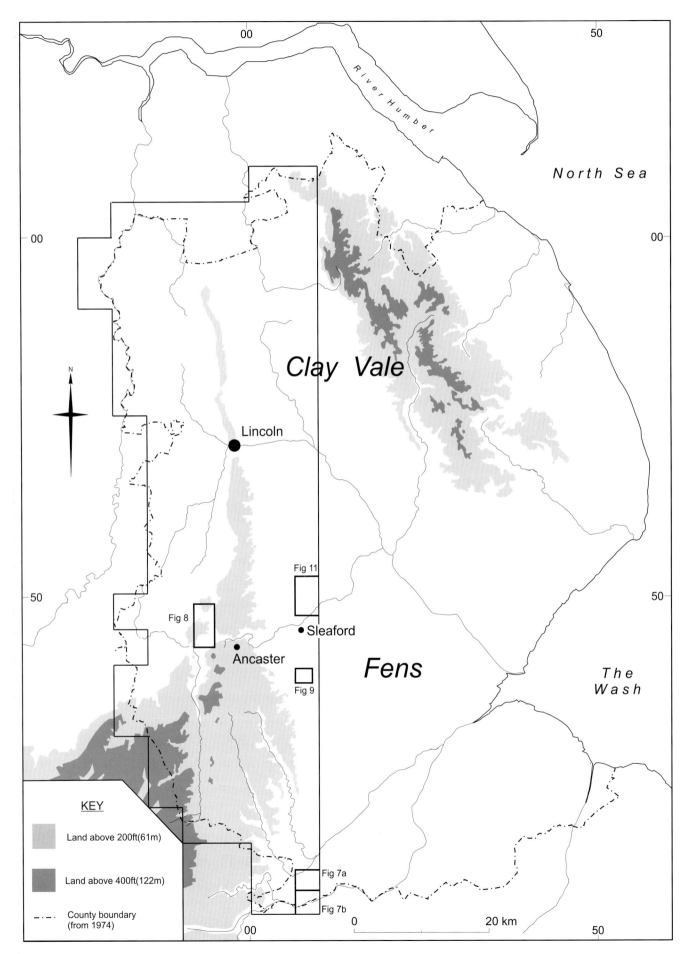

Fig.1. Map of the area defined in the text as 'west Lincolnshire' showing the location of the areas in Figs 7-9 and 11 (© Crown copyright. RCHME 1998).

therefore possible that occupation sites lie adjacent rather than within the enclosures or field systems recorded in this present survey.

The cropmarks of a settlement may represent only the latest phase of development, as at Holme Pierrepont, Nottinghamshire (O'Brien 1979, p.303, Fig.2, site 3) or alternatively cropmarks, comprised of several elements which appear as a single phase, may be a palimpsest of many contemporary, contiguous and separate phases. At the excavated settlement at Wakerley, Northamptonshire (Jackson

& Ambrose 1978, Fig.4) an unenclosed occupation area, adjacent to a possible stock enclosure, is later enclosed. This results in two apparently conjoined enclosures, of similar form, from different phases of development on the site. At Gamston, Nottinghamshire (Knight 1992, pp.83-84, Fig.4, plate 1) a series of apparently conjoined enclosures, visible as cropmarks, encompassed four phases of quite different forms of remains from the late first millennium BC to the mid first century AD. These comprised an open settlement, then an enclosure, and then a rectilinear boundary system and finally another

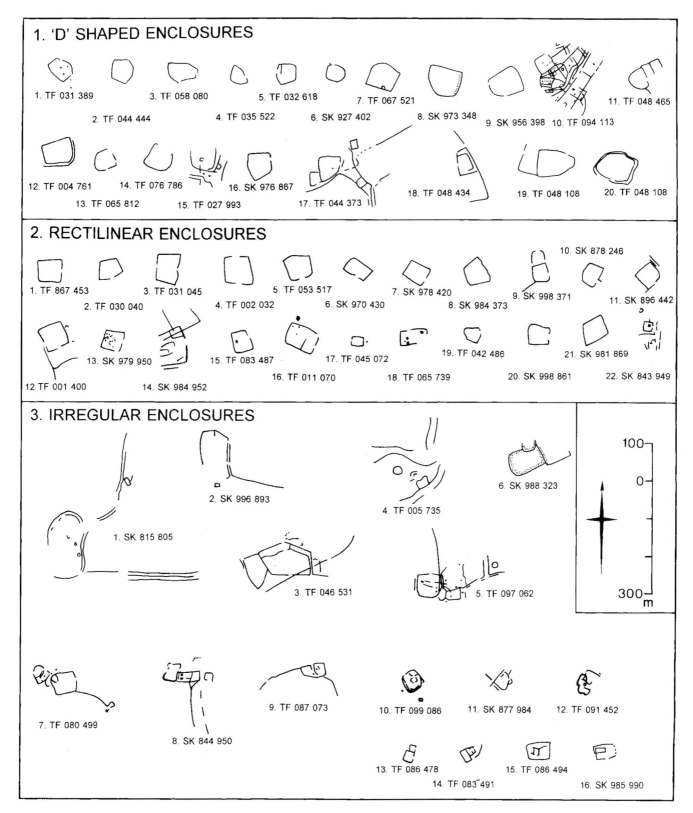

Fig.2. Examples of 'simple' possible Iron Age or Roman settlement enclosures (© Crown copyright. RCHME 1998).

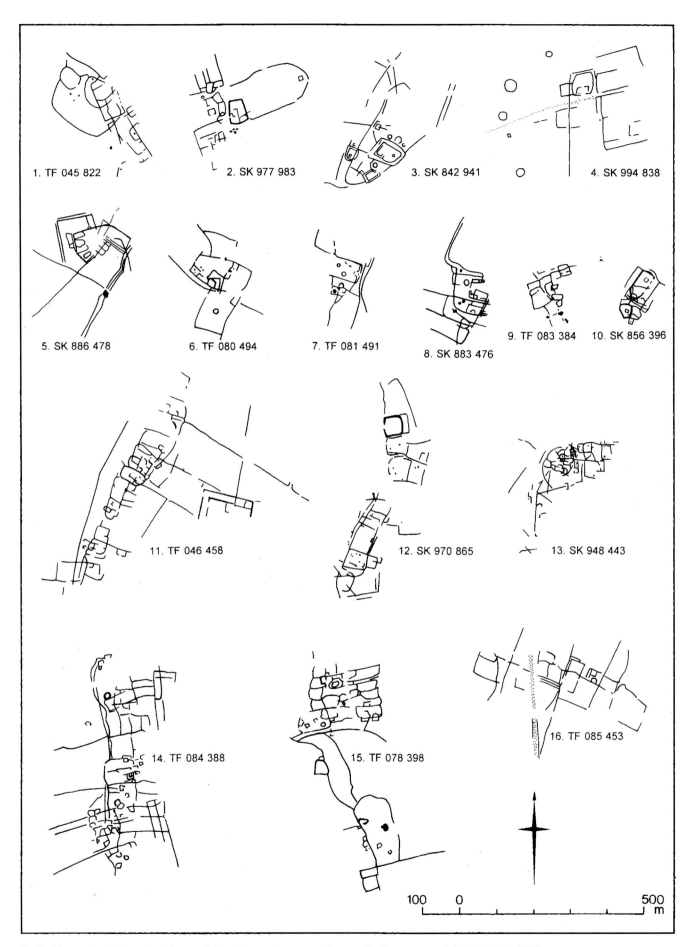

Fig.3. Examples of 'complex' forms of Iron Age or Roman settlement (© Crown copyright. RCHME 1998).

enclosure, all of which were on a similar alignment and possibly incorporated elements of previous phases, yet appeared as a single phase on aerial photographs. Complex plans may be the result of many phases of a long-lived settlement or of settlement shift over a long period of time. For example at an extensive cropmark complex at Clay Lane, Northamptonshire, excavation revealed that only small areas of the whole complex were occupied at any one time from the middle Iron Age through to the fourth century AD (Windell 1983, p.41). Therefore sites interpreted as complex settlements in the survey, could represent many phases of simple settlement forms.

Although one must be aware of the limiting factors of cropmark evidence much can still be done to suggest possible dates for certain types of monument. Few of the cropmarks in west Lincolnshire have readily available dating evidence as there is a poor correlation with existing finds evidence, available through the SMR and NMR. Relative chronologies for cropmark features can be proposed when they are in close proximity to other datable monuments, for example relationships to recognisable Roman features, as at Kirmington (Jones & Whitwell, 1991). However the majority of the enclosures recorded in this survey usually occurred in isolation from other cropmarks. Until further evidence is forthcoming, the only means of suggesting the possible date of these cropmarks is by morphological comparison with the plans of dated settlements (Palmer 1984, pp.9-11; Whimster 1989, pp.26-34, 66-68; Stoertz 1997, p.13).

Pre-Iron Age settlement.

There is a lack of evidence from aerial photographs for early prehistoric (Mesolithic and Palaeolithic) settlement. The evidence of Neolithic and Bronze Age activity, from this survey, appears to be restricted to the funerary or ritual class of monument. However it is possible that some of the cropmark enclosures do have a Bronze Age date. A cropmark site, excavated at Kirmond-le-Mire, on the Lincolnshire Wolds (Field & Knight 1992) comprised 'at least four sub-square enclosures', and although dating is problematic, has a possible date range from the late Bronze Age to the mid-first millennium BC. On excavation of a cropmark site at Billingborough, on the Lincolnshire Fen edge, four phases of occupation were identified from the early to mid Bronze Age, and of the features visible as cropmarks, three sides of a ditched rectilinear enclosure were thought to enclose an occupation area which was abandoned and replaced with a possible field system (Chowne 1978, 1980).

A possible predictive model for identifying Bronze Age enclosures from aerial photographs has been proposed for the Yorkshire Wolds based on topographical and morphological similarities to Bronze Age enclosures excavated in the area (Stoertz 1997, pp.46-47). However the variance in Lincolnshire in the excavated Bronze Age enclosures, in terms of shape, size and location, means that no single site type has yet been identified with which to classify potential Bronze Age enclosures in this survey.

Iron Age settlement.

A recognisable territory and material culture for the *Corieltauvi* is represented in the numismatic, ceramic and metalwork evidence in the East Midlands (May 1976a, pp.156-201; Cunliffe 1991, pp.175-77). The diversity in the evidence and plans of excavated Iron Age settlements in the east and south Midlands, is also found in the cropmark evidence in west Lincolnshire.

Simple Enclosures.

A number of single 'D'-shaped enclosures were identified (Fig.2.1), similar to the late Iron Age enclosures at

Colsterworth, Lincolnshire (May 1976a, p.192, Fig.96), and Enderby, Leicestershire (Clay 1992). Also recorded (Fig.2.2) were a number of enclosures with superficial similarities to the excavated irregular rectilinear Iron Age enclosures at Wakerley, Northamptonshire (Jackson & Ambrose 1978), Clay Lane, Northamptonshire (Windell 1983), Fisherwick, Staffordshire, (O'Brien 1979) or the many enclosures dated to the Iron Age in Warwickshire (Hingley 1989b, Fig.9.9).

Many of the 'simple' enclosures in figure 2 have a potentially wide date range, but based on excavated examples in the East Midlands the majority probably date from the Iron Age or early Roman period. The inclusion of some of these enclosure forms in apparently more complex settlements shows that the cropmarks of some of the simpler enclosures may represent only one phase in a complex. In particular the ditches defining many of the 'irregular' enclosures may be respecting features which are not visible as cropmarks, perhaps earlier settlements or linear features.

Complex settlements.

Based on excavated examples, there appears to have been an increase in material wealth at a number of sites, through the late second century BC to the first century AD (May 1976a, 1976b, 1984; Willis 1997). In certain cases this seems to have accompanied a corresponding increase in the complexity in the form of the settlements. At the settlement at Wakerley, Northamptonshire (Jackson & Ambrose 1978), two enclosures are constructed: the first, situated adjacent to the occupation area, in the first century BC, and the second, attached to the first and enclosing the occupation area, in the first century AD. At Weekley, Northamptonshire (Jackson & Dix 1987, Fig.4) the enclosures surrounding the various phases of occupation get progressively larger from the second century BC to the later second century AD. The final phase at Enderby, Leicestershire (Clay 1992, Fig.18) is the larger 'D' shaped enclosure. At Old Sleaford, Lincolnshire (Elsdon 1997, Fig.31) and Dragonby, Lincolnshire (May 1996, Fig.5.41) the periods with evidence of material prosperity in the later Iron Age are accompanied by complex ground plans with small enclosures flanking trackways. It is possible that the more complex settlements recorded in this survey, with comparable forms to the excavated examples have a similar date range.

The cropmarks of the possible complex settlements, which are perhaps datable to the late Iron Age, seem to fall into two groups.

Firstly there are enclosures of a similar form to the 'simple' enclosures, with complex arrangements of enclosures attached (Figs 3.1-10). Some of these seem to include elaborate entrances, which range from simple tapering or thickening of terminals to more complex forms like the funnel in figure 3.8. These complex access arrangements may be comparable to the increasing sophistication in settlement form seen in the construction of entrances at Wakerley, Northamptonshire (Jackson & Ambrose 1978, p.172) in the first century BC and at Aldwincle, Northamptonshire (Jackson 1977, p.13) in the second century BC to the first century AD. A similar example of this may be seen in figure 3.7 where short stretches of ditch flank a funnel-shaped access to an enclosure.

The second possible type of complex pre-Roman settlement recorded as cropmarks in this survey (Figs 3.11-16) has similarities to the complexes of small enclosures along trackways at the excavated Iron Age settlements at Dragonby (May 1996), Old Sleaford (Elsdon 1997) and Fengate (Pryor 1984). Until there is further investigation of these cropmark sites it will be difficult to ascertain if they are even contemporary or have a similar character to the large rural settlements like Dragonby and Fengate, or the possibly proto-urban nature of Sleaford.

The more complex settlements existed alongside smaller settlements, for example the enclosed and unenclosed first century AD settlement at Ancaster and Colsterworth

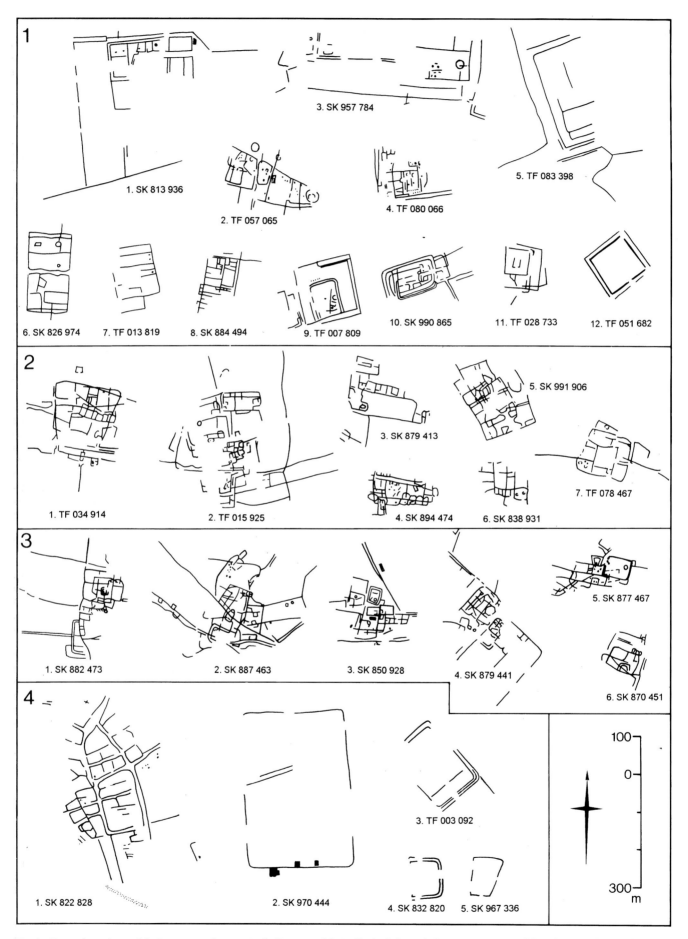

Fig.4. Examples of possible Roman settlement including possible 'villas' (1-3) and the Roman town of Segelocum *(4.1) and Roman camps and forts (4.2-5) (© Crown copyright. RCHME 1998).*

respectively (May 1976a, pp.133-41, 192). The remains of the apparently large settlements could therefore represent a pattern of small shifting settlements producing a large area of cropmarks of apparently contemporary, but in fact contiguous or overlapping, use of the site.

The inherent bias, in a survey based on aerial photographs, towards ditched enclosures should not be allowed to sway consideration of the types of site regarded as prevalent at any given period in the Iron Age. Open settlements co-existed with the enclosed settlements of the Iron Age, for example the two unenclosed settlements near Ancaster, one, at Castle Lime Pit, apparently occupied in the mid third century BC, and the other probably occupied in the first centuries BC and AD (May 1976a, pp.133-41, 175-77, Fig.68). Excavated evidence also suggests the presence of ditched enclosures from at least the second century BC to the mid first century AD. For example a ditched enclosure containing hut circles at Fisherwick, Staffordshire was dated to 180 BC $\pm$ 100 (Smith 1977, p.60) and the excavated enclosure containing hut circles at Colsterworth, Lincolnshire (May 1976a, p.192) flourished in the mid first century AD.

The diversity in the plans of the settlements transcribed as part of this project parallels that of the excavated Iron Age settlements in the East Midlands and no single type of Iron Age settlement appears to be predominant. Although cropmark sites of a similar extent to the large, possibly defended, enclosures (Whitwell 1982) already identified in Lincolnshire, were recorded during this survey (Figs 2.3.1-4) these remain to be shown to be Iron Age forts or large stock enclosures similar to the possible example at Tattershall Thorpe (Chowne *et al.* 1986, p.184). What has not been identified in this survey of west Lincolnshire, with any certainty, is 'open' settlement, or the type of site with a relatively small curvilinear enclosure large enough to enclose only one hut, such as that excavated at Brigstock and Draughton, Northamptonshire (Cunliffe 1991, p.235, Fig.12.14; Jackson 1983; Grimes 1961). In addition open settlements within areas of land division, as at Willington, Derbyshire (Wheeler 1979) or adjacent to a small enclosure, as at Twywell, Northamptonshire (Jackson 1975, Fig.3) may have existed in west Lincolnshire but have not been positively identified in this survey.

The problems of dating settlements to the Iron Age with certainty is compounded by the continuity of certain settlement forms into the Roman period.

Roman settlement.

The extent to which the indigenous population was already familiar with Roman culture and artefacts, through trade and other contacts with the continent, is not known but it is clear that there had been contact prior to the invasion. The Roman conquest undoubtedly brought changes to the region and man-made features of a different type did develop which can be identified from the air (Frere & St Joseph 1983).

Military activity.

The contribution of aerial photography to Roman military studies has been amply demonstrated by the numerous discoveries of forts and temporary camps in the British Isles (Frere & St Joseph 1983; Welfare & Swan 1995). The known military installations, in particular the forts at Ancaster, Great Casterton and Littleborough and the temporary camp at Ancaster were mapped as part of the project (all but the fort at Ancaster are illustrated in figure 4.4). The survey, however, did not add to the known military features in the survey area and it is becoming less likely that significant numbers of new military installations remain to be discovered from the air. Only one possible temporary camp was tentatively identified at the head of the Glen valley (Fig.4.4.5) but its attribution as a Roman military feature is doubtful.

Villas and rural settlements.

There was a poor correlation between cropmark sites thought to have a possible Roman date and Roman settlements already identified from finds and building material in west Lincolnshire.

The majority of the evidence for Roman villas in the survey is in the form of double-ditched enclosures. The association of a villa with a double-ditched enclosure is seen at Lockington, Leicestershire (Clay 1985, Fig.2), Cromwell, Nottinghamshire (Todd 1973, plate 21) and at Winterton, Lincolnshire (Todd 1973, plate 22). A number of similar examples were found in the survey (Fig.4.1) and these vary in form and completeness. Fragments of a possible double-ditched enclosure (Fig.4.1.3) were found associated with the excavated villa at Scampton (Whitwell 1970, pp.82-83), to the north of Lincoln.

The identification of Roman buildings from the air can be successful (Wilson 1974, p.256) but requires good conditions for the formation of cropmarks, especially when the building has no associated features or its location has not been previously identified by other means, for example by find scatters. The few buildings identified in this survey were all close to the river Welland, situated on soils very responsive to the formation of cropmarks. A single isolated building was recorded as a rectangular enclosure, to the north of Stamford, east of the excavated villa near Great Casterton which did not show as cropmarks. To the north-west of Barnack, a simple rectangular house divided into rooms possibly of the type referred to as a 'cottage house' (Hingley 1989a, Fig.15), was recorded and is apparently associated with a series of irregular enclosures (Fig.4.1.2). To the north-east of Barnack (Fig.4.1.4) cropmarks of a double row of pits, apparently associated with a number of rectilinear enclosures, (St Joseph 1973, plate XVa, Fig.1a), proved on excavation to be the remains of a third- to fourth-century AD basilican building (Simpson 1966, pp.22-23). A possible parallel to this (St Joseph 1973; Wilson 1974) is situated to the north-east of Barholm (Fig.2.1.10). This double row of pits appears to be enclosed by an 'Iron Age type' enclosure and is a further indication of the difficulty in dating and phasing complex sites.

Other possible villa sites are indicated by cropmarks of arrangements of more irregular double-ditched enclosures and small paddocks, often arranged around a central 'courtyard'. An example of this was partially excavated at Lynch Farm, Peterborough (Jones 1975, pp.132-34, Fig.2), where the main occupation appears to have been in the third century AD, perhaps with generations of the same family whose burial plots were adjacent to the settlement. Similar arrangements of enclosures to those at Lynch Farm have been identified during the survey (Fig.4.2) near the upper River Witham, and on the wind blown sands on the lower dipslope of the limestone scarp to the north of Lincoln. This type of settlement is common on the Wolds (Jones, this volume).

Based on the frequency of rectilinear double-ditched enclosures at Roman settlements, cropmarks have been interpreted as having a possible Roman phase (Fig.4.3) when they incorporate a double-ditched element, often as part of a complex of overlapping enclosures. The apparent great number of contiguous and contemporary phases, probably represented by the different alignments of overlapping enclosures, at these sites provides a contrast to some of the apparently regularly laid out villa sites (Fig.4.1). Further investigation could ascertain whether the regularly laid out sites do represent a new and/or single phase of development of a settlement.

Enclosures associated with villas or Roman rural settlements are not always rectilinear and/or double ditched. The villa excavated at Norton Disney, Lincolnshire (Oswald & Buxton 1937, plate XLV) was surrounded by two phases of a third- and fourth-century, curvilinear, double-ditched enclosure with a

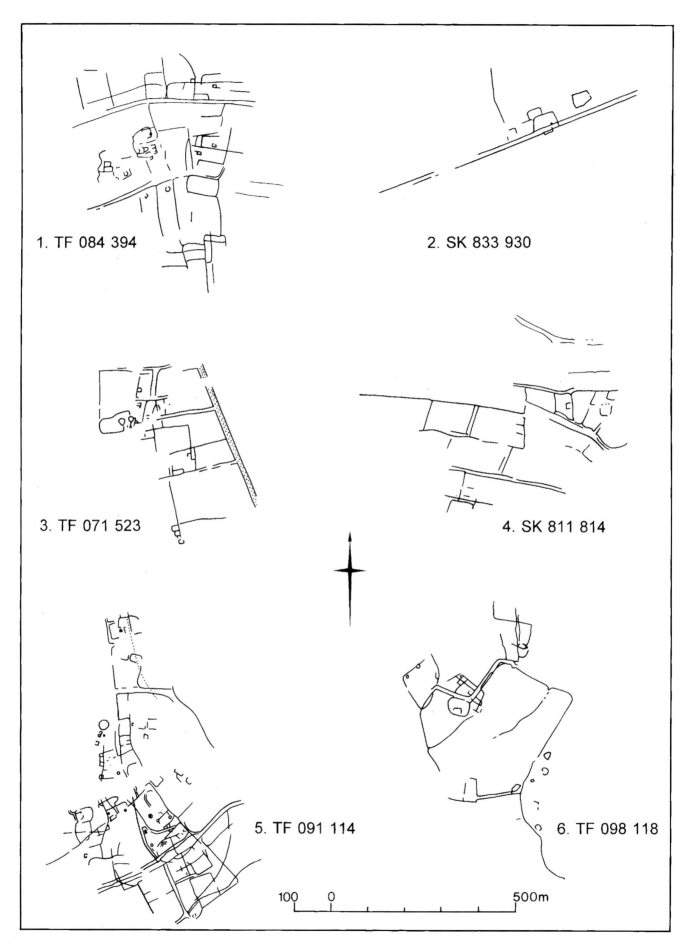

1. TF 084 394

2. SK 833 930

3. TF 071 523

4. SK 811 814

5. TF 091 114

6. TF 098 118

100   0   500m

Fig.5a. Examples of settlements associated with Roman roads (1-3), or focused on trackways (4-6) (© Crown copyright. RCHME 1998).

substantial gatehouse. If seen as a cropmark the enclosure could easily be confused with an Iron Age or non-villa settlement. Similarly at Mansfield Woodhouse, Nottinghamshire (Oswald 1949, p.2), stone buildings developed from a late first-century AD settlement consisting of wooden huts in a single-ditched enclosure.

Towns and small towns.

The cropmarks of the small town of *Segelocum* (Fig.4.4.1), near Littleborough, Nottinghamshire in the Trent valley (Riley *et al.*

1995) and parts of the Roman town defences at Great Casterton were mapped as part of the survey. A series of enclosures (Fig.3.16) apparently cut by a section of Roman road to the south east of Old Sleaford, could be part of the Roman phases of settlement there. However the majority of the small towns, roadside settlements (Whitwell 1982, 1995) or 'local centres' (Hingley 1989a, pp.25-29) identified in Lincolnshire have proved problematic to identify from aerial photographs. Excavated examples in the region of the survey area include Hibaldstow (Smith 1987 pp.25-29, 189-98, Figs 2-3, 10-14), Sapperton (Simmons 1995), and Thistleton (Lewis 1966, pp.84,

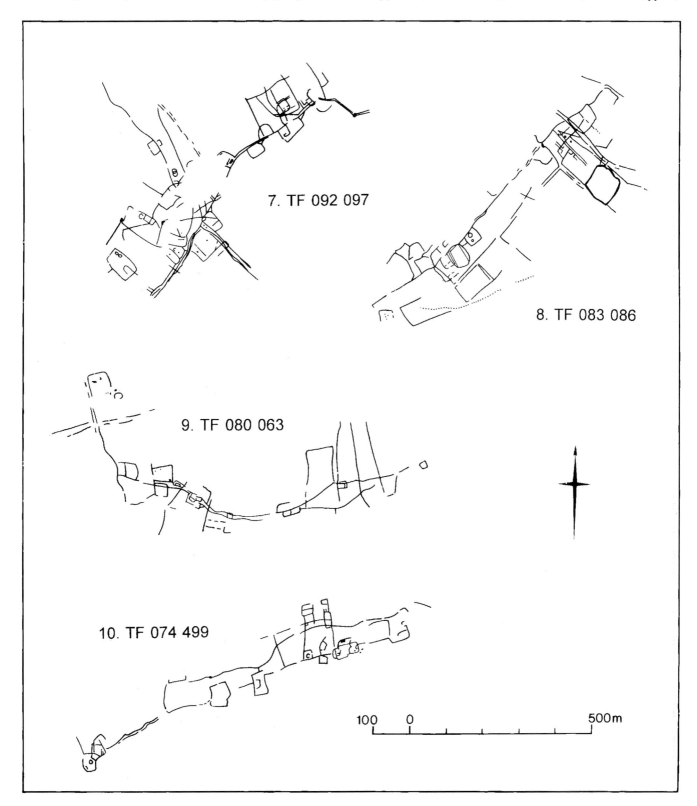

Fig.5b. Examples of settlements focused on trackways (7-10) (© Crown copyright. RCHME 1998).

93-94, 146) where the villa, temple and temenos ditch were revealed as cropmarks.

Roman roads and settlement.

Some of the possible settlements found in the survey have been dated to the Roman period because of direct associations with a Roman road. For example cropmarks of settlements linked by side roads to a Roman road were recorded during the survey, south of Sleaford, near Threekingham (Figs 5a.1 & 9), apparently attached to Mareham Lane (Margary 1973, pp.234-35, RR260), and also associated with Bloxholm Lane (Margary 1973, pp.234-35, RR260), near Ruskington to the north of Sleaford (Figs 5.3 & 11). On the same Roman road to the north of Sleaford, near Moor Farm, a side road extends west from the Roman road (Fig.11) perhaps indicating there is a settlement in the vicinity that is not visible on aerial photographs. Re-evaluation of the excavated sites near Tallington (Simpson 1966, p.21; Simpson *et al.* 1993, pp.67-68) has suggested that some of the enclosures and droveways which appeared to be associated with the Roman road King Street, and by implication of Roman date, have a date range from the late Bronze Age/early Iron Age to the middle Iron Age. As Pryor (Simpson *et al.* 1993, pp.67-68) points out in his discussion of the excavation this could indicate King Street is of prehistoric origin but until further work is carried out the relationships between these features will not be fully understood. The implications of the results at Tallington could be that the sites interpreted here, with a Roman date, could also have earlier origins than the Roman road and droveway to which they appear to relate.

A group of enclosures attached to a stretch of parallel ditches (Fig.5.2) to the south-west of Blyton, north of Gainsborough, may be an example of a roadside settlement but is not on a known stretch of Roman road. This has morphological similarities to a more extensive example recently photographed near Dry Doddington, near the Lincolnshire/Nottinghamshire border (Boutwood 1998). The settlements discovered in close proximity to Roman roads may be important, if placed at a strategic distance along a Roman road. A site near Owmby Cliff Farm on the limestone uplands, to the north of Lincoln and currently under investigation by English Heritage (Olivier 1996, pp.29-30), is strategically placed between Lincoln and the Humber. It has been identified as an important Iron Age and Roman settlement, largely because of the quantity and quality of finds recovered from the site (May 1976a, p.191; Whitwell 1970, pp.67-68). The site is, however, morphologically similar to Iron Age settlements and it is unclear to what extent they relate to activity in the Roman period (Fig.3.12).

Prehistoric and/or Roman features.

The difficulty in positively identifying many of the cropmark sites recorded in this survey as either late prehistoric or Roman has meant that a large class of settlements has been assigned a broad date. These features have been classified by their form for the purposes of analysis. The similarity in form could be an indication of similarity in function or character but this remains to be investigated.

Enclosures and trackways.

The trackways are often defined by double ditches, perhaps for drainage or controlling livestock, and differ from those of a Roman road in their irregularity of form and direction. The enclosures and trackways have a limited distribution in the very south of the survey area (Figs 5a.5-6, 5b.7-10) except figure 5b.10 which is near Ruskington to the north of Sleaford. These have similarities with the extensive systems of Roman settlements, linked by droveways, found on the Fenland, which although thought to be largely Roman in date may have earlier

origins (Palmer 1996, Fig.2). Figures 5.5-8 appear to form part of an extensive, possibly Roman, landscape of features (Figs 7a, 7b) which extends eastwards along similar alignments, around Langtoft, on the Fen edge; the parts outside the survey area have been mapped by R. Palmer (1996, p.5).

Part of the east end of the east-west ditch in figure 5b.9 has been excavated and a late Iron Age and early Roman date has been suggested (Pryor and French 1985, p.296). Cropmarks similar to those identified in this survey, and illustrated in figures 5b.9-10, were investigated at Alrewas, Staffordshire (Smith 1977, p.59, Fig.5). The features at Alrewas were the subject of intense field survey, and an absence of Romano-British finds possibly indicates an earlier date. Smith interprets the development of the droveways as an indication of a shift of emphasis away from arable farming towards stock farming, possibly as a result of the deteriorating climate at the end of the first millennium BC which appears to be confirmed by the pollen spectrum at Dragonby (Smith 1977, p.59). Although similarity of form is no guarantee of similar date, the model for development at Alrewas could possibly apply to the sites illustrated in figures 5.9-10 and be an indication of an emphasis on stock farming.

Enclosures and boundaries.

These features have been grouped (Fig.6) simply because they have a boundary attached but Boutwood (this volume) discusses the problems of dating linear features, and the assignment of simple enclosures to any phase of the prehistoric or Roman periods is equally difficult. There appear to be two groups: those consisting of a series of small enclosures attached to a ditched boundary (Fig.6.1), often referred to as 'washing lines', and those where fewer, and larger, enclosures are attached to a ditched boundary (Fig.6.2). Where a number of small enclosures are associated with a boundary, some appear attached and others overlie the boundary, perhaps representing a number of different chronological phases. This could indicate that the ditched boundary or the route of the boundary was a steady feature, and by implication important, along which the enclosures were constructed. At Willington, Derbyshire (Wheeler 1979), a number of phases of hut circles were associated within a steady system of boundaries which were re-cut and maintained.

An example of an enclosure attached to a pit alignment was found near the River Welland (Fig.6.2.8) to the north-east of Tallington. This could be similar to an excavated pit alignment attached to a settlement near Barnack in the Welland valley, (Mackreth & O'Neill 1979, p.23) which was middle Iron Age in date at the latest, and established before c.300 BC.

The possible relationships of settlement to the larger multiple boundaries are also discussed by Boutwood in this volume. Enclosures attached to apparently isolated boundaries raise questions of land allotment and 'ownership'. O'Brien suggests that Iron Age enclosures of the fourth to second century BC are stable landholdings within systems of firm land division. It is difficult to see how the linear boundaries with attached enclosures found in this survey function; these features (Fig.6.2) do not appear to have a direct relationship to local topography, such as cutting off the head of a valley or controlling access to a water supply. This could mean they are fragments of a larger system of land division organised without regard for the local topography and more elements of the system have yet to be discovered.

Field systems may provide evidence for arable farming, as the land divisions may have been used to protect crops or to provide drainage. A number of possible settlement enclosures have been recorded in close proximity to possible field systems, for example figure 11. It is hard to say in these cases if the land division systems are contemporary or associated with possible settlement enclosures unless specifically linked by a ditched boundary. It is possible that the kind of settlement associated with the small field systems may be characterised by features

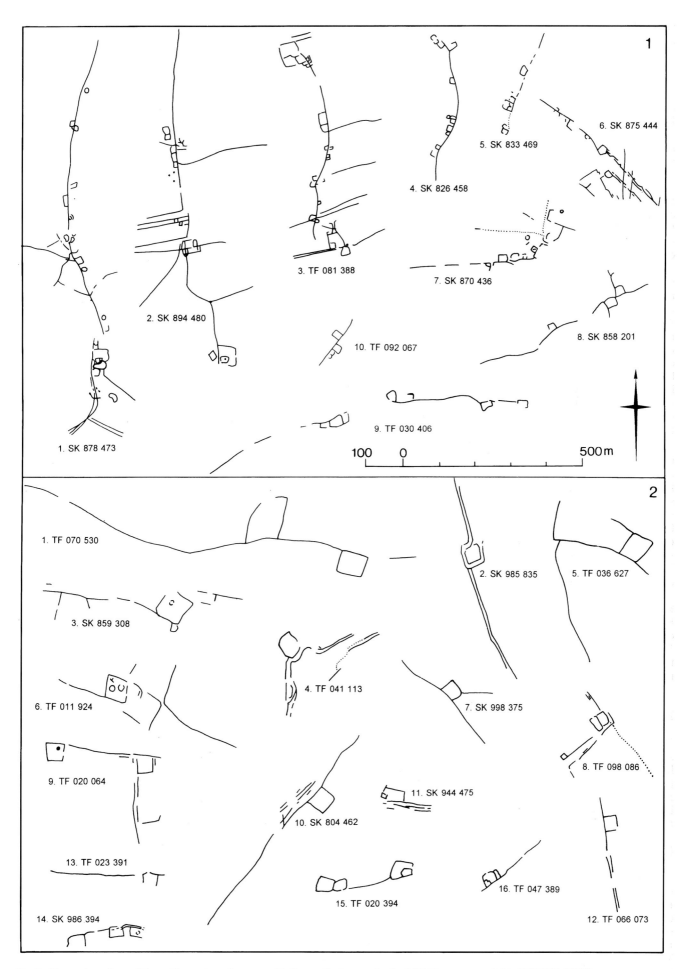

Fig.6. Examples of possible settlement enclosures with linear features attached (© Crown copyright. RCHME 1998).

that do not readily show as cropmarks. No features were recorded during the survey comparable to the 'brickwork' field systems found to the west in Nottinghamshire (Riley 1980; Deegan, forthcoming). Parts of an extensive field system were recorded on the western fringes (SK 80 80) of the survey area but these appear to form parts of systems of settlement and land division found in the Trent valley, and largely recorded as part of the RCHME Nottinghamshire NMP (Deegan, forthcoming).

Post-Roman settlement.

The settlement pattern established by the end of the Roman period has obvious implications for identification of transitional and post-Roman settlement patterns.

Identification of early medieval settlements is difficult, but not impossible from the air. The sunken featured structures associated with post-Roman settlement, can show as dark rectangular marks (Gates & O'Brien 1988) but none were positively identified in the survey. The cropmarks of the settlement at Riby cross roads (Steedman 1994, Illus.3-4) comprising a series of conjoined enclosures and pits may provide an idea of possible early medieval settlement form but would be difficult to distinguish from some of the possible Iron Age settlements. Sites similar to the Riby cross roads example found on the Yorkshire Wolds (Stoertz 1997, Fig.30) suggest these may be a particular type of post-Roman settlement. The difficulty in distinguishing these from Iron Age settlements has meant that nothing similar was positively identified in west Lincolnshire.

It is possible some of the apparently Roman settlements have a continuity of use at the site into the post-Roman period. Evidence of fifth-century activity at excavated late Roman settlements is scarce or only hinted at. Where there is evidence of Anglo-Saxon material on the site of Roman settlements it is often in the form of burials. For example at cemeteries at Great Casterton and Ancaster (Whitwell 1970, p.138), or the bodies, possibly of early medieval date found placed over the stone walls of the villa at Scampton (Whitwell 1970, pp.82-83), and similarly at Empingham in the Gwash valley (Cooper 1996, p.174, Fig.9). Cooper suggests that villa buildings survived, at least as ruins, and were considered significant enough to be a focus for burial. Finds of possible fifth- or sixth-century metalwork were found near the site of the villa at Kirmington and a possible post-Roman settlement was postulated, situated between the villa and the medieval settlement (Whitwell 1995, p.102). A similar settlement shift may have occurred at other Roman settlement sites in west Lincolnshire, including those visible as cropmarks. There is a difficulty in formulating theories of post-Roman settlement in relation to the possible Roman sites in this survey without further work. There does appear to be some consistency in the lack of evidence for post fourth-century activity at excavated late Roman settlements in the East Midlands which could be an indication of consolidation of landholdings and the resultant abandonment of certain settlements, for example Pasture Lodge Farm, Long Bennington Lincolnshire (Leary 1995), Mansfield Woodhouse, Nottinghamshire (Oswald 1949) and Norton Disney, Lincolnshire (Oswald & Buxton 1937).

Settlement in topographical context.

Distributions of archaeological data can be misleading and those derived from information on aerial photographs are no exception when influenced by non-archaeological factors (Carter, this volume). Lack of cropmarks in certain areas is quite clearly not an indication of lack of settlement, for example very few cropmarks have been found in the parish of Ropsley and Humby but fieldwalking recovered evidence of a considerable distribution of possible settlement sites (Lane 1995).

Regional contexts.

The cropmarks recorded in west Lincolnshire can be viewed in the context of other landscape zones mapped from aerial photographs. To the west of this survey area, parts of the Trent valley, surveyed as part of Nottinghamshire NMP (Deegan, forthcoming), show an extensive organised landscape of late prehistoric/Roman settlements apparently joined by large field systems. Cropmark landscapes on the Yorkshire Wolds are also characterised by linked systems of boundaries and settlement complexes (Stoertz 1997). In the Fenland, to the east of the southern portion of the survey area, cropmarks reveal extensive settlements and associated field systems linked by trackways (Palmer 1996). The character of the sites on the Lincolnshire Wolds, although in a topographically similar landscape zone appear to differ in that they consist of predominantly dispersed settlements, with fewer clusters or extensive settlements (Jones, this volume).

Within the area of the limestone edge, discussed in this paper, there appears to be no consistent distribution of the cropmarks relating to possible settlements (Carter, this volume). North of Lincoln in the areas where cropmarks occur, the pattern is that of dispersed settlements which even when found within a kilometre of each other seem unconnected. This contrasts with the south of Lincoln where the cropmarks also occur in dispersed locations but there are four areas where the cropmarks of settlements appear in closely grouped clusters and are often linked by boundaries or trackways (Figs 7-12).

Although the settlements and their distribution in west Lincolnshire, provide contrasts to the adjacent areas, many do have similarities in plan to settlements excavated elsewhere in the East Midlands, and the rest of England. However, the cropmark evidence suggests that west Lincolnshire did not have a landscape organised on a large scale, as is manifested by the extensive field systems and boundaries found elsewhere in the East Midlands. This could be because organisation of the landscape was not based on substantial physical links, such as large ditched linear boundaries, conducive to the formation of cropmarks.

It remains to be seen if the differences between the settlement patterns in west Lincolnshire and the adjacent landscape zones are significant, and a genuine indication of regional variety which could be a reflection of different land use and possibly even social organisation.

Local contexts.

The number of examples within the cropmark categories suggested in this paper, are mostly too small to provide a sufficient sample to indicate whether any one category has a preferred topographical location, such as proximity to a water supply or an upslope, or downslope, location. The 'simple' enclosures provide the single largest morphologically similar group but the problems of dating them make it meaningless to deduce anything from their overall distribution. Topographical factors governing the choice of location of settlements may have changed, for example the closer proximity of the coastline in the Iron Age, and the many advantages this may have brought to settlement on the Fen Edge (Simmons 1993, p.20) could have influenced the settlements on the eastern fringe of the survey area which look east to the Fen Edge. Social factors governing the organisation of the countryside may also have been a factor in the availability of land for settlement during the late prehistoric and Roman periods. The only unifying factor in the distribution of the cropmarks of possible settlement recorded in west Lincolnshire appears to be their location on soils conducive to cropmarks (Carter, this volume). It may therefore only be valid to compare the cropmarks within one particular type of geological zone, or on very similar soil types.

On the light soils associated with tops of the limestone escarpment to the south of Lincoln, there were few cropmarks of possible settlements, and these were usually in the form of ple enclosures (Figs 2.1.9, 2.2.9), in contrast to north of coln where simple and complex forms are found on the her ground (Figs 2.1.16, 3.12, 4.1.10). The soils are tively thin on the limestone uplands and were possibly only able for grazing or subsistence farming in the Iron Age and man periods. In the late eighteenth century, Arthur Young sidered them to be a prime candidate for improvement irsk 1957, p.80) and the associated heath placenames vive to the south of Lincoln to this day, for example lloughby, Caythorpe, Metheringham and Dunston heaths. poor soils and possible difficulty in digging into the estone may be reflected in the sparse and simple forms of losures. The variance in the forms of cropmarks found on limestone uplands north and south of Lincoln could be a ection of the different character of settlement or land use or y be the result of differing levels of evidence. The Ropsley Humby survey (Lane 1995), if the area is typical of other as south of Lincoln, would seem to suggest that the dscape was not dominated by ditched enclosures and ndaries which show as cropmarks but future aerial onnaissance may reveal further information.

Comparison of two smaller areas of similar soil type may be re appropriate for targeting future research priorities. To the th of Lincoln, to the west and east of the limestone ridge pectively, settlement clusters near Dry Doddington (Fig.8) north east of Osbournby (Fig.9) are each situated on a ket or band of drift sand and gravel amongst heavier clay s, in broad flat valleys surrounded by low hills. In both areas shing line' enclosures and boundaries appear to demarcate western limits of the settlement zone, parallel to a change in /geology type. This perhaps indicates that the settlements clustered on recognised units of land, and that whatever pens beyond the boundaries is different, whether that is re, but different, settlement, or a different type of land use. s could be an example of topographical conditions uencing the settlement distribution similar to the settlement land use patterns following the routes of the roddons in the land (Palmer 1996, Fig.6). The medieval parishes in west colnshire were often arranged to include several different types to accommodate different farming practices (Thirsk 7, p.80). The Ropsley and Humby survey (Lane 1995, p.25) nd some evidence of preference for Roman settlement ation near a change in soil or geological type. Although one st be careful not to extrapolate too much of later Iron Age Roman agricultural practices from medieval examples it is inconceivable that the boundaries at Dry Doddington and ournby could be the demarcation of different land uses or clustering could simply be the result of a preference for lements close to a variety of land types. Any future research ld concentrate on investigating the settlement patterns on the / soils around the pockets of light soils where the cropmarks ur to ascertain if the settlement pattern is significantly erent there.

haeological contexts.

relationships between features in the landscape are as ortant as the settlement sites themselves when investigating development of an area. Where cropmark features can be ed from their form, for example prehistoric funerary numents or Roman roads and villas, some phasing of the ures in a landscape can be made, as with the cropmark nplex at Kirmington (Jones & Whitwell 1991).

n the Welland valley there are complex relationships ween the funerary or 'ritual' monuments and the settlements .7). This area has already been the focus of intensive earch (Pryor & French 1985; Simpson et al. 1993). The lland valley was an area of considerable prehistoric activity uding a cursus, two causewayed enclosures and numerous nd barrows. These Neolithic and Bronze Age monuments a reminder that the settlements in the survey area did not

develop in an empty, untouched landscape. Some features appear to respect the earlier features, for example the enclosure with a barrow in its corner at TF 085 066. Other features run over the earlier features, for example the system of land division defined by pits and ditched boundaries which appear to run through the remains of barrows at TF 095 067. Adjacent to two Bronze Age/Neolithic barrow cemeteries, one incorporating a Neolithic cursus, are two villas (one is illustrated in figure 7 at TF 081 066). Settlements co-located with funerary monuments could either be interpreted as an indication of continuity of 'significant' locations or as an indication that earlier monuments had been flattened, or partially buried by later deposits.

The River Witham, where it cuts through the limestone escarpment at Lincoln appears to have been a similar focus of ritual activity, as indicated by the quantity and quality of finds retrieved from the river. There is a concentration of ritual or funerary monuments which are showing as cropmarks as the mounds of the round and long barrows stand proud of the eroding peat. However, any possible ditched enclosures which could be parts of settlements do not show as cropmarks because they are masked by the peat. Only a few possible settlements were visible on aerial photographs and these were situated on the limestone scarp where it overlooks the river valley (Figs 2.2.18, 2.3.4, 4.1.11).

The palimpsest of many periods of activity provided by the information on aerial photographs also provides an ideal opportunity for further research into the continuity and change of use of the landscape and settlement and boundary patterns.

Near Doddington Littlegate a number of boundaries appear to enclose and subdivide a roughly triangular area to the west of Temple Hill (Fig.8), and near Osbournby a similar system of boundaries appears to subdivide a roughly rectangular area (Fig.9). In both these areas the cropmarks of possible settlement enclosures appear to respect and/or mirror the alignment of the boundaries perhaps indicating a continuity of use of the boundary system. Both ends of the visible extent of a 'washing line' boundary situated to the east of Temple Hill (Fig.8) appear to be overlain by Roman settlement forms, in contrast to a similar boundary near Osbournby which appears to terminate in Iron Age type enclosures (Figs 9, 10). This could indicate that the land allotment associated with the boundaries east of Temple Hill was obsolete or deliberately ignored when the Roman settlements were established. Further investigation could attempt to ascertain the nature of the development of the boundary systems and their contemporaneity with any of the settlements and from this compare the land use patterns in these areas, in particular in the transitional phase from pre-Roman to Roman periods.

A more obvious effect of the Roman influence on the countryside, which can sometimes be seen in the cropmark evidence, is the construction of metalled roads. Almost five kilometres of the agger, side ditches and (possibly associated) quarry pits, of the Roman road, Bloxholm Lane, from Sleaford to Lincoln (Margary 1973, pp.234-35, RR260) is visible on aerial photographs between Sleaford and Ruskington (Figs 11, 12). The cropmark features around the road raise a number of questions about its position in the development of that landscape. Parts of some of the settlements are cut by the road, perhaps indicating they had gone out of use by the time the road had been built. Others appear to focus on it, or perhaps on an earlier route, and some are directly linked to the road by side-roads. The establishment of the nature of the relationships, if any, of the settlements with the road will have an important bearing on the understanding of the development of the area and the impact of Roman influence. It would also be useful to ascertain how the cropmark sites compare to other roadside settlements, for example those excavated at Hibaldstow and Sapperton, or those identified from finds at Navenby and Owmby Cliff (Smith 1987, pp.187-98, 202).

Investigation into the relationships between cropmark sites of

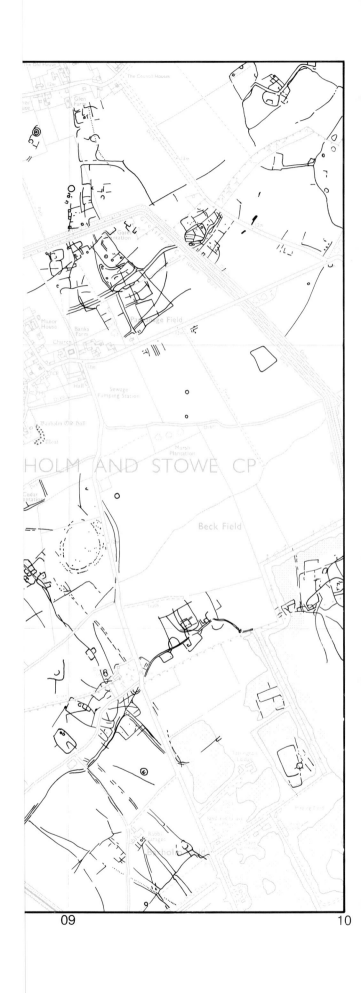

HOLM AND STOWE CP

Beck Field

09   10

E and TF 00 NE (© Crown copyright.) showing plans of cropmarks

Fig 7a over

Fig.7b. Extract from NMP overlay (original scale 1:10,000 © Cr
settlements and, ritual and funerary monuments extendin

Fig 7b over

apparently pre-Roman and Roman forms of settlement may also shed light on the development of settlement during these periods in west Lincolnshire.

Continuity of settlement may be represented at the sites where a Roman element appears to form one phase of activity for example those sites that contain a double ditched element as one phase (Figs 4.3.1-6), or the two sites in the Welland valley where possible Roman buildings appear to be situated in Iron Age type enclosures (Figs 4.1.2, 4.1.4). The development of villas on the same site as, or adjacent to, earlier settlement is found in the region and the rest of Britain (Wilson 1974, p.252).

Settlement shift could be represented by adjacent Roman and pre-Roman forms of settlement (Fig.9.). If the two forms of settlement were ever simultaneously occupied this raises questions about the social relations between them. At Lockington, Leicestershire it has been suggested that the Iron Age settlement could have continued as a 'servant' or 'tenant farmer' settlement to the adjacent Roman villa (Hingley 1989a, p.102; Clay 1985, p.25).

At some excavated sites in the East Midlands settlement shift involved the re-use of the Iron Age settlement areas for other activities, as at Wakerley (Jackson & Ambrose 1978, p.173) and Weekley (Jackson & Dix 1987, p.43), Northamptonshire and at Fengate (Pryor & Cranstone 1978, p.26). This could have been the case at the cropmark site at Osbournby (Fig.9) where the more rectilinear, and therefore possibly Roman, phases are located at the northern end of the site. This could indicate a settlement shift to the north, but the distribution of Roman material occurs over the whole area, including those with no cropmarks suggesting occupation or some other activity across the whole site.

Summary.

The systematic mapping carried out during this project provides a synthesis of over fifty years of aerial photography in Lincolnshire. The cropmarks of prehistoric and Roman settlements and associated features in west Lincolnshire, recorded as part of the NMP, are only one part of the available evidence on this topic but are a valuable resource for research. The production of multi-period overlays to modern maps means that the prehistoric and Roman settlements can be seen in the context of the developing man-made landscape from prehistory to the modern period.

As there is little or no dating evidence available for the cropmark sites in this survey, the classification of the sites on morphological grounds is useful for possible dating and for targeting future research priorities. The NMP data provide a corpus of plans of settlements and associated features which can be compared to new discoveries in the survey area and to other sites in the region.

The function or development of settlements could provide avenues for future research. Hingley (1989a, pp.6, 59-69) has suggested that the development of an extended family could be reflected in the plans of settlements. This could be applied, for example, to the more complex settlements in figures 3.1-10. The largest of the enclosures could be the original element in the settlement or the 'dominant' enclosure where the main activities and the main family group live, and as the group grows more enclosures might be added. Complex entrances or double ditches incorporated in a settlement could be interpreted as agricultural necessities, for the management of stock (Pryor 1996), or for prestige and defensive reasons, for example the entrances to the enclosures in figures 3.7 and 3.8 or the double ditched elements in the possible Roman settlements in figures 4.1-3.

Cropmarks often represent many phases of development of a site and future research could attempt to date and assess the differences between simple and complex forms. If simplicity or complexity of plan can be seen as an indication of low or high

status then the survey has recorded settlements ranging from humble farm to larger possible estate centres. Some of extensive cropmark complexes could be a genu representation of contemporary settlement features and if so of comparable extent to the 'major' settlements of the late Age identified in Lincolnshire (May 1976b, 1984). settlements near Osbournby (Fig.3.14) and in the Well valley (Fig.5.6-8) are similar, or greater, in extent to the m Iron Age settlements excavated at Dragonby (May 19 Fig.5.41) and Old Sleaford (Elsdon 1997, Fig.31).

The bias in the cropmark evidence towards ditcl enclosures should never be ignored. Future surveys using evidence provided by cropmarks of possible settlements co concentrate on comparing these with different types evidence, especially that of apparently unenclosed settlem provided by artefact scatters, as found in the Ropsley Humby survey (Lane 1995).

Excavation evidence has shown that the settlements in late prehistoric and Roman periods do not fit into any sir theory of predominant settlement types and land u Speculation on distributions of apparently similar 'types' settlement may only reflect the biases in the available evide (Carter, this volume). The emphasis on large 'fort' enclosures in analysis of Iron Age society in other areas England may not be applicable to the Iron Age societies of w Lincolnshire. The region is remarkable for having only a forts and the search for suitable candidates has produce group with little or no dating evidence, and a disparity of fc except where size and survival as earthworks is concern They have a limited distribution between the Witham and Welland (Whitwell 1982, p.20) and a potential date range fr the Bronze Age to the medieval period.

More accurate dating of settlements within the Iron age Roman periods is needed to compare the different categorie cropmark forms to see how the settlement patterns develop This is especially true when examining the effects of poss transitional periods in cultural and economic developmen the region between the early and late Iron Age, Iron Ag Roman and Roman to post-Roman periods.

Dating of cropmark sites simply from finds scatters can pr difficult as finds may not relate to the sub-surface depo forming the cropmarks (Palmer 1996, pp.14-15, Fig.7; Pryo French 1985, pp.296-97), and there is not always a correlat between concentrations of finds and concentrations cropmarks apparently relating to settlement features (Pal 1996, Fig.8; Crowther 1983, p.43).

Similarly field evaluation and excavation of cropmark si where possible, should be carefully targeted, as a feature r have been mapped from a photograph over fifty years old, subsequent activity may have removed all traces archaeological deposits relating to the cropmarks. E recently photographed cropmarks may have formed from very bottoms of ditches or residual remains of archaeological features which will not be detectable on ground.

Clusters of cropmarks could be compared to gain a fu understanding of the potential differences in the develop character of settlement across the survey area. A multi-pe landscape approach, which can be seen in the survey of Ropsley and Humby parish (Lane 1995) and in the survey of Welland valley (Simpson et al. 1993), using a number different archaeological survey techniques could, wh appropriate, use the NMP data to target research priorit Analysis of the cropmark sites as well as the areas immedia adjacent could provide further information on settlen change and continuity in a number of diverse topograph locations in west Lincolnshire.

Comparison could be made between the areas east and w of the limestone to the south of Lincoln (Figs 8, 9) wh clusters of cropmarks appear to show different patterns settlement. These could then be compared to a similar are

Fig 8 over

the north of Lincoln, for example the dispersed settlements and enclosures in an area approximately ten kilometres square near Blyton, which includes a possible villa (Fig.4.1.1), a number of possible Iron Age/Roman settlements (Figs 2.2.22, 2.3.8, 3.3, 4.2.6) and the enclosures ranged along a possible road or track (Fig.5a.2). Comparison of the limestone uplands north and south of Lincoln could include the cropmark evidence of simple dispersed enclosures found between Ancaster and Ropsley, and the cropmarks of more complex settlements found on the limestone uplands between the areas to the west of Owmby-by-Spital and Kirton-in-Lindsey.

The record of Iron Age and Roman settlement in west Lincolnshire could form one strand of a research strategy for Lincolnshire based on a multi-period and multi-method approach to archaeological investigation. The national scope of the NMP will, in future, allow the Lincolnshire material to be seen in its regional and national context. Further reconnaissance, field survey and other non-intrusive methods, such as geophysical survey, will identify new sites, outwith the present distribution of cropmarks, but investigation of the known archaeological landscapes is a high priority because the archaeological sites which have formed cropmarks are increasingly under threat.

Notes.

1. The Iron Age tribe has been referred to as the *Coritani* but epigraphical research has shown that *Corieltauvi* is probably the correct form (Tomlin 1983).

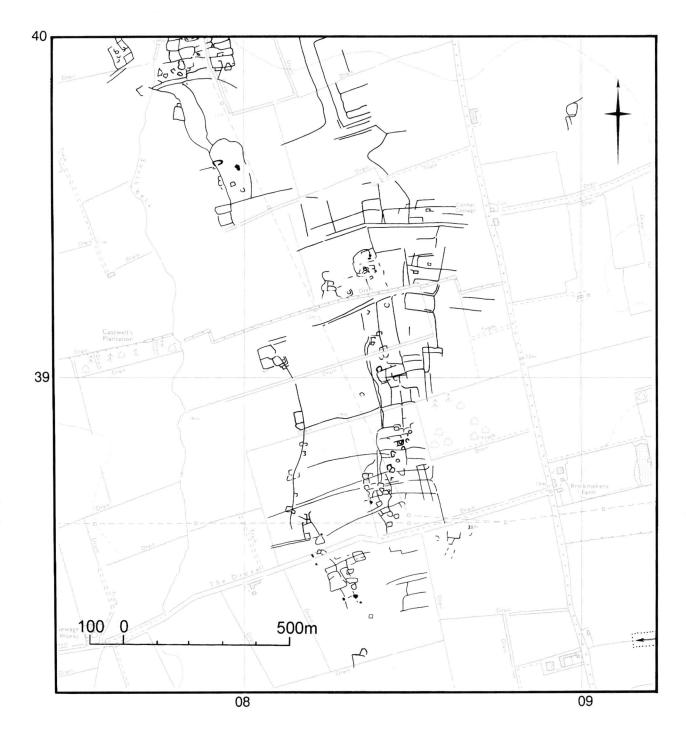

Fig.9. Extract from NMP overlays (original scale 1:10,000 © Crown copyright. RCHME 1998) to Ordnance Survey map TF 03 NE (© Crown copyright.) showing plans of extensive cropmarks of late prehistoric and Roman settlement.

2.   These features have a similar form to square barrows identified on the Yorkshire Wolds, where excavations at Wetwang Slack suggest the earliest form of square barrow, dated to the fourth and early third century BC, was typically a large square platform with a deep ditch and a shallow or absent grave pit (Stoertz 1997, p.36, Fig.1; Whimster 1981, p.195; Dent 1982, p.446). Similar features have been identified in the Welland valley (Pryor & French 1985, p.260, Fig.168) and at Aston-on-Trent, Derbyshire (May 1970).

Bibliography.

Bewley, R. H. and Jones, D. 1992. Aerial archaeology in Lincolnshire: 1991 and beyond. *Lincolnshire History and Archaeology*, vol.27, pp.43-44.

Boutwood, Y. 1998. Long Bennington, Lincolnshire. *Britannia*, vol.29, pp.307-09.

Chowne, P. 1978. Billingborough Bronze Age settlement: An interim note. *Lincolnshire History and Archaeology*, vol.13, pp.15-21.

Chowne, P. 1980. Bronze Age settlement in south Lincolnshire. In *Settlement and Society in the British Later Bronze Age*, edited by J. C. Barrett and R. J. Bradley, pp.295-395.

Chowne, P., Girling M. and Grieg J. 1986. Excavations at an Iron Age defended enclosure at Tattershall Thorpe, Lincolnshire. *Proceedings of the Prehistoric Society*, vol.52, pp.159-88.

Clay, P. 1985. A survey of two cropmark sites in Lockington-Hemington parish, Leicestershire. *Transactions of the Leicestershire Archaeological and Historical Society*, vol.61, pp.17-26.

Clay, P. 1992. An Iron Age farmstead at Grove Farm, Enderby, Leicestershire. *Transactions of the Leicestershire Archaeological and Historical Society*, vol.66, pp.1-82.

Cooper, N. J. 1996. Anglo-Saxon settlement in the Gwash valley, Rutland. In *Anglo-Saxon Landscapes of the East Midlands*, edited by J. Bourne, pp.165-279. Leicester.

Crowther, D. 1983. Old land surfaces and modern ploughsoil: Implications of recent work at Maxey, Cambs. *Scottish Archaeological Review*, vol.2:1, pp.31-44.

Cunliffe, B. W. 1991. *Iron Age Communities in Britain: An account of England, Scotland and Wales from the seventh century BC until the Roman conquest*, 3rd edition.

Deegan, A. forthcoming. *Nottinghamshire NMP report*. RCHME internal document.

Dent, J. S. 1982. Cemeteries and settlement patterns of the Iron Age on the Yorkshire Wolds. *Proceedings of the Prehistoric Society*, vol.32, pp.437-57.

Elsdon, S. M. 1997. *Old Sleaford Revealed, A Lincolnshire Settlement in Iron Age, Roman, Saxon and Medieval Times: Excavations 1882-1995*. Oxbow monograph 78, Nottingham Studies in Archaeology 2. Oxford.

Everson, P. 1977. Aerial reconnaissance in north Lincolnshire. *Lincolnshire History and Archaeology*, vol.12, p.83.

Everson, P. 1978. Aerial reconnaissance in north Lincolnshire. *Lincolnshire History and Archaeology*, vol.13, pp.82-83.

Everson, P. 1980. North Lincolnshire, aerial reconnaissance. *Lincolnshire History and Archaeology*, vol.15, p.80.

Everson, P. 1982. Recent results from aerial reconnaissance. *Lincolnshire History and Archaeology*, vol.17, pp.77-79.

Everson, P. and Hayes, T. 1984. Lincolnshire from the air. In *A Prospect of Lincolnshire*, edited by F. N. Field and A. J. White, pp.33-41. Lincoln.

Field, N. and Knight, D. 1992. A later Bronze Age site at Kirmond-le-Mire. *Lincolnshire History and Archaeology* vol.27, pp.43-45.

Frere S. S. and St Joseph, J. K. S. 1983. *Roman Britain from the Air*. Cambridge.

Gates, T. and O'Brien C. F. 1988. Cropmarks at Milfield and New Bewick and the recognition of *grubenhäuser* in Northumberland. *Archaeologia Aeliana* fifth series, vol.16, pp.1-9.

Grimes, W. F. 1961. Draughton, Colsterworth and Heathrow. In *The problems of the Iron Age in southern Britain*, edited by S. S. Frere, pp.21-28.

Hingley, R. 1989a. *Rural Settlement in Roman Britain*.

Hingley, R. 1989b. Iron Age society in central and southern Warwickshire: Directions for future research. In *Midlands Prehistory, Some recent researches into the prehistory of central England*, edited by A. Gibson,

British Archaeological Reports, British Series 204, pp.122-57. Oxford.

Jackson, D. A. 1975. An Iron Age site at Twywell, Northamptonshire. *Northamptonshire Archaeology*, vol.10, pp.31-93.

Jackson, D. A. 1977. Further excavations at Aldwincle 1969-71. *Northamptonshire Archaeology*, vol.12, pp.9-54.

Jackson, D. A. 1983. The excavation of an Iron Age site at Brigstock, Northamptonshire. *Northamptonshire Archaeology* vol.18, pp.7-32.

Jackson, D. A. and Ambrose, T. M. 1978. Excavations at Wakerley, Northants, 1972-1975. *Britannia*, vol.9, pp.115-242.

Jackson D. and Dix B. 1987. Late Iron Age and Roman settlement at Weekley, Northants. *Northamptonshire Archaeology*, vol.21, pp.41-94.

Jones, D. 1988. Aerial reconnaissance and prehistoric and Romano-British archaeology in northern Lincolnshire - A sample survey. *Lincolnshire History and Archaeology*, vol.23, pp.5-30.

Jones, D. 1998. Long barrows and Neolithic elongated enclosures in Lincolnshire: An analysis of the air photographic evidence. *Proceedings of the Prehistoric Society,* vol.64.

Jones, D. and Whitwell, J. B. 1991. Survey of the Roman fort and multi-period settlement complex at Kirmington on the Lincolnshire Wolds. *Lincolnshire History and Archaeology*, vol.26, pp.57-62.

Jones, R. 1975. The Romano-British farmstead and its cemetery at Lynch Farm, near Peterborough. *Northamptonshire Archaeology*, vol.10, pp.94-137.

Knight, D. 1992. Excavations of an Iron Age settlement at Gamston, Nottinghamshire. *Transactions of the Thoroton Society of Nottinghamshire*, vol.96, pp.16-90.

Lane, T. W. 1995. *The Archaeology and Developing Landscape of Ropsley and Humby, Lincolnshire*. Lincolnshire Archaeology and Heritage Reports Series, No.2. Heckington.

Leary R. S. 1995. *Excavations at the Romano-British Settlement at Pasture Lodge Farm, Long Bennington, Lincolnshire, 1975-77, by H. M. Wheeler*. Occasional Papers in Lincolnshire History and Archaeology, No.10. Lincoln.

Lewis M. J. T. 1966. *Temples in Roman Britain*. Cambridge.

Mackreth, D. and O'Neill F. 1979. Barnack 1978-79. *Durobrivae* vol.7, pp.23-25.

Margery, I. D. 1973. *Roman Roads in Britain*. 3rd edition.

May, J. 1970. An Iron Age enclosure at Aston upon Trent, Derbyshire: A report on excavations in 1967. *Derbyshire Archaeological Journal*, vol.40, pp.10-21.

May, J. 1976a. *Prehistoric Lincolnshire*. History of Lincolnshire I. Lincoln.

May, J. 1976b. The growth of settlements in the later Iron Age in Lincolnshire. In *Oppida: The Beginnings of Urbanisation in Barbarian Europe*, edited by B. Cunliffe and T. Rowley. British Archaeological Reports, Supplementary Series II. pp.163-80.

May, J. 1984. The major settlements of the later Iron Age in Lincolnshire. In *A Prospect of Lincolnshire*, edited by F. N. Field and A. J. White, pp.18-22. Lincoln.

May, J. 1996. *Dragonby, Report on excavations at an Iron Age and Romano-British settlement in north Lincolnshire*. Oxbow Monograph 61, 2 vols. Oxford.

O'Brien, C. 1979. Iron Age and Romano-British settlement in the Trent Basin. In *Invasion and Response, the Case of Roman Britain*, edited by B. C. Burnham and H. B. Johnson, British Archaeological Reports, British Series 73, pp.299-314. Oxford.

Olivier, A. 1996. *English Heritage Archaeological Review 1995-6*.

Oswald, A. 1949. A re-excavation of the Roman villa at Mansfield Woodhouse, Nottinghamshire, 1936-39. *Transactions of the Thoroton Society of Nottinghamshire*, vol.53, pp.1-14.

Oswald, A. and Buxton, L. H. D. 1937. A Roman fortified villa at Norton Disney, Lincs. *Antiquaries Journal*, vol.17, pp.138-78.

Palmer, R. 1984. *Danebury An Iron Age Hillfort in Hampshire, An Aerial Photographic Interpretation of its Environs*. RCHME Supplementary Series No.6.

Palmer, R. 1996. Air photo interpretation and the Lincolnshire Fenland. *Landscape History* vol.18, pp.5-16.

Pickering, J. 1979. Aerial archaeology and the prehistoric landscape. *Landscape History* vol.1, pp.10-15.

Pickering, J. 1989. Discovering the prehistoric Midlands. In *Midlands Prehistory, Some Recent Researches into the Prehistory of Central England*, edited by A. Gibson. British Archaeological Reports, British Series 204, pp.106-10. Oxford.

Fig.10. Possible Iron Age settlement (centre of photograph) near the village of Osbournby. In the top left of the photograph cropmarks of a large, late prehistoric, and/or Roman, settlement are faintly visible (NMR TF0838/39 3118/358 24 July 1986, © Crown copyright. RCHME).

Pickering, J. 1995. 'A Lincolnshire villa' and 'Sleaford', *Current Archaeology* No.145, vol.13:1, pp.21-25.

Pryor, F. 1984. *Exacavation at Fengate Peterborough, England: Fourth report*. Northamptonshire Archaeological Society Monograph 2, Royal Ontario Museum Archaeology Monograph 7. Toronto and Northampton.

Pryor, F. 1996. Sheep, stockyards and field systems: Bronze Age livestock and populations of the fenlands of eastern England. *Antiquity*, vol.70, pp.313-24.

Pryor, F. and Cranstone D. 1978. An interim report on the excavations at Fengate 1975-79. *Northamptonshire Archaeology*, vol.13, pp.9-27.

Pryor, F. M. M. and French, C. A. J. 1985. *Cambridgeshire: The Fenland Project No.1: Archaeology and Environment in the Lower Welland Valley*. East Anglian Archaeology, Report No.27. Cambridge.

Riley, D. N. 1980. *Early Landscapes from the Air: Studies of Cropmarks in South Yorkshire and north Nottinghamshire*. Sheffield.

Riley, D. N., Buckland, P. C. and Wade, J. S. 1995. Aerial reconnaissance and excavation at Littleborough-on-Trent, Notts. *Britannia*, vol.26, pp.253-84.

Sharman, J. and Clay, P. 1991. Leicester Lane, Enderby: An archaeological evaluation. *Transactions of the Leicestershire Archaeological and Historical Society*, vol.65, pp.1-11.

Simmons, B. B. 1993. Iron Age and Roman coasts around the wash, II: Archaeology. In *An Historical Atlas of Lincolnshire*, edited by S. Bennett and N. Bennett, pp.20-21. Hull.

Simmons, B. B. 1995. Sapperton. In *Roman Small Towns in Eastern England and Beyond*, edited by A. E. Brown. Oxbow Monograph 52, pp.157-66. Oxford.

Simpson, W. G. 1966. Romano-British settlement on the Welland Gravels. In *Rural Settlement in Roman Britain*, edited by C. Thomas. Council for British Archaeology, Research Report 7, pp.15-25.

Simpson, W. G., Gurney, D. A., Neve, J. and Pryor, F. M. M. 1993. *Fenland: The Fenland Project No.7: Excavations in Peterborough and the Lower Welland Valley 1960-69*. East Anglian Archaeology, Report No.61. Peterborough.

Smith, C. 1977. The valleys of the Tame and middle Trent - their populations and ecology during the late first millennium B.C. In *The Iron Age in Britain - A Review*, edited by J. Collis, pp.51-61. Sheffield.

Smith, R. F. 1987. *Roadside Settlements in Lowland Britain*. British Archaeological Reports, British Series 157. Oxford.

Fig 11 over

Fig.12. Part of the Roman road illustrated in figure 11 crosses the photograph from right to left. Three settlements linked by a linear ditch are visible in the foreground (NMR TF0849/23 3118/342 24 July 1986, © Crown copyright. RCHME).

St Joseph, J. K. 1973. Air reconnaissance: recent results 30. *Archaeological Journal*, vol.47, pp.145-46.

Stead, I. M. 1991. *Iron Age Cemeteries in East Yorkshire*. English Heritage Archaeological Report 22.

Steedman, K. 1994. Excavation of a Saxon site at Riby Crossroads, Lincolnshire. *Archaeological Journal,* vol.151, pp.212-306.

Stoertz, C. 1997. *Ancient Landscapes of the Yorkshire Wolds: Aerial Photographic Transcription and Analysis*. Swindon.

Taylor C. 1975. Roman settlement in the Nene valley. In *Recent Work in Rural Archaeology*, edited by P. J. Fowler, pp.107-19. Bradford-on-Avon.

Taylor, G. 1996. Deeping St James: Welland Bank Pit. *Lincolnshire History and Archaeology*, vol.31, pp.63-64.

Thirsk, J. 1957. *English Peasant Farming, The Agrarian History of Lincolnshire from Tudor to Recent Times*.

Todd, M. 1973. *The Coritani*.

Todd, M. 1975. The Romano-British rural settlement at Staunton, Nottinghamshire. *Transactions of the Thoroton Society of Nottinghamshire*, vol.79, pp.29-39.

Tomlin, R. 1983. *Non Coritani sed Corieltauvi*. *Antiquaries Journal*, vol.63, p.353.

Welfare, H. and Swan, V. 1995. *Roman Camps in England, The Field Archaeology*.

Wheeler, H. 1979. Excavation at Willington, Derbyshire, 1970-1972. *Derbyshire Archaeological Journal*, vol.99, pp.58-220.

Whimster, R. P. 1981. *Burial Practices in Iron Age Britain*. British Archaeological Reports, British Series 90. Oxford.

Whimster, R. P. 1989. *The Emerging Past, Air Photography and the Buried Landscape*.

Whitwell, J. B. 1970. *Roman Lincolnshire*. History of Lincolnshire II. Lincoln.

Whitwell, J. B. 1982. *The Coritani: Some Aspects of the Iron Age Tribe and the Roman Civitas*. British Archaeological Reports, British Series 99. Oxford.

Whitwell, J. B. 1995. Some Roman small towns in north Lincolnshire and south Humberside. In *Roman Small Towns in Eastern England and Beyond*, edited by A. E. Brown. Oxbow Monograph 52, pp.95-102. Oxford.

Willis, S. 1997. Settlement, materiality and landscape in the Iron Age of the East Midlands: Evidence, interpretation and wider resonance. In *Reconstructing Iron Age Societies*, edited by A. Gwilt and C. Haselgrove. Oxbow Monograph 71, pp.205-15. Oxford.

Wilson, D. R. 1974. Romano-British villas from the air. *Britannia*, vol.5, pp.251-61.

Windell, D. 1983. Clay Lane 1980: Interim Report, An Iron Age and Roman rural settlement at Clay Lane, Earls Barton. *Northamptonshire Archaeology* vol.18, pp.33-42.

Romano-British Settlements on the Lincolnshire Wolds.

Dilwyn Jones

Introduction.

The standard work on the archaeology of the Roman period in the county is Whitwell (1970; revised edition, 1992). A regional overview by the same author (1982) considered the county in the wider context of the East Midlands in Roman times. However, neither study was able to discuss the aerial photographic evidence because systematic examination of the material had not been completed by the RCHME at that time. The potential contribution of this evidence to Roman studies in Lincolnshire had been underlined by the results of two sampling exercises undertaken by RCHME (Jones 1988; 1989) which investigated the evidence from two landscape blocks at the northern end of the Wolds.

This present article attempts to provide an overview of Roman settlement of the whole chalkland massif, including that part in the north which from 1974 to 1996, constituted part of south Humberside. The purpose of this contribution is not to produce an exhaustive survey of all cropmark sites assigned to the Roman period but to identify the main settlement forms of that period on the Wolds, and to consider the nature and main trends in settlement recorded on aerial photographs. Potential topics for research have been identified, and comparisons have been made with the published evidence from other cropmark-responsive landscapes in the western half of the county (Jones 1988; Winton, this volume).

The distribution of Romano-British cropmark sites (Fig.1).

Cropmark sites attributed a Roman date either by virtue of their rectilinear (or sub-rectilinear) form or association with finds show a very dispersed pattern of distribution across the Lincolnshire Wolds. The distribution of these cropmark sites suggests a sparsely populated landscape with large areas apparently devoid of settlements or only showing a thin scatter of sites. Seven possible major settlements are found in 1125 square kilometres of chalk, a density of 1 per 160.7 square kilometres. The distribution of findspots of the period from the Wolds shows a higher number of potential sites but indicates a similar dispersed pattern of settlement. There are some areas, such as the upper Lymn Valley and the western edge of the Wolds between Ludford and Caistor, which have a particularly high concentration of sites.

In terms of their topographical location cropmark sites of the Roman period usually occupy the higher ground, being found more often on the crests of spurs or upper valley slopes, and less frequently in valley bottom locations. Our ability to record the pattern of distribution of settlement may be affected by the position of later, medieval villages in valley bottoms which have obscured sites of earlier date. Villa sites identified from findspots at Kirmond-le-Mire, Thoresway and a possible example identified from cropmarks at Edlington with Wispington, in the Bain Valley, indicate settlement extended over the lower ground in places in the Roman period.

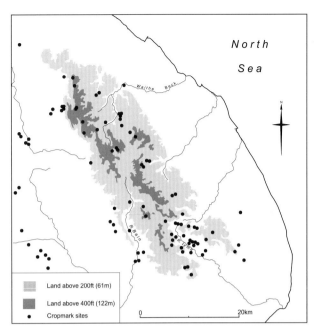

Fig.1. Distribution of cropmark sites attributed a Roman date on the Lincolnshire Wolds and adjacent areas (© Crown copyright. RCHME 1998).

Site classifications.

The morphology of settlements represented on the Wolds is rectilinear (or sub-rectilinear) in plan. The variation in size and shape is a reflection of the type of settlement. From an analysis of the cropmark evidence it has been possible to identify a hierarchy of sites, broadly divisible into three basic types: major settlements, villas and minor farmsteads.

Major settlements (Fig.2).

The first century BC saw the development in the East Midlands of a group of nucleated, 'open' or undefended settlements in the territory of the *Corieltauvi* (May 1984). These are known from surface scatters to have multi-period occupation with origins in the Iron Age, and to cover extensive areas of between ten and thirty hectares. On the Lincolnshire Wolds, settlements in this category have been identified at Kirmington, Ludford, Horncastle, Ulceby Cross and Spilsby. In the Roman period they served as major centres of population. The walled towns of Caistor and Horncastle enclose areas of approximately five and eight hectares respectively, by comparison.

The extensive plan of the settlement (and fort) at Kirmington in North Lincolnshire (Jones & Whitwell 1991) shows a multi-period palimpsest of features. The civil settlement in the Roman period displays an 'open', unenclosed plan, with enclosures focused on a network of forked roads. Examples of round houses of possibly Iron Age date are found at Kirmington (and at Ludford, Ulceby Cross and Aswardby) as well as a shrine with origins in the Iron Age (Leahy 1980). The cropmark evidence for Ludford and Ulceby Cross is less complete, but hints at settlements of similar form; there is none for the settlement at Spilsby.

The scale and morphology of a site at Aswardby (Fig.3) in the Lymn Valley suggests it belongs to this class. In plan the settlement has close analogies with a large 'village' recorded at Hacconby Fen, in the Lincolnshire Fens (Taylor 1983). Aswardby shows the characteristic accretion of enclosures along a network of roadways (in this case ditched, unmetalled lanes) typical of other major settlements on the Wolds. It covers an area of, at most, twenty hectares which at its western extremity, where the lanes fork, contains a possible temple enclosure. Cursory ground examination (not under ideal

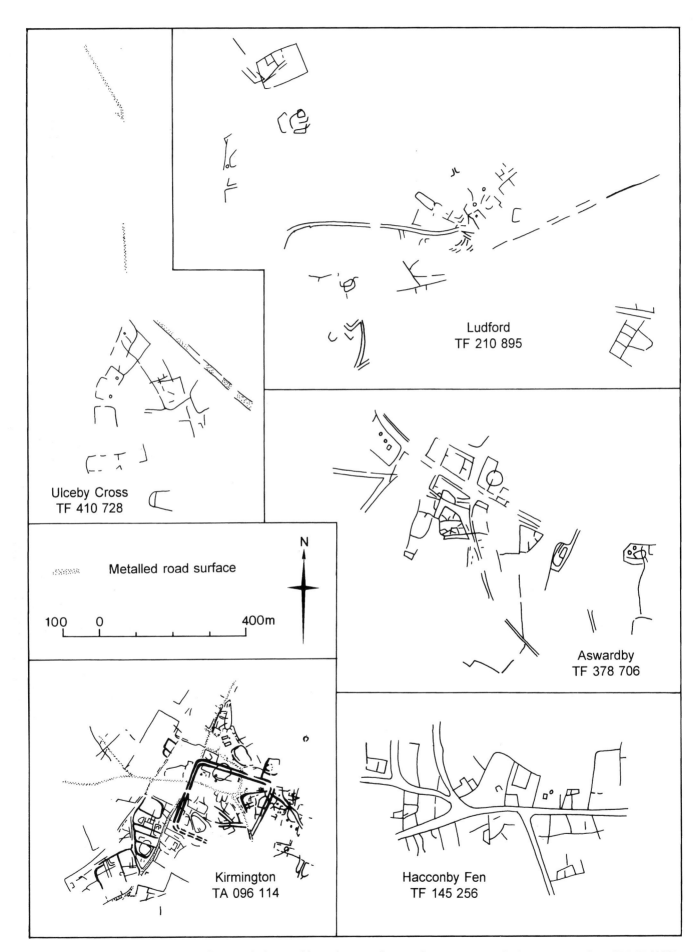

Fig.2. Plans of major settlements on the Lincolnshire Wolds, and Hacconby Fen, for comparison (© Crown copyright. RCHME 1998).

Fig.3. Aswardby, a major Romano-British settlement in the Lymn Valley viewed from the north-west. Enclosures flank ditched trackways or roads, which are forked at their extremities. (NMR TF 3770/52, © Crown copyright. RCHME 1996).

conditions) of the Aswardby site in November 1993 yielded a sparse scatter of Romano-British greyware potsherds, together with a mortarium rim fragment (possibly a Mancetter type, dated from c.250 to c.350 AD, K. Hartley personal communication).

A similar attribution is given to a site located at Nettleton Top, adjacent to the High Street ridgeway between Caistor and Ludford. This displays a typical plan (derived mainly from geophysical survey) where enclosures flank possible lanes; traces of occupation cover at least nine hectares. Finds indicated a complex Iron Age and Roman site, which may have contained an Iron Age shrine as well as a later Roman temple (Bonnor & Griffiths 1993).

Villa sites (Fig.4).

A total of six villas have been recorded on the Wolds, at Horkstow, Worlaby, Bigby, Claxby, Walesby and at Kirmond-

le-Mire. Of these only Walesby has produced cropmarks of sufficient detail to enable a plan to be drawn up of its layout. As a result of this NMP survey another dozen potential villa sites have been identified on the Wolds, principally on the basis of their distinctive morphology.

In the East Midlands the villa residences recorded at Cromwell, Nottinghamshire (Wilson 1974, p.253, pl.XXIII) and Lockington, Leicestershire (Clay 1985), are located within enclosures delimited by double-ditches. This is a feature of the Kirmond-le-Mire villa, and of a number of rectilinear cropmark complexes on the Lincolnshire Wolds to which a similar interpretation may be applied, even though actual buildings cannot be identified on the aerial photographs.

Cropmark complexes of this kind, where limits are defined by a pair of ditches, or where double-ditched enclosures form an integral element, are recorded at Ashby Puerorum, Asterby, Edlington, Scamblesby, Somersby and Welton-le-Wold. Evidence to support a villa interpretation comes from the site at

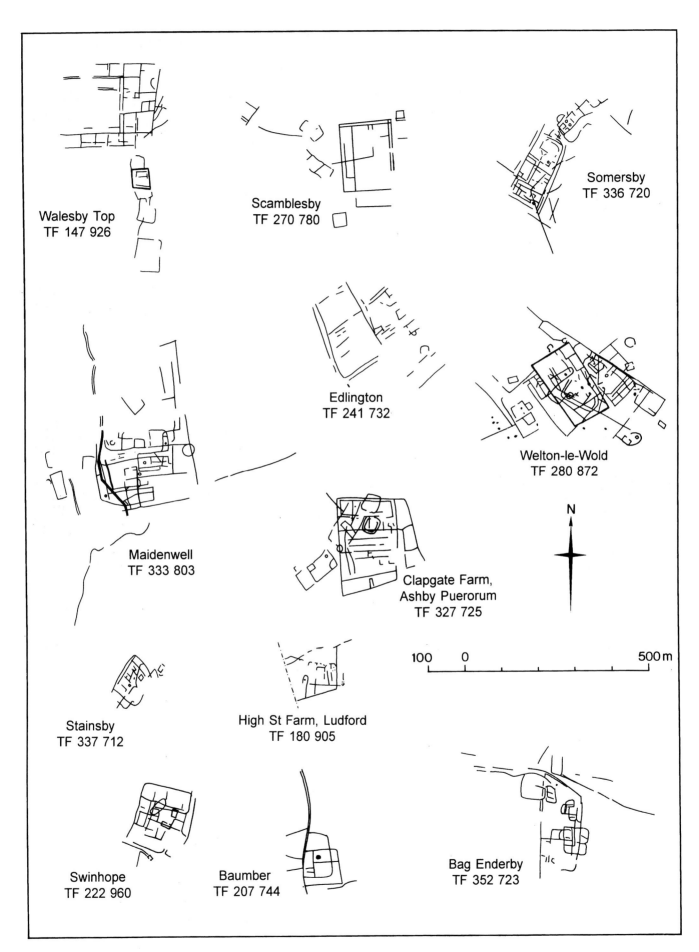

Fig.4. Roman villa sites on the Wolds (© Crown copyright. RCHME 1998).

Fig.5. Edlington. A probable villa complex defined by a double-ditched enclosure which shows internal divisions. Archaeological features extend along the valley floor and geological periglacial stripes show on the slopes. (NMR TF 2473/9, © Crown copyright. RCHME 1996).

Edlington in the Bain Valley (Fig.5) which has yielded Roman building remains, pottery and a coin hoard of late third-century date (NMR TF 27 SW 8).

In addition, Romano-British pottery, oyster shells and possible tile fragments are recorded from the central area at Welton-le-Wold (NMR TF 28 NE 8). At this site the double-ditched enclosure is located within a large rectangular shaped enclosure defined by a single ditch, comparable to the villa-enclosure at Allington Hill, Bottisham, Cambridgeshire (Wilson 1974, pl.XXIV B). At Maidenwell where the cropmark complex is contained within a single-ditched boundary of rectilinear plan, a villa enclosure can be postulated.

At Swinhope (Bewley & Jones 1992); High Street Farm, Ludford; Stainsby; Baumber and Bag Enderby are found examples of settlements of nucleated form, with well-defined limits, that lack the strict rectilinearity of villa sites, but which may, nevertheless, be attributed villa status. In terms of their morphology the complexes conform with three villa-type sites from the Ancholme Valley which form a distinct sub-group within the 'irregular rectilinear complex' type identified by Jones (1988, pp.16-17, 24-25). The difference in form of the two types may reflect a difference in status and function. On this point special mention must be made of the Walesby villa, the plan of which is unique among the villa sites on the Wolds.

At Walesby cropmarks reveal a rectilinear complex of enclosures in a very regular arrangement with wings enclosing an open, central area. The results of excavations in 1861 indicated a villa of high status (Philpot 1861). The plan of the complex, derived from aerial photographs, emphasises its atypical character and indicates the site deserves further study. Whitwell (1982, pp.131-32) has suggested a possible tenurial connection between the villa at Winterton on the Jurassic limestone in North Lincolnshire and the nearby iron smelting site at Thealby. A similar relationship may have existed between the Walesby villa and the iron-working and pottery industries on Otby Moor (Jones 1988, pp.26-27).

Villas in a landscape context (Fig.6).

The potential villas at Scamblesby, Swinhope and Welton-le-Wold form part of larger cropmark landscapes which contain sites that are rectilinear in shape and probably contemporary with the villas. The chronology of these sites needs further investigation in terms of fieldwork and small scale excavation.

Scamblesby, TF 27 78. The villa-like enclosure at Scamblesby is rectilinear in plan and measures 180m by 140m. Two of the sides are double-ditched. The enclosure forms part of a dispersed scatter of minor enclosures of rectilinear form at the head of the valley of a tributary of the Bain. The Roman road to Ulceby Cross runs across the high ground 1.6 kilometres to the south. To the north of the villa enclosure, at Asterby, there is a small group of enclosures flanked by lanes which may be associated with the nearby villa site.

Swinhope, TF 22 96. The villa at Swinhope occupies a prominent position on the slopes of a spur on the east side of the valley of the Waithe Beck. Cropmarks of intersecting linear field boundaries are found to the east, and several undated

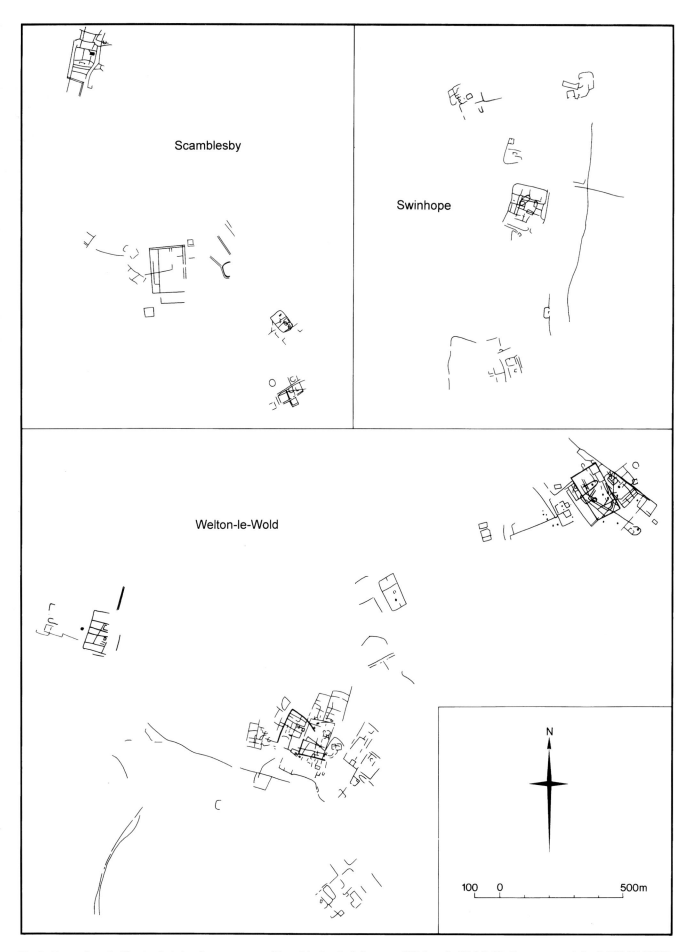

Fig.6. Examples of villas in their landscape context (Scamblesby, Swinhope and Welton-le-Wold) (© Crown copyright. RCHME 1998).

enclosure groups, thought to be Roman in date, have been recorded within a radius of 600 metres to the north and south. Romano-British potsherds, together with prehistoric lithic material, are recorded from the field (Phillips 1989, part ii, pp.71-72). The latter finds are associated with a plough-levelled long barrow, with an oval ditch plan, situated towards the centre of the complex (Bewley & Jones 1992, p.42, Fig.4).

Welton-le-Wold, TF 28 87. Well-defined soilmarks at Welton-le-Wold (Figs 4 & 7) point to a complex pattern of overlapping enclosures on different alignments with associated features. The soilmarks extend over an area 650m by 300m, and are centred on a large rectangular enclosure, measuring 200m by 100m, within which there occurs a large, double-ditched, open D-shaped enclosure. Romano-British pottery, oyster-shells and possible tile fragments have been recorded from the central area. This site forms part of a more extensive cropmark landscape of Romano-British date running up the valley for some two kilometres from Welton towards the Bluestone Heath ridgeway at Gayton Top.

Apart from the villa complex the major component in this landscape comprises an irregularly shaped group of rectilinear accreted enclosures, covering an area 500m by 400m which has produced Romano-British pottery and a beehive quern (NMR TF 28 NE 3). The nature of the site is uncertain, but it may represent a dependent village of the Welton villa estate; compare, for example, sites on Cross Lane in the Ancholme Valley (Jones 1988, Fig.19). The village site at Welton-le-Wold appears to have affinities in terms of its size and form with the undated enclosure complex at Binbrook Walk House (Jones 1987).

The landscape of the Lymn Valley (Fig.8).

The density of settlements in the Lymn Valley is exceptional for the Wolds suggesting it was important during the Roman period. The strong funerary and ritual elements recorded in the area suggest it was also important in the prehistoric period. The area is not served by a Roman road, the nearest being situated three kilometres to the north, running along the summit of the Wolds in a south-easterly direction towards Ulceby Cross.

Towards the southern end of the valley lies the major settlement at Aswardby (Fig.3). From here a ditched trackway runs westward in the general direction of a possible villa site at Bag Enderby which has produced undiagnostic Romano-British wares. Two further possible villa sites may be identified at the head of the valley at Clapgate Farm, Ashby Puerorum, and Somersby. The latter has produced pottery of third- to fourth-century date. The Clapgate Farm site shows more than one phase of development, the main enclosure, which has a trapezoidal shape, partly overlies a group of small, more irregularly-shaped enclosures of unknown date. Comparisons can be made with the Cromwell villa (Wilson 1974) and the line of conjoined enclosures of unknown date which extends downslope from the Walesby Top villa. Lower down the Lymn Valley from Harrington Wood, near Aswardby, a coin of Domitian (AD81-96) has been recorded.

Minor settlements or farmsteads (Fig.9).

Minor enclosures found either as isolated single features, or forming small groups of conjoined enclosures are common on the Wolds. In terms of their morphology the enclosures are predominantly rectilinear and probably of Roman date, while a few display a more curvilinear ditch plan, which may be indicative of Iron Age origins, for example Swinhope Hill, Binbrook. Few enclosures of simple form incorporate a round house structure (indicative of settlement) with only a dozen examples recorded to date. Examples are found at a number of villa complexes, for example at Welton-le-Wold, and at major settlements like Ludford and Ulceby Cross. They may be an indication of Iron Age occupation. Fieldwalking of a farmstead

Fig.7. Welton-le-Wold villa site. Soilmarks reveal a group of overlapping rectilinear enclosures of different size, and orientation. A double-ditched D-shaped enclosure lies at the centre. The whole is overlaid by the parallel lines of medieval ridge-and-furrow. BHL 42, 28 October 1971 (Cambridge University Collection of Air Photographs: copyright reserved).

with enclosures of rectilinear plan in Normanby-le-Wold parish produced part of a large quernstone and a sherd of samian ware.

The most common minor settlement or farmstead form in the Midlands in the Iron Age and Roman periods is a rectilinear enclosure with a single entrance (Dark & Dark 1997, pp.56-58). Enclosures of this type, of varying dimensions, are found as components of irregularly-shaped enclosure clusters, and as isolated sites on the chalklands, but are not particularly numerous. One example, measuring 30m by 20m, is found associated with a group of rectilinear enclosures at Churn Water Heads, Tealby, which has produced Romano-British greywares, including a carinated bowl of late second- to early third-century date. A cluster of overlapping enclosures situated on the lower slope of the spur, some 200 metres to the south-east, has produced pottery of similar date and evidence of buildings. An enclosure of similar dimensions (20m by 20m) with a single entrance, occurs at Belchford and, like the Tealby site, shows a similar cluster of overlapping rectilinear enclosures in its immediate vicinity.

A much larger example of this enclosure type, measuring 65m by 60m, and which has yielded pottery of Iron Age date, is known from Skendleby (Fig.10) at the southern tip of the Wolds. On the exterior the enclosure is partly encompassed by a slight palisade ditch and shows an internal subdivision in the south-west corner. A slightly larger, undated example, without an outer ditch and also with internal subdivisions, occurs at Brocklesby in the northern Wolds, to the east of the major settlement complex at Kirmington.

Near Ruckland, in Maidenwell parish (Fig.9), is a unique type of enclosure for the Wolds, with a single entrance and an irregular curvilinear form. Although the form may be an indication of an earlier date, a date in the Roman period should

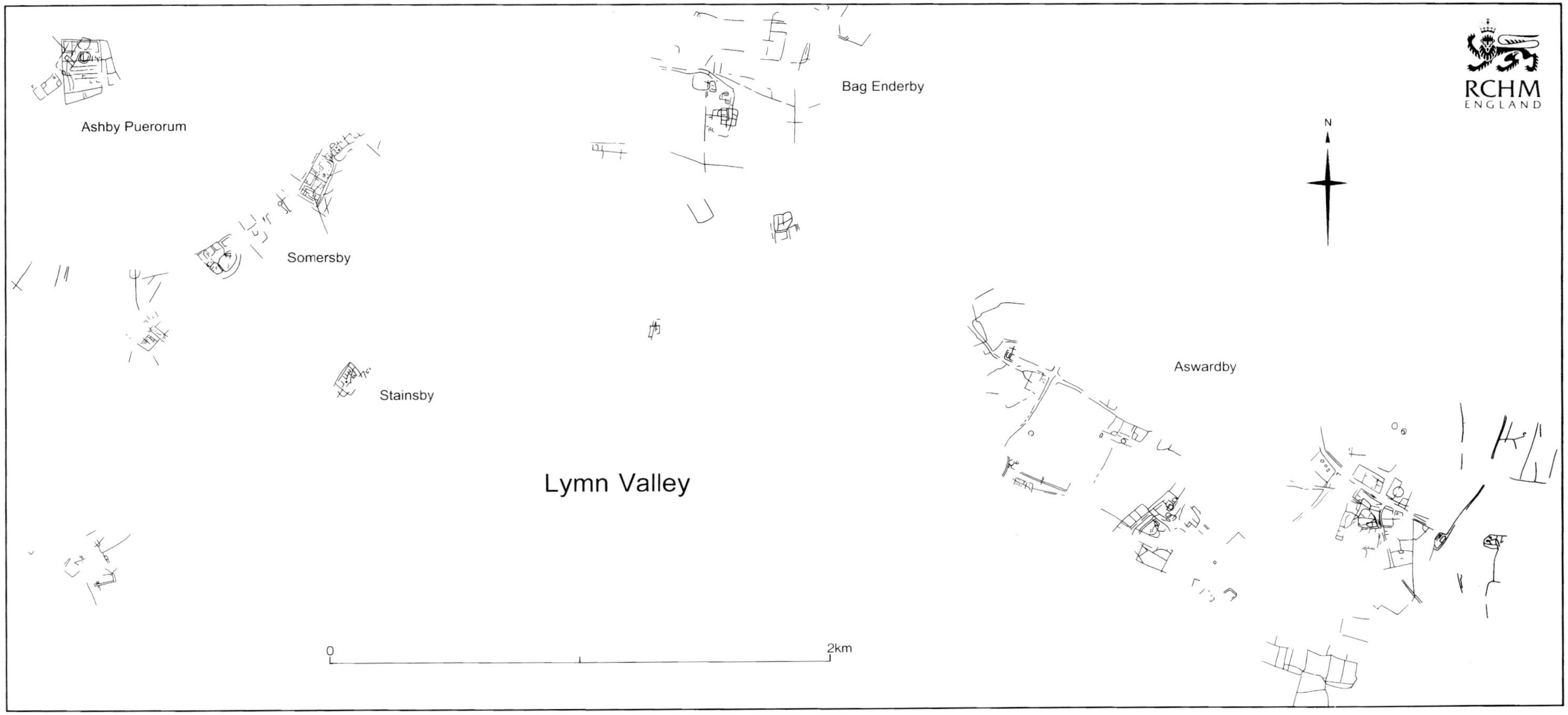

Fig.8. The cropmark landscape of the Lymn Valley, Lincolnshire (© Crown copyright. RCHME 1998).

not be dismissed. What function the enclosure served is uncertain, but the inturned entrance, taken together with the internal subdivisions may indicate usage in animal husbandry.

Other enclosure forms (Fig.11).

Among the cropmark sites recorded on the Wolds which do not readily fit into any class, attention can be drawn to two distinct forms of unknown function which deserve further study.

Ladder enclosures (Fig.11a).

In the valley of the Waithe Beck in the northern Wolds there are several examples of large rectilinear enclosures with a very regular plan, previously referred to as 'ladder enclosures' (Jones 1988, pp.25-26), all of which display internal subdivisions at regular intervals. The fieldwalking evidence suggested a Roman date, but there is no evidence of their purpose. The sites lie in the vicinity of the Kirmond-le-Mire villa and it is possible that there is a link with the agricultural economy of that villa. Where enclosures of this type are found elsewhere on the Wolds they appear to have similar spatial associations. One example occurs at Gayton Top, not far from the site of the villa at Welton-le-Wold, and one at Flint Hill, near the Scamblesby cropmark villa site. Another possible example is found on the eastern outskirts of the major settlement at Ludford. The examples at Scamblesby and Ludford lie alongside a Roman road. One other possible enclosure of the type, the full extent of which is not known, is found as an isolated feature on a ridge summit at Langton-by-Spilsby, adjacent to where Romano-British pottery has been recorded (NMR TF 37 SE 5).

Enclosures appended to linear features (Fig.11b).

Four possible examples are identified on the Wolds of sites where enclosures are appended to a single linear ditch reminiscent of a 'washing-line' plan. The lack of archaeological material from the sites makes dating uncertain, but the morphology of the enclosures and the spatial associations at two sites hints at a Roman date. The site at Stenigot in the Bain Valley is attached to small irregularly-shaped and overlapping enclosures where Romano-British potsherds together with prehistoric lithic material have been found (NMR TF 28 SW 16). The 'washing-line' site in Maidenwell parish (TF 32 80) represents a detached feature, situated 600 metres west of a large cropmark complex, interpreted as a possible villa and which has produced a thin scatter of Romano-British potsherds from a cursory field examination. Other longer examples of linear features with appended enclosures occur in the Trent Valley to the south, with a marked concentration found in the Long Bennington-Dry Doddington-Foston-Allington areas (Boutwood, this volume; Winton, this volume).

Roman roads (Fig.12).

One of the notable features of the chalklands is the lack of evidence for roads linking the major settlements of the hinterland with the coast. A Roman road running in a north-easterly direction from Lincoln (Margary 1973, pp.238-40) divides in two in the region of Langworth. One arm branches off north-eastwards in the direction of Grainthorpe Haven on the coast, the other south-eastwards in the direction of Ulceby Cross and Burgh-le-Marsh beyond. Portions of the latter road are recorded on aerial photographs at Belchford, Tetford and

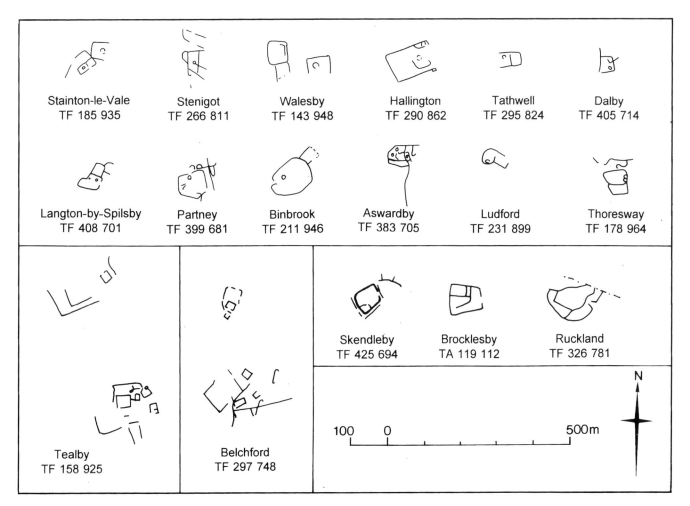

Fig.9. Minor settlements or farmsteads on the Lincolnshire Wolds (© Crown copyright. RCHME 1998).

Brinkhill (where it survives as an earthwork) (Fig.13), and Ulceby Cross (where it makes a realignment southwards). At Platts Lane, Tetford, an undated rectilinear enclosure, 160m by 60m, with other elements attached, flanks the route of the road. The road follows a course to the north of the Lymn Valley into which there does not appear to be a connecting branch road.

At the roadside settlement at Ludford, on the High Street between Caistor and Horncastle a fork occurs in a short section of road on the eastern side of the settlement. One section heads north-east in the general direction of Grainthorpe Haven, the other due east to an unknown destination.

A new, possible Roman road, traced for 900 metres, and following an east-west orientation has been recorded on the Wolds to the east of Binbrook village. A minor enclosure, which produced Romano-British pottery lies immediately adjacent to it, and a settlement type complex at Binbrook Walk House, is situated approximately two kilometres to the south-east at the nearest point to the road (Jones 1987).

On the west side of the Wolds are found the walled towns of Caistor and Horncastle that are not linked by a road. The towns lie on a ridgeway, running along the western escarpment, that would have formed a natural route between the two. A short section of possible Roman road has been identified on the eastern outskirts of Caistor, running northwards for a short distance to connect with the present A1173 road, and perhaps leading via Fonaby Top to Kirmington. A short section of road, approximately 200 metres long, runs eastwards from Kirmington in the direction of Mere Hill, Little Limber, from a point where the B1210 changes alignment towards the Memorial Arch. These potential new routes need to be confirmed by field investigation.

Discussion.

Sites interpreted as settlements in this survey are widespread but thinly dispersed across the Lincolnshire Wolds. The distribution of sites is uneven with higher concentrations forming more extensive spreads in certain areas; the concentration of sites in the Lymn Valley is conspicuous. A clustering of sites is evident also in the vicinity of the suggested villas at Scamblesby, Swinhope, Welton-le-Wold and along the High Street between Ludford and Caistor.

Very notable in the cropmark record is the lack of evidence for field systems accompanying settlements. With the exception of the Fenlands, this absence of evidence is common to the rest of the county (Boutwood, this volume; Winton, this volume). On the Wolds, one area where the landscape may show an element of deliberate planning, albeit on a very limited, minor scale, occurs in the upper Lymn Valley to the west of Aswardby. Here there is a ditched trackway, one kilometre long, flanked in places by rectilinear enclosures. On the south side of this trackway there occurs a large, square-shaped area of land, 400m by 350m, defined by a single ditch, which may well represent a field. Further up the valley at Bag Enderby there is cropmark evidence of trackways with associated settlement enclosures which appear to form part of the same Romano-British landscape.

The Lincolnshire Wolds has a different pattern of sites and a different form of sites when compared to the cropmark landscapes of adjacent areas. To the north, on the chalklands of the Yorkshire Wolds, on the opposite side of the Humber, extended linear, or ribbon-like settlements with integral field systems are more typical (Stoertz 1997). A similar picture is seen in the Fenlands to the south (Palmer 1996) where settlements have a nucleated form and are set within field systems. This is also true of the landscape of the Trent Valley to the west in South Yorkshire and north Nottinghamshire, which is characterised by extensive field systems of very regular plan (Riley 1980; Deegan, forthcoming).

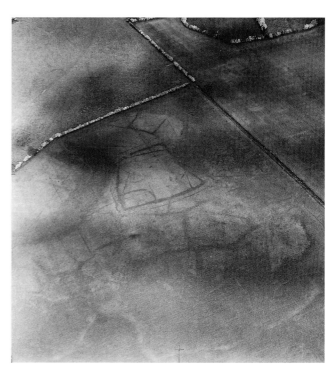

Fig.10. Skendleby enclosure, a minor farmstead, with a surrounding palisade ditch. EW 67, 3 June 1950 (Cambridge University Collection of Air Photographs, © Crown copyright/MOD).

There are, however, parallels for the settlement forms encountered on the Lincolnshire Wolds in these adjacent regions. The sites at Asterby, Bag Enderby and Maidenwell, are similar to those on the Yorkshire Wolds. Examples of ladder-type enclosures are known from the Trent Valley in Nottinghamshire and on the Yorkshire Wolds. A parallel for the large settlement at Aswardby may be found at Hacconby, in the Fens, near Bourne. The principal difference between these areas and the Lincolnshire Wolds is the lack of evidence for field systems on the latter.

Farming in lowland areas during the Roman period probably formed a mixed economy. Wilson (1993) has suggested that the lack of evidence of ditched field boundaries to protect crops from stock in some areas can be explained by the use of other types of barrier, such as chalk banks surmounted by a thorn hedge, that have left no traces. Though ditched field systems are conspicuously absent from the aerial record of the Wolds, other evidence occurs which indicates that cereal production formed part of the agricultural economy of this region. Excavations at Ludford (N. Field, personal communication) have revealed evidence of grain production in the form of a corn-drying kiln. Other examples of corn drying kilns have been uncovered along the route of a gas pipeline in Scamblesby parish where remote sensing (geophysics) also recorded the existence of an extensive network of field enclosures.

The evidence for animal husbandry on the Wolds is far less tangible due to the limited number of excavations of rural sites. That stock rearing played a prominent role in the economy can be inferred from the form of the enclosures which are sometimes incorporated in villa complexes. One of the principal components of the Welton-le-Wold villa complex, and noted at others both on the Lincolnshire Wolds and elsewhere, is a double-ditched enclosure which does not appear to fulfil any defensive role. The ditches may have been dug to facilitate drainage. However, more likely uses could have been to contain stock, to act as a barrier to feed-animals or to protect crops from both feral and domestic animals. There is an undated, large, double-ditched, rectilinear enclosure within the Romano-British landscape on Otby Moor, that possesses a funnel or channelled entrance at one corner which strongly suggests use in stock control or stock rearing (Jones 1988, Fig.15).

This interpretation may also apply to the isolated, undated, irregularly-shaped and curvilinear enclosure with an inturned entrance, recorded at Ruckland (Fig.9) on the summit of the Wolds. This enclosure is similar to the excavated, concentric, Iron Age stock-enclosure at Tattershall Thorpe (Chowne 1986).

Where villa enclosures are double-ditched, or include major components which are double-ditched, it is suggested that the villas functioned principally as stock farms or ranches. This would also help explain the apparent lack of field systems accompanying settlements on the Wolds in Roman times, when the landscape may have largely formed open range.

Bibliography.

Bewley, R. H. and Jones, D. 1992. Aerial archaeology in Lincolnshire: 1991 and beyond. *Lincolnshire History and Archaeology*, vol.27, pp.41-43.

Bonnor, L. D. and Griffiths, D. W. 1993. *Archaeological Report on British Gas Skitter to Hatton (1050mm diameter) Pipeline*. Unpublished. Copy of typescript deposited with Lincolnshire County Council, Sites and Monuments Record.

Chowne, P. 1986. Excavations at an Iron Age defended enclosure at Tattershall Thorpe, Lincolnshire. *Proceedings of the Prehistoric Society*, vol.52, pp.159-88.

Clay, P. 1985. A survey of two cropmark sites in Lockington-Hemington parish, Leicestershire. *Transactions of the Leicestershire Archaeological and Historical Society*, vol.59, pp.17-26.

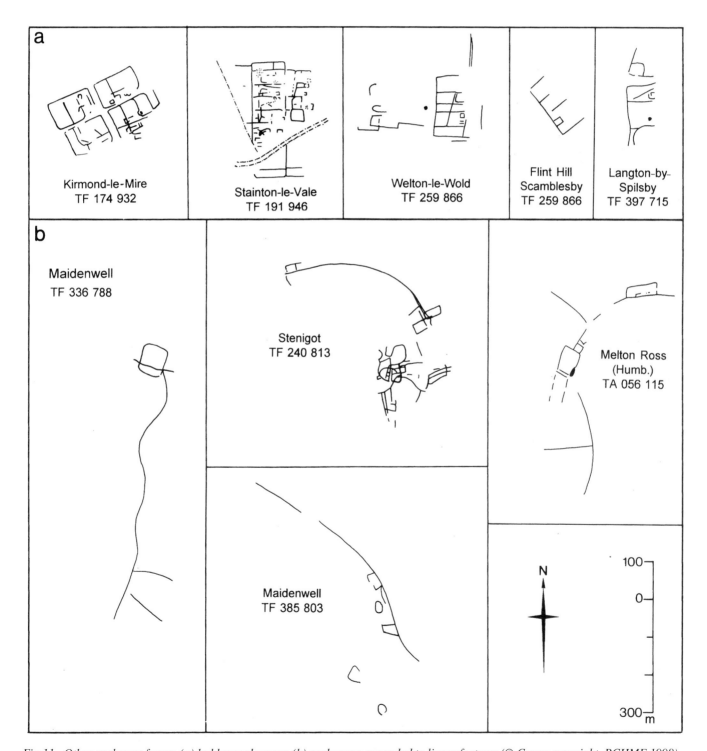

Fig.11. Other enclosure forms: (a) ladder enclosures; (b) enclosures appended to linear features (© Crown copyright. RCHME 1998).

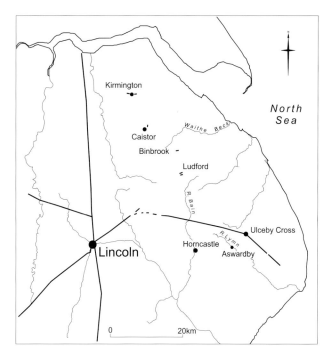

Fig.12. Roman roads in Lincolnshire (© Crown copyright. RCHME 1998).

Dark, K. and Dark, P. 1997. *The Landscape of Roman Britain*.

Deegan, A., forthcoming. *Nottinghamshire NMP Project*. RCHME internal report.

Jones, D. 1987. North Lincolnshire transect survey: a summary. *Lincolnshire History and Archaeology*, vol.22, pp.41-42.

Jones, D. 1988. Aerial reconnaissance and prehistoric and Romano-British archaeology in northern Lincolnshire - A sample survey. *Lincolnshire History and Archaeology*, vol.23, pp.5-30.

Jones, D. 1989. Aerial evidence from the survey area and its environs. In P. Phillips (ed.) 1989, part ii, pp.2-25.

Jones, D. and Whitwell, J. B. 1991. Survey of the Roman fort and multi-period settlement complex at Kirmington on the Lincolnshire Wolds. *Lincolnshire History and Archaeology*, vol.26, pp.57-62.

Leahy, K. A. 1980. Votive models from Kirmington, South Humberside. *Britannia*, vol.11, pp.326-30.

Margary, I. D. 1973. *Roman Roads in Britain*. 3rd edition.

May, J. 1984. The major settlements of the later Iron Age in Lincolnshire. In *A Prospect of Lincolnshire*, edited by F. N. Field and A. J. White, pp.18-22. Lincoln.

Palmer, R. 1996. Air photo interpretation and the Lincolnshire Fenland. *Landscape History* vol.18, pp.5-16.

Phillips, P. (ed.) 1989. *Archaeology and Landscape Studies in North Lincolnshire*. British Archaeological Reports, British Series 208 two volumes. Oxford.

Philpot, W. B. 1861. The remains of the Roman villa in the parish of Walesby. *Associated Architectural Societies' Reports and Papers*, vol.6:1, pp.135-38.

Riley, D. N. 1980. *Early Landscapes from the Air: Studies of Cropmarks in South Yorkshire and north Nottinghamshire*. Sheffield.

Stoertz, C. 1997. *Ancient Landscapes of the Yorkshire Wolds: Aerial Photographic Transcription and Analysis*. Swindon.

Taylor, C. 1983. *Village and Farmstead, A History of Rural Settlement in England*.

Whitwell, J. B. 1970, revised edition 1992. *Roman Lincolnshire*. History of Lincolnshire II. Lincoln.

Whitwell, J. B. 1982. *The Coritani: Some Aspects of the Iron Age Tribe and the Roman Civitas*. British Archaeological Reports, British Series 99. Oxford.

Wilson, D. R. 1974. Romano-British villas from the air. *Britannia*, vol.5, pp.251-61.

Wilson, D. R. 1993. Some thoughts on field archaeology. *AARGnews* (the Newsletter of the Aerial Archaeology Research Group), no.6, March 1993, pp.7-9.

Winton, H. 1995. *Owmby Cliff, Lincolnshire: Air Photograph Interpretation*. RCHME internal report. York.

Fig.13. Brinkhill. A stretch of the Roman road surviving as an earthwork next to a medieval moated site. The road can be traced in the field above as a soilmark. NMR TF3773/17/33, 13 January 1980, photograph P. Everson (© Crown copyright. RCHME).

Medieval and Post-Medieval Salt Extraction in North-East Lincolnshire.

Damian M. Grady

Introduction.

Human beings have no need for additional salt in their diet, yet the diet of the late twentieth century contains a high salt intake (Carter 1975). Why this paradox? One reason could be that we have grown accustomed to the taste of salt because of its previous use as a preservative. For all human communities the preservation of food, especially through the winter months, has been vital for survival. Before refrigeration became commonplace, the main methods for preserving food were drying, smoking and salting. In Lincolnshire the exploitation of sea water to produce salt has been important in most periods of the county's history. The focus of this paper is the presentation of the material remains of the medieval and post-medieval salt industry in the Outmarsh area between Humberston and Saltfleet in north-east Lincolnshire (Fig.1) and an assessment of the evidence for understanding the origins of this industry in the early medieval period.

The salt industry in the area mapped by the project has inspired much academic interest, mainly from historians and geographers. This paper will assess the information from this previous research, in light of the archaeological evidence visible on aerial photographs. Four themes will be considered: the current understanding of how salt was made at this time will be outlined, with special emphasis on the method, known as sand-washing, used in north-east Lincolnshire; the evidence visible on aerial photographs for sand-washing will be examined; the relationship between other features in the landscape, the coastline, sea banks, settlement and havens will be used to highlight some of the earliest physical remains of salt extraction in the area; and a discussion of the origins of medieval salt extraction and suggestions for further research.

Methods of extracting salt from sea water in the medieval/post-medieval periods.

The open pan process.

The easiest way of extracting salt from sea water involved boiling the sea water in a large lead or iron pan after it had been channelled into some form of collecting tank or pit. Medieval and post-medieval sites of this nature are not very common, with the Parsons Drove site in Cambridgeshire (French 1992) being one of the few medieval sites to have been excavated. However, it is still a method used to this day in Maldon, Essex. The open pan method was used more extensively in the prehistoric and Roman periods. In Bronze Age contexts natural pools were exploited for collecting the sea water (Palmer-Brown 1993), while in the Iron Age and Roman periods clay lined tanks were constructed to allow silt and sand to sink to the bottom before the sea water was boiled. In Essex the settling tanks consisted of a series of connected sub-circular pits (Fawn et al. 1990, p.8) and in the Lincolnshire Fens sea water was channelled off roddons to the settling tanks (Palmer 1996, p.10). The sea water was then boiled in an open pan of clay which was raised above a hearth by clay stands. The numerous clay artifacts involved in this process are generally known as briquetage. The broken briquetage was the main waste product and built up to form mounds with a characteristic red colour, which in Essex have become known as Red Hills. Although there has been a number of variations of the open pan process over time and in different parts of the country, the basic principle of the direct boiling of sea water remained the same.

Solar evaporation.

The most common method of salt extraction from sea water in medieval Europe was by the solar evaporation method. This technique is illustrated in Georgius Agricola's book De Re Metallica (1556), which depicts sea water being channelled through a series of shallow evaporation tanks. After exposure to the sun, the salt left behind can then be scraped up and dried. Salt made by this method became known as Bay salt, after a major production area in France called Borgneuf Bay, at the mouth of the Loire valley where the sites, at which the technique was used, were called sunworks. As this technique required no fuel for boiling, Bay salt was much cheaper to produce than other methods, although the quality of the salt was thought to be inferior to boiled salt.

A variation of this technique was used in some places along the English coast during the post-medieval period, most notably at Lymington in Hampshire (Lloyd 1967). At Lymington windmills were used to pump sea water from one evaporation tank to another, but even on the south coast of England the weather was generally not hot enough to totally evaporate the water, so the process had to be finished off by boiling.

The existence of a sunworks has been proposed at Sutton-on-Sea in Lincolnshire. The site which is situated in the inter-tidal zone at Sutton, has been known for some time, but became most prominent following the Great Storm of 1953. The storm ripped all the sand off the beach, some of which was deposited inland, revealing a complex arrangement of shallow rectangular features that extended from Sutton to Mablethorpe. Rudkin found post-medieval pottery in the vicinity of the rectangular features, which led to her interpretation of the site being a sunworks (Rudkin 1975, pp.39-40).

The rectangular features at Sutton show some resemblances to sunworks such as Lymington, but there is a lack of any documentary evidence for such a site. Other factors also count against Rudkin's interpretation. The east coast in the post-medieval period in Lincolnshire would have been even colder than Lymington and is not likely to have been hot enough, for long enough periods, to evaporate vast quantities of sea water, even if evaporation was finished off with boiling.

An important feature of the Lymington site is that it is situated on a relatively stable coastline. Sutton is not. Owen (1993, pp.39-41) has demonstrated how Sutton formerly had a large area of land beyond the modern shore-line. The post-medieval pottery found by Rudkin on the beach at Sutton, probably derives from the village which was washed away by the sea along with its church (Owen 1952, p.334).

The alternative explanation for the rectangular features is that they are remains of clay extraction for building and repairing sea defences. Some of the pits are the result of using clay to pack the foundations of nineteenth- and twentieth-century groynes (Betty Kirkham personal communication). However, not all the pits can relate to this recent activity, as some of the groynes overlie the pits. Many are likely to date back to at least the seventeenth century, when people in the district had a duty to help build and repair sea banks, with one of the tasks including collecting clay from the locality and transporting it to the new banks on sledges (Owen 1963, pp.26-27).

Sand-Washing.

The most extensively used method to extract salt from sea water in the medieval period was sand-washing, also known as

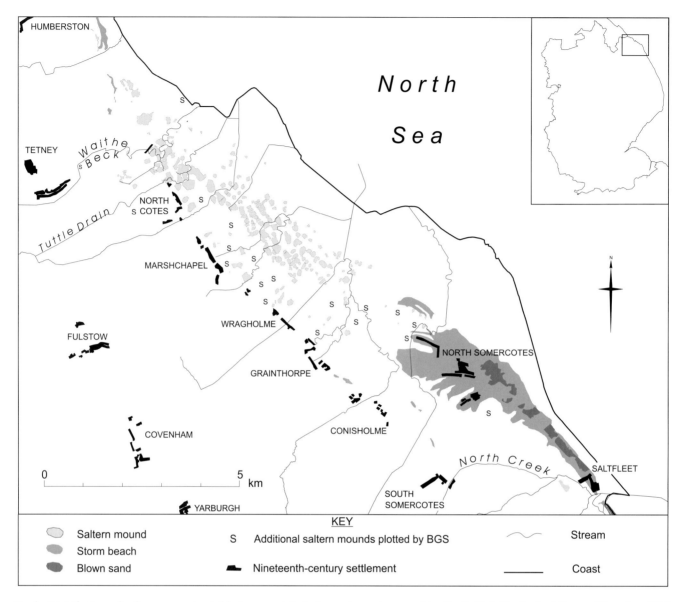

Fig.1. Distribution of saltern mounds visible from aerial photographs and mapped by the British Geological Survey (Based on BGS sheet 91 © NERC) (© Crown copyright. RCHME 1998).

sleeching. Current understanding of this method is based on a seminal paper by Rudkin and Owen (1960). Their article relied on monastic records and probate inventories from north-east Lincolnshire and post-medieval accounts of other salt making areas in Cumbria, the Solway Firth and excavations in Kent (Thompson 1956). Confirmation of Rudkin and Owen's theories on the method of salt production has come from excavations in the south of Lincolnshire, at Bicker Haven (Healey 1975, forthcoming), Wrangle Toft (Bannister 1983) and Wainfleet St Mary (McAvoy 1994), as well as other parts of England, such as Sussex (Holden & Hudson 1981).

This sand-washing method has left extensive remains in the area covered by the project. In order to fully understand the impact of salt extraction on the landscape in north-east Lincolnshire, it is first necessary to summarise what is known about the processes involved.

Gathering mould.

Following spring tides the sun and wind evaporated the surface moisture off the beach, leaving salt crystals on the surface of the sand. This top layer of sand was scraped off, possibly using a similar device to that used by salt makers in the Solway Firth, which was a horse-drawn, sledge-like implement, known as a *hap* (Duncan 1812, p.527). The resulting salt-impregnated sand

was called *mould or mouldefang* (Rudkin & Owen 1960, p.83), and was taken, by sledge, to the salt making site and stored as mounds, which were covered and protected by faggots (Sturman 1984, p.51).

Filtration.

The next stage involved separating the salt from the sand using a device, known in Cumbria as a *kinch* (Rudkin & Owen 1960, p.83), but following excavations at Wainfleet St Mary these have become known as filtration units (McAvoy 1994). The Wainfleet filtration units consisted of a shallow, rectangular, clay-lined pit, with a layer of peat at the bottom, upon which a timber box was placed. The mould was then placed in the box and had water poured over it. The peat acted as a filter allowing the salt to trickle through, in the form of brine. The bottom of the filter-bed sloped gently towards a clay- and turf-lined circular vat, where the brine collected. Small-scale excavations at Wrangle Toft found similar filtration units which had been constructed with blue clay, which would not have discoloured the salt as much as the red clay used at Wainfleet (Bannister 1983, pp.104-05).

The salt maker knew that all the salt had been extracted from the mould when the brine in the collecting vessel started to weaken. The strength of the brine was tested using a fresh egg.

Fig.2. An indication of what a Marshchapel saltcote may have looked like in 1595 can be seen in this reconstruction drawing by Wally Day. Note the cart bringing the salt-impregnated sand from the shore, the brine boiling away inside the saltcote and the salt drying outside. Reproduced with kind permission of David N. Robinson from The Book of the Lincolnshire Seaside.

An egg will float in a strong solution of salt but as the solution weakens the egg will sink, thereby indicating to the salt maker to stop washing the mould and move on to the next stage, of boiling the brine.

Boiling Brine.

Documentary sources describe the use of shallow lead pans for boiling the brine. No complete lead pans have been found in Lincolnshire, which is no surprise, as the lead would have been a valuable commodity. However, lead offcuts were found in areas of burning, assumed to be hearths, at Wainfleet St Mary (McAvoy 1994, p.142). The pans would have sat on top of a peat-fired hearth, such as the ones at Bicker Haven measuring 1.37m by 0.45m by 0.38m (Healey 1975, forthcoming).

The boiling of brine was a skilful task, carried out by people called *wellers* (Owen 1975b, p.43). There are six different salts in sea water, which are not equally soluble; the least soluble crystallize first when boiled. The main salt required was *sodium chloride*, which was the third salt to crystallize (Bridbury 1955, p.7). The remaining salts were collectively known as *bittern* and included *magnesium sulphate* (more commonly known as Epsom salts). It was crucial that the weller removed the required salt crystals at the appropriate time. The bittern was either reboiled, so that the other salts could be removed and used for other purposes, or thrown away. The amount of bittern could be reduced by using fresh water, rather than sea water, for washing the mould.

In addition to the bittern, the weller had to remove other material from the brine, such as silt, peat, *etc.*, which may not have been removed at the filtration stage. To help remove this material, various ingredients were added to the brine, in the belief that they would combine with the unwanted material and form a scum, which could be scraped off the top. The additives used tended to vary according to local custom, and could include sheep blood, flour or beer.

Saltcotes.

The whole boiling process took place in a building known as a saltcote. In the Lincolnshire Fens these buildings were made of mud walls, with timber doors and windows, and a roof of timber and reed thatch (Hallam 1960, p.98). Once the salt was scooped out of the pans it was placed in wicker baskets and hung up to dry, before it was taken away to be sold (Fig.2).

Fuel.

The filtration of mould would appear to be an unnecessarily complex and labour-intensive process, compared to the direct boiling of sea water. However, the major advantage of boiling concentrated brine from the sand-washing process over boiling of sea water, was the fact that it saved fuel.

Peat was the main fuel used. The nearest peat deposits available in the Outmarsh were in Grainthorpe and Conisholme Fens, but the quantities were so insubstantial that they have not appeared on the geological or soil maps. Therefore, peat had to be shipped in from elsewhere. A number of monasteries which owned salterns in north-east Lincolnshire held turbary (peat cutting) rights in the Humber Headlands, from where they shipped peat to their salterns (Sturman 1984, p.54; Pawley 1993, p.56). In some parts of the county, such as Wainfleet and Wrangle, the granting of turbary rights appears to have been a necessary requirement for salt production to be possible (Owen, forthcoming). Later, peat appears to have been replaced by coal as the main fuel (Rudkin & Owen 1960, p.80).

Waste.

The waste material from the filtration and boiling processes was disposed of close to the production areas and gradually built up to form mounds. These mounds are the dominant features in the landscape, with many being clearly visible on aerial photographs (Fig.3), and this project mapped over 200 individual mounds between Humberston and Saltfleet in an area sixteen kilometres long by about three kilometres wide (Fig.1). All these features relating to salt production, mounds, saltcotes, *etc.*, are known collectively as salterns.

Identifying the sand-washing process from the air.

Waste mounds.

Although the mounds come in many different sizes and shapes, they all have similar characteristics. When ploughed, the edges of the mounds show up as a lighter mark, compared to the centre of the mound (Fig.3). The mounds also have a distinctive outline which Healey (forthcoming) describes as *floriform*. This describes the bulbous outline and dark, possibly wetter centre. The dark centre could be where the filtration took place, with the waste being dumped to one side creating one of the protrusions of the mound. However, until excavations are carried out on these mounds, these observations are preliminary.

In some areas the shape of the mounds has been determined by their position near meandering tidal streams; these mounds tend to be elongated and irregular, especially those in North Coates[1] and Tetney near Waithe Beck and Tuttle Drain. The large group of mounds in Marshchapel and Grainthorpe are slightly less elongated and irregular. This is possibly a reflection of their original position, facing out to the open sea, and the manner in which the salt marsh in front of the active salterns was divided up. In the Lincolnshire Fens, the salt marsh was divided by boundaries to form an area called a *greva* or *sandacre* (Hallam 1960, pp.109-10). Similar salt-marsh boundaries can be seen on a map of Marshchapel made in 1595 by William Haiwarde (Beresford & St Joseph 1958, p.263). Some of the boundaries are still traceable today, in the form of the straight dykes and roads between the village of Marshchapel and the 1638 sea bank.

Of the salterns that have been mapped from aerial photographs there appears to be a concentration extending from the first Grainthorpe Haven to the south-east side of North Coates parish. However, from brief ground observation and examination of the British Geological Survey map (BGS 1990), it is clear that there are a number of salterns which have not been plotted, lying between the apparent concentration and the settlement to the west (Fig.1). The main reason for this is that the majority of these mounds are overlain by ridge-and-furrow. This has had the affect of obscuring the outline of the mounds and smoothing their edges, so that they now appear to merge into 'an undulating plateau' (Pattison & Williamson 1986, p.78), which makes individual mounds difficult to see on aerial photographs.

Mould.

While the waste mounds are relatively easy features to identify on aerial photographs, the other salt production features are more difficult to interpret. According to the probate inventories of the sixteenth and seventeenth centuries for the area, the mould was one of the most valuable items belonging to a salt maker (Sturman 1984, p.53), and so mould mounds are unlikely to have been abandoned.

Filtration units.

If it is assumed that similar filtration units to the Wainfleet examples were used in north-east Lincolnshire they would be very difficult to detect on aerial photographs, due to their relatively short length (3.42m) and shallow depth (0.28m). The same would be true even if they were a similar size (6m long) to those described by Brownrigg (1748, pp.135-37) in eighteenth-century Cumbria. One of the mounds (TA 3709 0018) in Marshchapel parish contains a pit with a diameter of one or two metres next to a rectangular pit surrounded by banks. This possible filtration unit, visible on RAF verticals taken in 1946, is difficult to see even with a stereoscope, so this interpretation should be treated with caution.

The Wainfleet excavations also revealed a series of pipes connected to pits, which were interpreted as sumps for the collection of sea water. The sea water would have been used for washing the mould. No such features have been identified in north-east Lincolnshire, but again their small size would make them difficult to spot on aerial photographs and they are likely to have been covered by later waste.

It is tempting to believe that any features associated with the mounds could be related to the salt industry, but this would be too simplistic. Many mounds have ridge-and-furrow covering them, which, in turn, is cut by circular and rectilinear enclosures. There are similar looking enclosures on mounds not covered by ridge-and-furrow. These enclosures are likely to relate to the period of land use following the abandonment of the mounds.

Saltcotes.

Haiwarde's map of Marshchapel made in 1595 (Walshaw 1935) shows buildings on many of the easternmost mounds, with the cartouche stating that they were 'presente in use for salt'. The buildings shown by Haiwarde were not visible on aerial photographs, but other mounds further west appear to contain remnants of buildings, which are visible mainly on 1940s and 1950s RAF verticals, before they were ploughed down (Fig.3). Most of the potential buildings only appear, at best, as two sides of a rectangular enclosure, or an amalgamation of overlapping, earth-covered foundations. If it is accepted that these are indeed buildings, there is no direct evidence to suggest that they are contemporary with salt manufacture. They could indicate later use as barns or farms which have been abandoned. However, Haiwarde's map depicts the active saltcotes in the middle and near the edge of the mounds so the buildings on the edge of the mounds visible on aerial photographs could be saltcotes. A further complication is the fact that Haiwarde's map also shows how many of the active mounds appear to have been split up and owned by more than one person. As Haiwarde's map is remarkably accurate in most respects, it is safe to assume that any saltcotes that can be identified to the west of those depicted by Haiwarde are likely to have been abandoned before 1595.

Boiling hearths.

A feature which may have been a boiling hearth was excavated at the beginning of the century on a mound in North Somercotes parish (Longley 1900). Longley states that:

> a mound which was circular in shape, stood out from the surrounding level to a height of five or six foot, the top being saucer shaped with a dip of about 2 foot 6 inches [0.75m] and measuring 21 feet [6.4m] across from brim to brim. On digging into this depression I found a kind of pan about 12 inches [0.3m] thick following roughly the curvature of the outer surface, and formed apparently of puddled clay, which on the underside had certainly been exposed to the action of fire, being quite vitreous in some places.

Longley goes on to describe how farmers had ploughed up other similar features on top of other mounds. Unfortunately there is no indication as to which mound was excavated. The feature described by Longley was possibly a boiling hearth, on top of which a lead pan would have been placed (David

Fig.3. Vertical photograph of Marshchapel and North Coates parishes showing some saltern mounds in pasture and others with the characteristic pale outline, which have been ploughed. Several of the mounds in pasture may have saltcotes on their edges. North is to the bottom of the photograph (RAF CPE UK/746 frame 5012, 21 Sept.1946, MOD © Crown Copyright).

Robinson, personal communication). The dimensions, given by Longley, of the top of the mound have been used as the dimensions of the pan itself (Rudkin & Owen 1960, p.80). While the vagueness of Longley's description makes this a possible interpretation, a pan 21 feet (6.4m) in diameter seems a little too large. The true size of the pan may be reflected in an earlier reference in Longley's article, to an excavation in Tetney by Bishop Trollope who found a similar feature which was 5 feet (1.5m) in diameter.

No circular depressions have been found on aerial photographs, which, even if Longley's dimensions are correct, are possibly too shallow and wide to be seen as earthworks. Excavation will be the only way of finding Longley's clay pans and testing whether the other features tentatively suggested to be contemporary with the mounds are indeed saltcotes and filtration units. Two suggested boiling pits at Tetney Lock have been proven to be a drinking pond and plover decoy respectively (David Robinson, personal communication).

Salt in the landscape: The relationship of salterns to other landscape features.

Having described the different ways to extract salt, it is worth pointing out one main difference between two of the methods used. No evidence for a phase of filtering salt-impregnated sand before boiling, has been recognised in prehistoric or Roman contexts. However, it must be noted that there is a lack of recent large-scale excavations of prehistoric and Roman salt working sites and most work, especially in Lincolnshire, has concentrated on the collection and dating of briquetage (Hayes & Lane 1992, pp.218-29). On available evidence, there does not appear to have been anything similar to the sand-washing process in the prehistoric or Roman periods. But when was the sand-washing method first used in north-east Lincolnshire? Without evidence from excavation this is difficult to say. Merely identifying salterns will not provide the answers. What may be useful, is an understanding of the relationship between salterns and other landscape features to help highlight some of the earliest sand-washing mounds in this area. But before these points in the landscape can be revealed, certain assumptions have to be stated about changes in the coastline and the relationship between salterns and sea banks.

Coastline changes.

Firstly, the saltern mounds furthest away from the sea are likely to be older than those closest to it. This is based, in part, on research on coastal evolution in north-east Lincolnshire (Swinnerton 1931; Robinson 1956, 1970) and partly on information about the salt industry from Haiwarde's 1595 map of Marshchapel and Fulstow (Walshaw 1935).

Since the last glaciation there have been a number of changes in the coastline of north-east Lincolnshire, but for the purposes of this paper the changes from the end of the Roman period are the most important. From this time there was a rise in sea level, resulting in higher tides which led to greater erosion of Holderness and a former offshore barrier (Swinnerton 1931, pp.371-72). Although the barrier was being eroded, it helped lessen the effect of heavy seas. Eventually the deposition of silt negated the impact of the higher tides and subsequently salt marshes developed and the coastline moved gradually seawards. The silting resulted in the river Lud forming three major distributaries. The natural deposition of sand and silt produced the ideal conditions for making salt by the sand-washing method, since the sand removed for mould was soon replaced.

In the thirteenth century weather conditions appeared to worsen (Owen 1952; Bailey 1989) with the result that the off-shore barrier was overtopped by rising sea levels. The debris created during this so called 'stormy century', possibly formed

the core of the storm beaches and sand dunes (blown sand in Fig.4) in Humberston and Somercotes. From the fourteenth century the coast was accreting faster than it was sinking and by the end of the sixteenth century the bulk of the accretion had been accomplished (Robinson 1956, pp.11-12). From the sixteenth century onwards, any changes in the coastline tended to be the result of deliberate man-made reclamation.

As has already been mentioned, the salt makers took advantage of the natural deposition of sand and silt, but the waste mounds also helped to consolidate the natural reclamation that was taking place. This is illustrated by Haiwarde's map, on which he tells us that when the mounds became too big for making salt, the salt makers moved closer to the sea, with the old mounds becoming pasture (Walshaw 1935, p.198).

The development of land from saltern to pasture can also be seen on Haiwarde's map. The active salterns, nearest the sea, appear as islands within the salt marsh. The older mounds, which have been turned into pasture, provide the impetus for reclamation to take place between the mounds, resulting in the formation of enclosed fields on the seaward side of the village of Marshchapel. An indication that these fields enclose mounds, comes from the field names, as most contain the *holme* element. *Holme* comes from the Old Norse *holmr*, meaning high drier ground amid the marshes (Sturman 1984, p.52).

Salterns and sea banks.

The second assumption is that saltern mounds behind, and incorporated into, sea banks, must have been abandoned when the banks were built. This is based on the fact that the construction of a barrier would inhibit the transfer of mould from the beach to the salt making site (Owen 1984, p.46). Where documentary evidence mentions a sea bank and a saltern in the same entry the saltern is said to lie outside the sea bank (Hallam 1960, p.110; Rudkin & Owen 1960, p.83). Therefore, if it is possible to date the construction of a sea bank, this date will provide a *terminus ante quem* for the abandonment of the mounds.

The truth of this assumption can be demonstrated by examining the sea bank built in 1638 (Rudkin & Owen 1960, p.80) in the parishes of Grainthorpe, Marshchapel and North Coates. The bank can be traced in part, as earthworks, cropmarks and field boundaries, from Seven Towns North Eau to Horse Shoe Point and then to the east of Tetney Lock (Fig.4). This sea bank enclosed a large area of salt marsh and incorporated a number of salterns along its course. The documentary evidence amassed by Rudkin and Owen (1960) makes it clear that just before this bank was built, the salt industry in these parishes had come to an end. This was due in part to the import of cheaper salt from the continent and, more importantly, from Scotland and Newcastle. Although the relatively labour intensive sand-washing process required less fuel than boiling sea water, the Scottish and Newcastle salt makers had easy access to cheap coal, which lowered the cost of production considerably (Sturman 1984, pp.54-55). Scottish salt makers were also given certain tax advantages when James I came to the throne. Conversely, Lincolnshire salt makers had to import coal at the beginning of the seventeenth century, with the result that the salt from the labour intensive sand-washing process became too expensive.

In North Somercotes a similar situation occurs. Documentary evidence suggests that salt making had ceased at the beginning of the seventeenth century, with the result that Sir Endymion Porter was able to begin the reclamation of the area to the north of the salterns in 1632. By 1638, when the reclamation was complete, the area became known as Porter's Marsh (Robinson 1981, p.28).

The only other sea bank that can be dated with any confidence lies in Tetney. In 1570 there was a major storm which affected the whole of the Lincolnshire coast (Owen

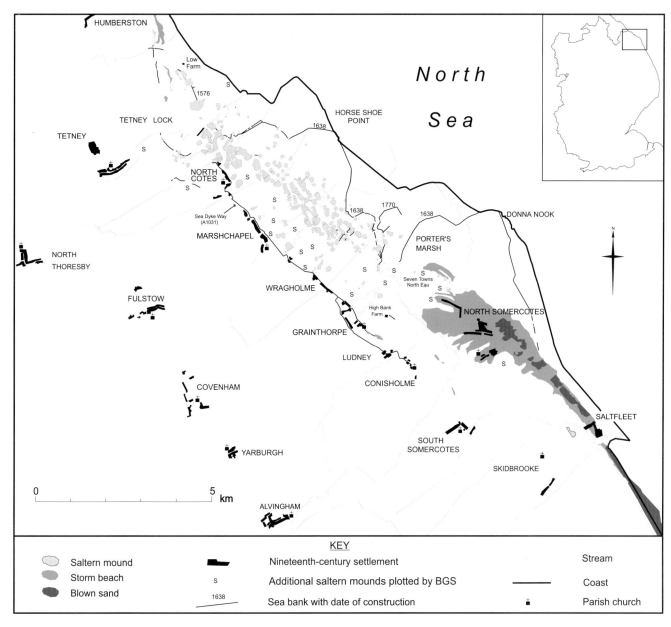

Fig.4. Saltern mounds in relation to sea banks and settlements (Based on BGS sheet 91 © NERC) (© Crown copyright. RCHME 1998).

1996) and resulted in the destruction of many saltcotes (Rudkin & Owen 1960, pp.79-80). The sea overran areas of Tetney because the sea bank, known as Eastseadyke, was 'no bigger than a plough furrow' (Robinson 1981, p.27) and was unable to cope with the floods. By 1576 the Eastseadyke was replaced by a more substantial bank and linked a number of salterns, which enabled the areas known as Newton, Lescastles and South Marshes to be reclaimed. A bank linking a number of salterns is visible on aerial photographs between Low Farm and Tetney Lock. This bank lies to the east of areas known as Newton Marsh, The Castles and South Marsh (Russell & Russell 1983, p.97), so presumably this is the 1576 sea bank. Therefore, it is safe to assume that the salterns incorporated into this bank must have been abandoned before 1576 (Fig.4).

In the few centuries before 1570 there appears to be no mention in documentary sources of the construction of new sea banks in the area. Either documents on the subject have not survived, or sea banks were not deemed necessary. It is notable that from the sea banks already discussed, the need to reclaim land may have been more important than protection from floods. For two or three hundred years before 1570 the seaward advance of the salterns themselves may have provided enough reclaimed land, thereby making sea banks unnecessary. This

idea may be supported by the fact that in the thirteenth century, a period which is known to have been very stormy (Bailey 1989), there were no major sea banks constructed in this area. However, a lack of documentary evidence does not provide proof and also there is one bank, in Grainthorpe parish to the east of High Bank Farm (Fig.4), for which no dating evidence has presented itself and which could, possibly, date from this time.

Salterns, sea banks and settlement.

Despite the lack of evidence for the construction of earlier sea banks, the existence of one can be inferred from understanding the relationship between the salterns and the origins of the settlements between North Cotes and Conisholme. The complex relationship between salterns, sea bank and settlement is based on the interpretations of documentary evidence by historians and geographers and can be summarised as follows.

Sometime before Domesday, salt makers set up their saltcotes in the area now covered by the settlements between North Cotes and Conisholme (Fig.4). The temporary nature of these early dwellings may be reflected in place-names such as North Cotes, meaning 'the huts to the north' (Cameron 1996, p.143). As more use was made of the abandoned salterns and surrounding salt marsh for pasture, there was an increasing need for a sea bank to protect the land. This sea bank incorporated some of the most westerly salterns, many of which can still be seen today within the modern villages. The sea bank, probably built in stages, is marked roughly by the line of the road that now connects all these villages. The earliest documentary reference to a sea bank in the area occurs in 1198 in Grainthorpe parish (Owen 1975a, p.50), but it is not known when the bank was constructed. Grainthorpe was the only one of the settlements to be named in Domesday: the remaining settlements, North Cotes, Marshchapel, Wragholme, Ludney and Conisholme are not mentioned individually. However, the settlements and their salterns are assumed to have been in existence, being incorporated in the entries for North Thoresby, Fulstow, the Covenhams and Alvingham, which are situated too far inland for salt production to be possible (Robinson 1970, p.63; Rudkin & Owen 1960, pp.76-79). In the case of Conisholme this assumption may be correct, in that there is a late pre-Conquest cross-head at Conisholme church, which would normally be taken to imply a church with burial rights (Everson & Stocker, forthcoming).

While the early sea bank may not appear very substantial, there are signs that it has had an important impact on village topography. For example in Marshchapel there are two distinct areas of settlement; the main street Sea Dyke Way, and the area around the church. Sea Dyke Way probably marks the position of the sea bank. It is conceivable that the area around the church, which is built on a saltern (BGS 1990), could mark the position of one element, at least, of an earlier settlement pattern. Haiwarde's map (Walshaw 1935, p.200) depicts the majority of settlement built against the west side of Sea Dyke Way, clearly demonstrating the impact of the bank on village development. It also demonstrates that the bank was constructed prior to construction of the buildings on its west flank.

This development from salterns, to sea bank to permanent settlement, cannot be proved or disproved by aerial photographic evidence, which cannot provide dates for each phase either. However, it is not inconsistent with what is known about the relationship between later salterns and sea banks.

A key area for determining the origins of sand-washing is in North Coates and Tetney parishes. Some of the most westerly saltern mounds are situated in these parishes, two of which (at TA 326 015 and TA 336 005, marked by an S in Fig.5) were not visible on aerial photographs but were mapped by BGS (1990). The latter mound, to the west of North Cotes, may also be associated with another sea bank. Two sections of bank are visible on aerial photographs, but are interpreted as being one sea bank. The point at which the bank cannot be traced from aerial photographs coincides with the seaward side of the mound mapped by BGS (1990), from which it is possible to conjecture that the mound had been abandoned before the bank was built. When the bank was built cannot be determined, but its position in the landscape appears to make it earlier than the North Cotes-Conisholme sea bank.

To the north of the mound and sea bank just described is a group of salterns near Riverside Farm (Fig.5). The appearance of these salterns is slightly different from the majority of other salterns. Though this is due mainly to the effects of later ploughing, the significant point is that they have ditches surrounding them. Salterns with surrounding ditches are common in Sussex, where the ditches are believed to have been formed by the effects of water running off the mounds (Holden & Hudson 1981, p.129). This is one possible reason for the ditches in the Riverside Farm example. However, there have been so many changes in the drainage pattern, due to the combined effects of natural deposition, the close proximity to the Tetney Blow Wells and the construction of the Louth Canal, that streams will have meandered around the mounds. Despite the effects of ridge-and-furrow and later ploughing, the mounds were still distinctive enough in the eighteenth century to be marked as individual fields on enclosure award maps (Russell & Russell 1983, p.97).

The Riverside Farm salterns are also incorporated into a sea bank. The bank is visible on early vertical photographs as an earthwork and on later ones as a cropmark. In many places the bank is cut by later stream channels and extends from the salterns to the southern end of Newton Marsh Lane. The line of the sea bank probably continues north, following the line of Newton Marsh Lane. The eastern section of this lane follows a sinuous course, which is similar to other medieval sea banks to the south of Sutton-on-Sea (Arthur Owen, personal communication). At the point where the lane turns east, the sea bank continues on its northern course and can be traced as an earthwork as far as another saltern in Humberston parish.

A small excavation was carried out on this last section of bank by Lindsey Archaeological Services (Tann 1995), but no dating evidence was found and the excavator thought that the bank was not substantial enough to have been a sea defence (Geoff Tann, personal communication). This is not an unreasonable observation, as other medieval sea banks elsewhere in the county are quite substantial. Despite this, the original interpretation of this being a sea bank is probably still valid as there are a number of ways in which it may have been reduced in size. Some of the sea banks which have been examined in this area have been seriously damaged by later farming practices. In other parts of Lincolnshire such as Theddlethorpe, the Commissioner for Sewers in the nineteenth century was concerned that local people were levelling old sea banks (Owen 1953, p.25). This and the lack of maintenance of many sea banks, especially the precursor of the 1576 one in Tetney, demonstrates that sea banks may appear, at times, to be quite insubstantial.

The bank from Humberston to the Riverside Farm salterns, is also difficult to date. It could be a continuation of the Conisholme-North Cotes sea bank, but this is a little speculative, especially as the aerial photographic evidence does not show the two actually connecting. However, from its position in the landscape, the Riverside Farm-Humberston sea bank is earlier than the 1576 bank to the east and is on the landward side of a line of old storm beaches (BGS 1990), which could indicate that the sea bank is earlier than the storm beaches. The development of the storm beach on the seaward side of the Humberston saltern would have prevented easy access to the salt marsh and so could have been the cause for the abandonment of the saltern. Robinson (1970) has proposed a late twelfth- to early fourteenth-century date for the storm beaches based on Owen's (1952) documentary research on Lincolnshire coastal erosion. If this is correct then the Humberston-Riverside Farm sea bank could be thirteenth century or earlier and the salterns incorporated into the sea bank earlier still. Tetney had thirteen active salterns at the time of Domesday. Whether the Riverside Farm salterns and the one to the west are those of Domesday is debateable, but worth testing, as is the date of the saltern and earlier sea bank to the south. However, can all the old storm beaches be assumed to date to around the thirteenth century? Examining the relationship between salterns, storm beaches, sand dunes and settlement between Saltfleet and North Somercotes suggests that in some cases it can and in others possibly not.

Salterns, old storm beaches and havens.

Between Saltfleet and the western end of North Somercotes village is a continuous area of storm beach (Fig.6). The southern end of the beach is less than one hundred metres wide, but to the north it 'consists in plan of at least seventeen separate fingers, some of which are straight and others recurved' (Pattison 1988a). Covering the storm beach is a veneer of blown sand, which in places form sand dunes up to ten metres high.

Towards the southern end of the storm beach is a saltern (Fig.6), which although it is situated behind the storm beach, is

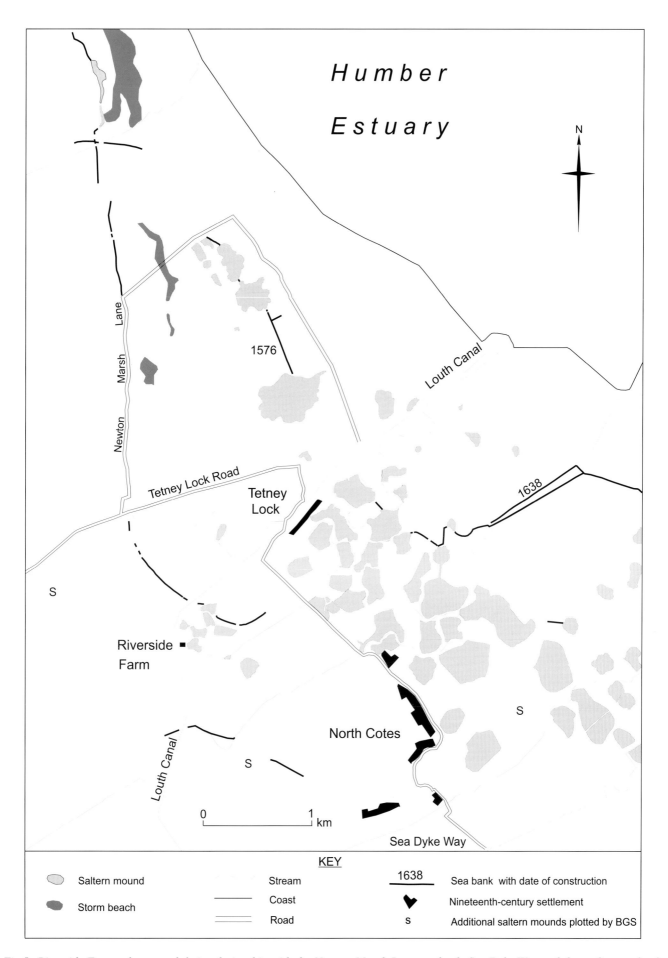

Fig.5. Riverside Farm salterns and their relationship with the Newton Marsh Lane sea bank, Sea Dyke Way and the earlier sea bank in North Coates (Based on BGS sheet 91 © NERC) (© Crown copyright. RCHME 1998).

not necessarily earlier than the beach. This is due to its position near the former course of North Creek, the southern distributary of the river Lud, which is one of the streams that flows into Saltfleet Haven and is likely to have been tidal, thereby making it possible for salt marsh to develop and allowing salt making to continue behind the storm beach.

The modern Saltfleet Haven has not changed its position much since it was mentioned in the Domesday Book, although the courses of the streams that enter the haven have been altered to stop it silting up (Owen 1954, pp.91-100). In more recent times a haven is classed as a place for ships and boats to shelter at times of poor weather (Smyth 1867, p.372). In the medieval period havens were also used for a limited amount of trade (Pawley 1993, p.56).

Another haven also mentioned in the same Domesday entry as Saltfleet Haven, is Mar Haven. This last haven has long since disappeared, but was situated where there is now a gap in the sand dunes near Skidbrooke Farm (Fig.6), where the parish boundaries of North and South Somercotes and Skidbrooke with Saltfleet converge on the coast (Owen 1954, pp.89-90). There are no references to salterns at Skidbrooke in Domesday, but by the twelfth century salt making appears to be well established in the parish, though no more is known beyond the thirteenth century, when documents refer to an abandoned saltern which had reverted to pasture, close to Mar harbour (Rudkin & Owen 1960, p.79).

In this area it would seem that at the end of the twelfth century Mar Haven went out of use (Owen 1954, p.90) possibly due to the development of the storm beach, with the abandoned salterns situated underneath or behind the storm beach. Although no salterns were visible on aerial photographs in this area, the BGS (1990) mapped a large group of salterns behind the storm beach and between North Somercotes church and Skidbrooke Farm. Unlike the saltern near Saltfleet, there is no sign of a tidal creek that could have kept the salterns as viable concerns once the storm beach developed and prevented access to the sea at Mar Haven. Such was the impact of the storm beach that the outfall of the Seven Towns South Eau, the central distributary of the river Lud, changed its position from Mar Haven to its current outfall near Donna Nook.

To the north west of Mar Haven the storm beach broadens out considerably and is now the location of the present village of North Somercotes (Fig.6). In the Domesday book no references are made to North or South Somercotes, just Somercotes. This and the creation of the storm beach has led to the assumption that Somercotes did not develop into North and South Somercotes until the thirteenth or fourteenth centuries (Robinson 1956, p.6). On the first edition Ordnance Survey map (XXXII.SW and XLI.NW) of 1891 North Somercotes is depicted with three nuclei. The southern nucleus is centred around the parish church and might be expected to have an early origin. The middle nucleus is centred on Keeling Street, which forms part of the road which links North Somercotes with Conisholme, and is assumed to be a continuation of the North Cotes-Conisholme sea bank (Owen 1975a, p.48). An alternative candidate for a sea bank is the northern settlement nucleus centred on an area called The Bank. The settlement in this area is situated to the south of a road called Bank End. Salterns plotted from aerial photographs lie to the north of this road. Where Bank End comes to a stop, its line is continued for 400 metres to the west by another saltern plotted by BGS (1990). The position of this mound suggests that it is one of the earliest salterns in the parish and determining the relationship between the possible banks and salterns will again help in dating the beginnings of the salt industry in the parish.

The identification of the latest salterns in North Somercotes parish is confused by the presence of a large storm beach. As has already been stated, salt making in North Somercotes came to an end at the beginning of the sixteenth century. By comparison with the salterns further north, the last salterns in the parish should be those closest to the sea. On the aerial photographs and geology map (BGS 1990) the nearest salterns to the sea lie between Bank End and Porter's Marsh, but on their seaward side is a kilometre long storm beach, which should, in theory, date the salterns to the thirteenth century or earlier. Two conclusions could be drawn from this. If the storm beach is thirteenth century then the sixteenth-century salterns await discovery by other survey techniques, or the salterns could be early sixteenth century with the storm beach developing sometime between the abandonment of the salterns and the creation of Porter's Marsh between 1632 and 1638.

If the second conclusion is correct, this demonstrates the need to test the assumption that all storm beaches in the vicinity are thirteenth century. This could be particularly important for dating the small isolated areas of storm beach between North and South Somercotes (Fig.6) and to the west of Conisholme church and in understanding their relationship with areas of settlement earthworks identified on aerial photographs near The Poplars, Eau Bridge Farm and to the east of Conisholme church. Add to this further areas of settlement earthworks at Skidbrooke Farm, the south-east side of South Somercotes and the area to the west of Skidbrooke church, where tenth century pottery has been found, this whole area highlights a degree of complexity in the landscape which is difficult to understand and beyond the narrow confines of attempting to understand the origins of sand-washing.

Grainthorpe and its havens.

The prominence of Grainthorpe among the North Cotes-Conisholme settlements as the only one named in Domesday is notable and persists through to the later medieval period. Why was this? One of the reasons could be the fact that it is a kilometre to the south-east of the end of a Roman road (Margary 1973, p.241 road number 272), called Salter's Lane which linked the coast with Lincoln in the medieval and post-medieval periods (Fig.7). Another reason is its relationship with a haven. Grainthorpe could have been a collection and redistribution point for both land and sea transport of salt and other commodities.

The existing Grainthorpe Haven consists of a channel dug into tidal mud flats at the outfall of Seven Towns North Eau, and was built in the nineteenth century (second GH in Fig.7). This replaced an earlier haven constructed in the seventeenth century (Foster & Longley 1924, pp.lxiii-lxiv) that can be traced as a funnel formed by the sea banks built in 1638 and 1770 near Sea Farm (first GH in Fig.7). This in turn replaced an earlier haven called Swine Haven, which is mentioned in the Domesday Book. Foster and Longley (1924, p.lxiii) locate the Domesday Swinehaven close to the point where Swine Dyke and the northern distributary of the river Lud, Seven Towns North Eau, converge. Between this point and the first Grainthorpe Haven, there are more banks between the salterns, which together form another funnel. From Foster and Longley's description it is tempting to believe that these banks are related to the Domesday Swinehaven. However, they could be related to the water management of the later havens.

Proving the exact position of Swinehaven would be very useful for dating the salterns in Grainthorpe and understanding the relationship between sea banks and the development of the settlement. The plan of the existing settlement of Grainthorpe is based on two parallel roads, both of which could follow the line of a sea bank. However, the most easterly road, High Street, has the most complex landscape relationships. At the north-east end of the village, High Street sits on top of the most westerly salterns in the parish (BGS 1990), and where High Street comes to an end, near the parish church, a track then a footpath may continue the line of the bank as far as Ludney. Determining the exact line of this last section of bank and indeed whether it is a sea bank or not, will also be important for dating three, small areas of storm beach. The most northerly storm beach lies

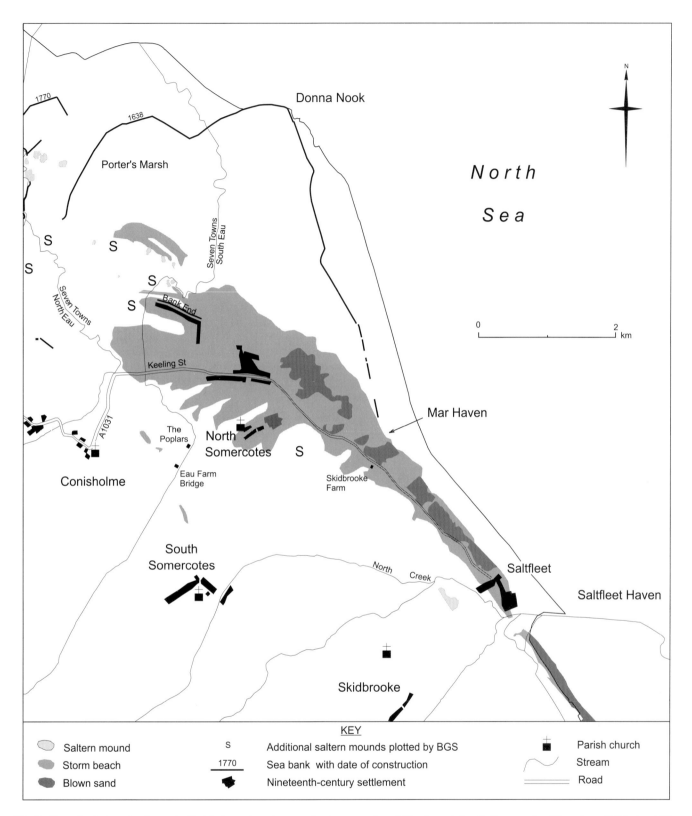

Fig.6. Map depicting the impact of old storm beaches on the topography of North and South Somercotes (Based on BGS sheet 91 © NERC) (© Crown copyright. RCHME 1998).

beneath the parish church, the middle one is situated behind the proposed line of the sea bank, with the most southerly one on either side of the bank. Are all three contemporary and do they date to the thirteenth century as suggested by BGS (Pattison 1988b)? Add to this another possible sea bank to the north-east of Grainthorpe, near High Bank Farm, and it is clear that, like the Somercotes parishes, Grainthorpe is a key area, not only for understanding the development of the salt industry, but also the date and nature of settlement and trade in the area.

Discussion and future research.

At present the examination of these complex landscape relationships can only provide a relative chronology for dating the phases of the salt industry in north-east Lincolnshire. The earliest date that can be used with any confidence is that of Domesday, but exactly which salterns were in use at this time is not clear. However, it is safe to assume that salt extraction was well under way before 1086, not only in this part of the country,

91

but also at over twelve hundred places where salterns are recorded in Domesday on the south and east coasts (Keen 1988, p.140). There are earlier references in Anglo-Saxon documents to sea-salt production in the south of England (Keen 1988, pp.134-36), although what method was used is not clear. The earliest use of the sand-washing method could conceivably have originated in other parts of the British Isles which were not recorded in Domesday, such as Cumbria (Martin 1975) and Dumfriesshire (Duncan 1812), which are known to have used the method a little later. Where the origins of the sand-washing process have been considered, it is assumed to have been brought in by Anglo-Saxon immigrants (Holden & Hudson 1981, p.123), yet researchers in this country have not been able to identify an early medieval sand-washing site on the continent. It is well known that sand-washing was practised in Normandy in the eighteenth century (Brownrigg 1748, p.135; Sturman 1984, pp.50-52), but from the published (translated) literature, there is no evidence for earlier sand-washing.

The main type of medieval sea-salt extraction on the continent, other than solar evaporation, was the burning of salt impregnated peat. This technique was mainly carried out in Belgium and Holland and does not appear to have found its way in to the British Isles. Although evidence for sand-washing has not been determined in early medieval contexts on the continent, there is some evidence of it in prehistory. Nenquin (1961, p.105) states that Pliny the Elder, in book thirty-one of his *Naturalis Historia*, refers to the use of sand-washing, but the evidence is not clear. However, evidence of Iron Age sand-washing has been found at La Panne in Belgium (Professor Thoen, personal communication).

Regardless of whether the sand-washing technique was brought from the continent in the early medieval period or not, what was the stimulus that led to its development in Lincolnshire? Excavations at Droitwich have demonstrated that, because of its inland brine springs with their greater purity, it was a major producer of salt from the post-Roman period through to the medieval period (Hurst 1997) and is likely to have dominated the salt market over a large area of the Midlands. What was the relationship between the inland salt production centres and those on the coast? Did an increase in population provide the stimulus for the less efficient and more costly sand-washing process to develop? Or did the political divisions brought by the Scandinavian settlement upset established trade patterns and lead to the establishment of local salt production centres.

Most of these questions are difficult to answer without material evidence of pre-Domesday salt extraction. Therefore, the identification of the early salterns in Tetney and North Coates could prove significant in understanding the origins of the sand-washing process.

It has already been demonstrated that saltern remains cannot be studied without taking into account other features in the landscape. Therefore, any future work in this area must go beyond considering the narrow question of the origins of sand-washing, especially as there is a possibility that it was a technique brought in from the continent. Understanding and dating the changes in the settlement pattern of the outer marshland and the origins and trade role of the Domesday havens would therefore be important. The recent publication of the Medieval Settlement Research Group (1997) research agenda highlights a number of topics, such as the influence of the natural environment on settlement. The regional patterning of nucleated and dispersed settlement undertaken by Roberts and Wrathmell (1995) identifies the Lindsey marshland as an area with an intensity of dispersal that sets it outside their Central Province of predominant nucleation. The historical origins of that pattern and its relationship to the specialised local land-use and economy are the key issues for this area.

In tackling these issues any future work must be multidisciplinary. To begin with, more detailed work could be

carried out on aerial photographs, possibly using photogrammetric techniques to produce contour maps, especially in the areas where salterns were not mapped by NMP, so that the relationships between salterns and other landscape features can be examined in more detail.

Further detailed aerial photographic interpretation should be followed by fieldwork, to find any remaining salterns and determine their exact relationship with settlement, sea banks, storm beaches and havens. This could then be combined with detailed topographical analysis of the settlement pattern, to determine suitable areas for excavation.

Any excavation strategy should be designed to determine the date of the salterns, to test the theory about the relationship between the earliest salterns, sea banks, storm beaches and settlement, and to examine the method of production of these early mounds. The assumptions that the majority of the old storm beaches are thirteenth century and that the sand-washing technique was used at the time of Domesday also need to be tested.

It is worth bearing in mind that the description of the sand-washing process in this paper has relied on excavations of comparative sites at Bicker Haven, Wrangle and Wainfleet St Mary. The Wainfleet site is the only one which has had large scale excavation, and as the elongated waste mounds at the site are atypical of mounds from sand-washing, there is a possibility that the other excavated features are also atypical. The excavator believed the shape of the mounds was due to the 'particular coastal circumstances' in which the salterns operated (McAvoy 1994, pp.160-61). Having said this Rudkin and Owen's documentary evidence for salt making techniques fits with the excavated evidence at Wainfleet. However, there does seem to be a difference between Wainfleet and other salt making areas in the manner of waste disposal and the scale of production.

Excavation may also prove useful in determining the relationship between the Domesday havens of Swine and Mar, not only to help to understand their relationship to the salterns, but also to determine the nature of small ports at, and before, Domesday. This paper has not looked at the prehistoric and Roman landscapes in this area as this is covered elsewhere (Robinson 1956), but any excavation is likely to reveal environmental information about these periods, if not material remains.

All this should be done in parallel with further documentary research to help date the physical remains. The documentary research carried out by Rudkin and Owen (1960) appears to show salt production to have been more or less continuous from Domesday to the early sixteenth century. This contradicts the evidence presented by Bridbury, who describes a decline in salt manufacture, from the fourteenth century, as a result of competition from continental Bay salt (1955, pp.101-05). This decline is true of certain areas, such as Sussex (Holden & Hudson 1981, pp.141-42), but not in north-east Lincolnshire. Bridbury appears to have concentrated on salt trade between nations and ignored the importance of regional and local trade in salt. There are bound to have been peaks and troughs in the Lincolnshire salt trade, but further documentary research would be useful in determining the nature of this local trade.

Any documentary research should include a reassessment of Haiwarde's 1595 map of Fulstow and Marshchapel and its accompanying field books, and the proposal to produce a facsimile publication by the Lincoln Record Society is a welcome first step (Arthur Owen, personal communication). This map, now sadly faded, is notable for its accuracy, especially in the area of the salterns, and is a key document for understanding the medieval salt industry.

More extensive study of the Continental literature on salt production in the early medieval period should test the assumption that sand-washing was brought to Britain during the

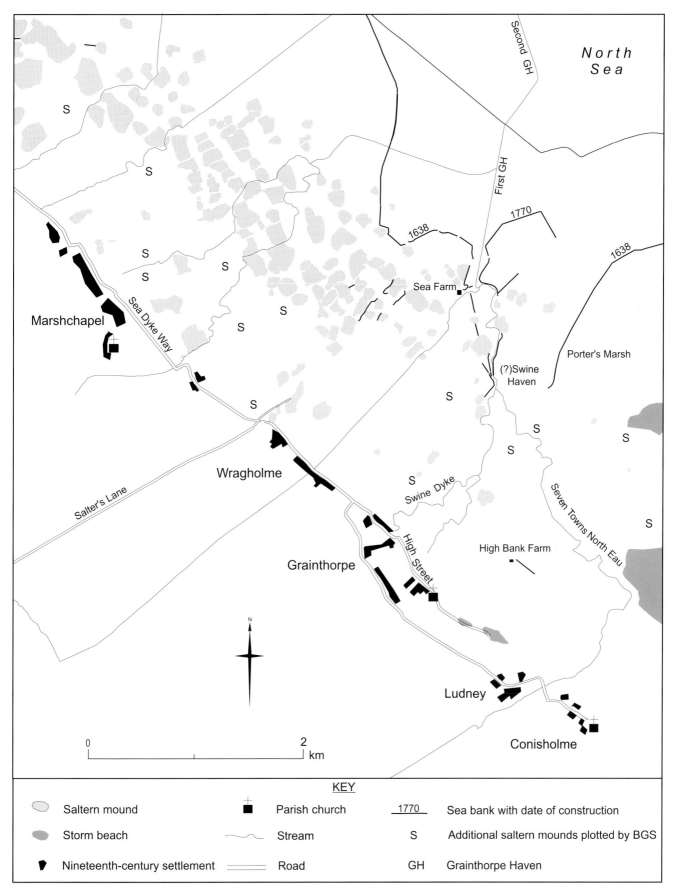

Fig.7. Map showing the relationship between the havens in Grainthorpe, Salter's Lane, salterns, sea banks, settlement and old storm beaches (Based on BGS sheet 91 © NERC) (© Crown copyright. RCHME 1998).

migration period, and provide a context in which to assess the similarities and differences between Continental and British methods of production.

Conclusion.

While the main aim of NMP is to record archaeological features visible on aerial photographs, in certain circumstances it is possible to go further than providing a simple record of the visible archaeology. Providing an assessment of the relationship between features in the landscape can furnish a better understanding of the archaeological sites and their development. In this instance the task has been made easier by the previous research of Dorothy and Arthur Owen, David Robinson, Ethel Rudkin and Christopher Sturman. This paper has probably raised more questions than answers about the origins of sea salt extraction, but it is hoped that this landscape approach will provide a framework for future research on a number of inter-related topics.

Note.

1.   On Ordnance Survey maps the settlement of North Cotes is spelt differently to the parish name, which is North Coates. For the purposes of this paper the different spellings will be maintained.

Bibliography.

Agricola, G. 1556. *De Re Metallica*, translated by H. C. Hoover and L. H. Hoover. New York, 1950.

Bailey, M. 1989. *Per impetum maris*: Natural disaster and economic decline in eastern England 1275-1350. In *Before the Black Death: Studies in the 'Crisis' of the Early Fourteenth Century*, edited by B. M. Campbell, pp.184-208. Manchester.

Bannister, R. T. 1983. Wrangle Toft. *Lincolnshire History and Archaeology*, vol.18, pp.104-05.

Beresford, M. V. and St Joseph, K. 1958. *Medieval England: An Aerial Survey*. Cambridge.

Bridbury, A. R. 1955. *England and the Salt Trade in the Later Middle Ages*, Oxford.

British Geological Survey. 1990. *Grimsby, England and Wales Sheet 90/91, Solid and Drift Geology 1:50,000 Series, Sheet 90/91 Solid and Drift Edition 1:50 000 Series*, Keyworth, Nottingham.

Brownrigg, W. 1748. *On the Art of Making Common Salt*.

Cameron, K. 1996. *The Place-Names of Lincolnshire. Part Four: The Wapentakes of Ludborough and Haverstoe*. English Place-Name Society, Volume 71. Nottingham.

Carter, C. O. 1975. Man's Need of Salt. In *Salt: the Study of an Ancient Industry*, edited by K. W. de Brisay and K. A. Evans, p.13. Colchester.

Duncan, H. 1812. On the Mode of Manufacturing Salt From Sea-Sand or Sleech, Practised in Annadale, Along the Coast of the Solway Firth. In *General View of the Agriculture, State of Property and Improvements in the County of Dumfries*, by Dr Singer, pp.527-33. Edinburgh.

Everson, P. E. and Stocker, D., forthcoming. *Corpus of Anglo-Saxon Stone Sculpture. Volume 5 Lincolnshire*.

Fawn, A. J., Evans, K. A., McMaster, I. and Davies, G. M. R. 1990. *The Red Hills of Essex: Salt making in Antiquity*. Colchester.

Foster, C. W. and Longley, T. 1924. *The Lincolnshire Domesday and the Lindsey Survey*, Lincoln Record Society vol.19. Lincoln.

French, C. A. I. 1992. Excavation at Parsons Drove Site 15, Cambridgeshire. *Fenland Research*, vol.7, pp.62-64.

Hallam, H. E. 1960. Salt-Making in the Lincolnshire Fenland during the Middle Ages. *Lincolnshire Architectural and Archaeological Society Reports and Papers*, vol.8, pp.85-112.

Hayes, P. P. and Lane, T. 1992. *The Fenland Project Number 5: Lincolnshire Survey, The South-West Fens*. East Anglian Archaeology, Report No.55. Sleaford.

Healey, R. H. 1975. A medieval salt-making site in Bicker Haven, Lincolnshire. In *Salt: the Study of an Ancient Industry*, edited by K. W. de Brisay and K. A. Evans, p.36. Colchester.

Healey, R. H., forthcoming. *A Medieval Salt-Making Site in Bicker Haven, Lincolnshire*.

Holden, E. W. and Hudson, T. P. 1981. Salt-Making in the Adur Valley, Sussex. *Sussex Archaeological Collections* vol.119, pp.117-48.

Hurst, J. D. 1997. *A Multi-Period Salt Production Site at Droitwich: Excavations at Upwich* Council for British Archaeology, Research Report No.107. York.

Keen, L. 1988. Coastal salt production in Norman England. In *Anglo-Norman Studies*, vol.11, pp.133-79.

Lloyd, A. T. 1967. The Salterns of the Lymington Area. *Proceedings of the Hampshire Field Club and Archaeological Society*, vol.24, pp.86-102.

Longley, T. 1900. Paper read before members of the Louth Naturalists' and Antiquarian Society. *Louth Advertiser*, 7 April 1900.

Margary, I. D. 1973. *Roman Roads in Britain*. 3rd edition.

Martin, J. J. 1975. Collected notes on the salt industry of the Cumbrian Solway Coast. In *Salt: the Study of an Ancient Industry*, edited by K. W. de Brisay and K. A. Evans, pp.71-76. Colchester.

McAvoy, F. 1994. Marine salt extraction of salterns at Wainfleet St Mary, Lincolnshire. *Medieval Archaeology*, vol.38, pp.134-63.

Medieval Settlement Research Group. 1997. *Medieval Rural Settlements – A Policy on their Research, Survey, Conservation and Excavation*.

Nenquin, J. 1961. Salt: a study in economic prehistory. In *Dissertationes Archaeologica Gandenses*, vol.6, edited by S. J. de Laet. Bruges: de Tempel.

Owen, A. E. B. 1952. Coastal erosion in east Lincolnshire. *Lincolnshire Historian*, vol.1, no.9, pp.330-41.

Owen, A. E. B. 1953. The Roman Bank. *Lincolnshire Poacher* vol.1, no.3, pp.25-27.

Owen, A. E. B. 1954. The early history of Saltfleet Haven. *Lincolnshire Architectural and Archaeological Society Reports and Papers*, vol.5, pp.87-100.

Owen, A. E. B. 1963. The upkeep of the Lindsey sea defences, 1550-1650. *The Lincolnshire Historian*, vol.2, no.10, pp.23-33.

Owen, A. E. B. 1975a. Hafdic: a Lindsey name and its implications. *The English Place-Name Society Journal*, vol.7, pp.45-56.

Owen, A. E. B. 1975b. Medieval salt making and the coastline in Cambridgeshire and north-west Norfolk. In *Salt: the Study of an Ancient Industry*, edited by K. W. de Brisay and K. A. Evans, pp.42-44. Colchester.

Owen, A. E. B. 1984. Salt, sea banks and medieval settlement on the Lindsey coast. In *A Prospect of Lincolnshire*, edited by F. N. Field and A. J. White, pp.46-49. Lincoln.

Owen, A. E. B. 1993. Beyond the sea bank: sheep on the Huttoft outmarsh in the early thirteenth century. *Lincolnshire History and Archaeology*, vol.28, pp.39-41.

Owen, A. E. B. 1996. Chapel St Leonards and the flood of 5 October 1570. In *Lincolnshire People and Places: Essays in Memory of Terence R. Leach*, edited by C. Sturman, pp.87-90. Lincoln.

Owen, A. E. B., forthcoming. Saint Edmund in Lincolnshire: the Abbey's lands at Wainfleet and Wrangle. In *Transactions of the British Archaeological Associations 1994 Bury St Edmunds Conference*.

Palmer, R. 1996. Air Photo Interpretation and the Lincolnshire Fenland. *Landscape History*, vol.18, pp.5-16.

Palmer-Brown, C. 1993. Bronze Age salt production in Tetney. *Current Archaeology* No.136, vol.12:4, pp.143-45.

Pattison, J. 1988a. *Geological notes and local details for 1:10000 sheets TF 49 NW and NE (and the northern areas of TF 49 SW and SE): North Somercotes and Saltfleet. Part of 1:50000 Sheets 90 (Grimsby) and 91 (Saltfleet)*. Technical Report WA/88/21. Keyworth, Nottingham.

Pattison, J. 1988b. *Geological notes and local details for 1:10000 sheets TF 39 NW and NE (and the northern areas of TF 39 SW and SE): Fulstow and Grainthorpe. Part of 1:50000 Sheet 90 (Grimsby)*. Technical Report WA/88/20. Keyworth, Nottingham.

Pattison, J. and Williamson, I. T. 1986. The saltern mounds of north-east Lincolnshire. *Proceedings of the Yorkshire Geological Society*, vol.46:1, pp.77-83.

Pawley, S. 1993. Maritime trade and fishing in the Middle Ages. In *An Historical Atlas of Lincolnshire*, edited by S. Bennett and N. Bennett, pp.56-57. Hull.

Roberts, B. K. and Wrathmell, S. 1995. *Terrain and Rural Settlement Mapping. The Methodology and Preliminary Results.*

Robinson, D. N. 1956. *The North-East coast of Lincolnshire: A Study in Coastal Evolution.* Unpublished MSc thesis, University of Nottingham.

Robinson, D. N. 1970. Coastal evolution in north-east Lincolnshire. *The East Midland Geographer*, vol 5; pts 1 & 2, nos 33 and 34, pp.62-70.

Robinson, D. N. 1981. *The Book of the Lincolnshire Seaside.* Buckingham.

Rudkin, E. H. 1975. Medieval salt making in Lincolnshire. In *Salt: the Study of an Ancient Industry*, edited by K. W. de Brisay and K. A. Evans, pp.37-40. Colchester.

Rudkin, E. H. and Owen, D. M. 1960. The medieval salt industry in the Lindsey marshland. *Lincolnshire Architectural and Archaeological Society Reports and Papers*, vol.8, pp.76-84.

Russell, E. and Russell, R. C. 1983. *Making New Landscapes in Lincolnshire: The Enclosures of Thirty-Four Parishes.* Lincolnshire History Series, No.5. Lincoln.

Smyth, W. H. 1867. *The Sailor's Word-Book: An Alphabetical Digest of Nautical Terms.* Facsimile reprint 1991.

Sturman, C. J. 1984. Salt-Making in the Lindsey marshland in the 16th and early 17th centuries. In *A Prospect of Lincolnshire*, edited by F. N. Field and A. J. White, pp.50-56. Lincoln.

Swinnerton, H. H. 1931. The post-glacial deposits of the Lincolnshire coast. *Quarterly Journal of the Geological Society*, vol.87:2, pp.360-72.

Tann, G. 1995. *Newton Marsh Treatment Works, Tetney, Lincolnshire.* Lindsey Archaeological Services. Unpublished report.

Thompson, M. W. 1956. A group of mounds on Seasalter Level, near Whitstable and the medieval imbanking in this area. *Archaeologia Cantiana*, vol.70, pp.44-67.

Walshaw, G. R. 1935. An ancient Lincolnshire map. *The Lincolnshire Magazine*, vol.2:7, pp.196-206.

The Contribution of Aerial Survey: Understanding the Results.

Ann Carter

The results of any aerial photographic survey need an explanation because they are never a true picture of the distribution of archaeological remains, but merely a reflection of those areas where this type of survey is able to make an effective contribution. Aerial survey has its limitations and the resulting record will inevitably be biased by a number of factors. The conditions of land use, such as extensive woodland and urban or industrial landscapes, may make this particular method of survey unfeasible in certain areas. The distribution of available photographs may be influenced by the activities of those involved in taking the photographs, whether in a positive or negative way, through concentrating on a particular area or avoiding an area because of flying restrictions. Finally, the conditions may not exist to favour the creation of cropmarks, which by differential growth and ripening reveal the presence of sub-surface features, and which form the basis for a majority of the records in Lincolnshire resulting from aerial survey. All these factors may influence the apparent distribution patterns, and need to be considered before we can feel convinced that sufficient reconnaissance has been done. When this stage has been reached, other survey techniques may be required before an area might be considered archaeologically blank.

Lincolnshire is particularly fortunate in many respects because the factors which limit the area available to aerial survey, such as industrial or urban landscapes, are relatively few and woodland represents only approximately 4% of the county. Around 75% of Lincolnshire is arable land and, as this might also suggest, a large proportion of the soils are light and the terrain is generally gentle. Furthermore, this is a part of the country which receives relatively low rainfall and together these factors make this an area where cropmarks can be expected in most years. Unfortunately some of the factors in Lincolnshire's favour, the gentle terrain and relatively small amount of industrial and built-up areas, have influenced the establishment of numerous airfields, particularly a concentration of military airfields. The line of large airfields which includes the Royal Air Force College at Cranwell, and the former home of the Red Arrows aerobatic team at Scampton is ranged down the western side of the county along the limestone plateau. Because of the controlled airspace surrounding them, the existence of these airfields has a negative effect on aerial reconnaissance undertaken for archaeological purposes (Fig.1). Although it is not necessarily impossible to enter Military Air Traffic Zones (MATZ), attempts to do so can be difficult and may need to be pre-arranged; this inevitably results in much less frequent and intense coverage. When the controlled airspace of a number of airfields is contiguous, as is the case in this part of Lincolnshire, it is not surprising if the entire area is given a wide berth. The presence of civil airfields affects smaller areas, but the increasing activities in recent years of gliders, parachutists and microlights causes cautious pilots to steer well clear of these areas also. Users of information resulting from the present survey, when assessing distribution patterns, need to be aware of this potentially major factor hindering the contribution of aerial survey.

Over the years, a number of different individuals have taken photographs in Lincolnshire for archaeological purposes. The bulk of photography has been taken by two bodies which aim at national coverage: the Cambridge University Committee for Aerial Photography and the Royal Commission on the Historical Monuments of England (RCHME), and by two individuals flying locally, Jim Pickering and Paul Everson. The coverage of the two individual flyers is roughly complementary, Paul Everson concentrating on the northern half of the county and Jim Pickering on the south. Together, their photography fills in some of the larger gaps in the coverage of the national bodies and generally reinforces the broad pattern of their flying. The earliest example of this specialist photography of Lincolnshire which is held by RCHME in its National Monuments Record dates from the 1930s. RCHME holds over 1,000 photographs, taken for archaeological purposes, in the decade 1950-1959. There is a drop in the numbers taken in the 1960s, but since then numbers have continued to rise: almost 5,000 photographs were taken in the 1970s, and over 7,500 in the 1980s. The figures for the first half of the current decade indicate that there is no sign of a drop in the quantities of photographs being taken.

Cropmarks, whether they are formed over archaeological or natural deposits, or the remains of man's more recent activities, are usually recorded on shallow, well-drained soils where the sub-soil material is permeable to water. The appearance of cropmarks is caused by a contrast in conditions between the deposit and those of the surrounding area. This may be a difference in soil depth, an impenetrable barrier to rooting, or other conditions affecting permeability, all of which alter the inter-relationship between moisture and nutrient supply to the crop. The result is a difference in the growth and ripening time of the crop growing over the deposits, compared with that growing over the rest of the field. Marks can result either when there is an excess of water to the crop or when there is a shortage. However, they most commonly result from a shortage of moisture to the majority of the crop, contrasting with more favourable conditions over the deposits. The relationship between rainfall and a plant's estimated requirements for transpiration and evaporation is known as a Soil Moisture Deficit (SMD). Figures which show the potential SMD can be obtained from the Meteorological Office and used as a guide to the likelihood of crops becoming affected by water shortage. The potential SMD figures, available at weekly intervals and covering areas of forty kilometre squares, are only a general guide and there may be variations locally. A heavy shower of rain, for instance, can encourage new shoots which will tend to obscure any cropmarks which might already have formed. A report on investigations into cropmarks at twenty-six locations in Britain found that the growth of crops begins to be affected when the SMD figures are greater than fifty millimetres and cropmarks can become very distinct when they reach in excess of one hundred millimetres (Jones & Evans 1975). In Lincolnshire, and in the rest of eastern and south-eastern England, SMD figures reach this level in most years. Marks can develop in crops grown on many different soil types but because of the way heavier soils release water more gradually, rather than their actual capacity to hold more water, marks appear on these soils more slowly. On sandy soils, where all water is readily available, the effect of a water shortage is more dramatic and can result in the sudden appearance of well defined marks. Cereal crops are the most susceptible to stress as a result of water shortage and barley, because of its larger leaf area, has been found to show the clearest cropmarks. The effect on the crop will depend on its stage of growth and so may vary in adjacent fields as a result of different sowing dates. The period prior to the development of the ears of corn is the time when the cereal crop is most vulnerable to stress; after the plant has matured, water shortage has little effect. Grassland appears to require SMD figures ten to twenty millimetres greater than cereals before it becomes affected (Jones & Evans 1975). Marks may also be seen in crops of linseed and peas, and some root crops, particularly sugar beet, where they appear later in the season than in cereals. The large leaf area of these plants

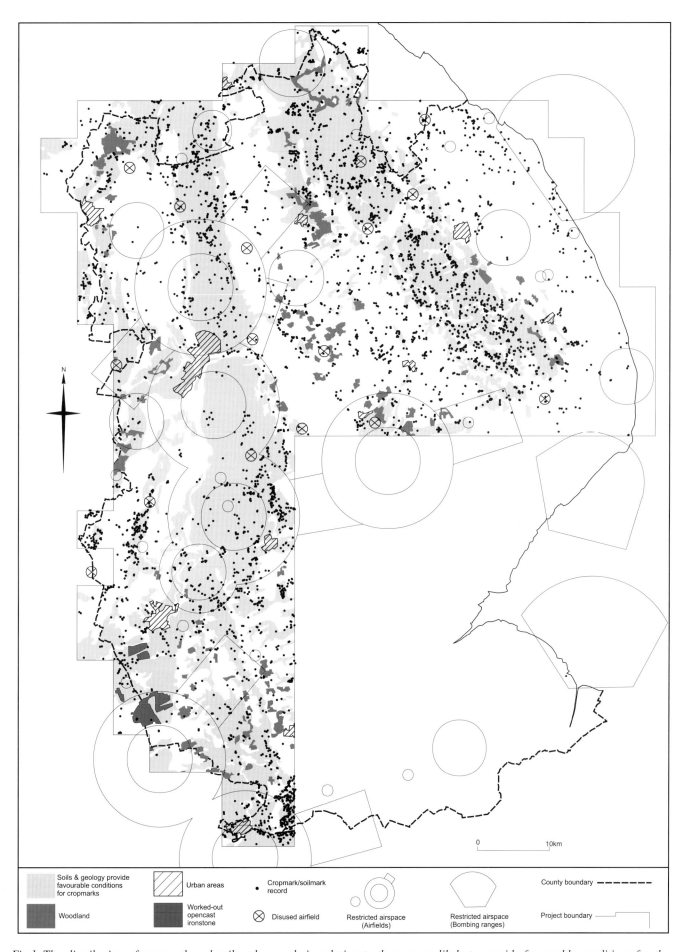

Fig.1. The distribution of cropmark and soilmark records in relation to those areas likely to provide favourable conditions for the appearance of cropmarks. (© Crown copyright. RCHME 1998).

makes them particularly prone to wilting, and marks in these crops are often noticed towards the end of the day.

Figure 1 shows the distribution of cropmark and soilmark records which result from this Lincolnshire National Mapping Programme (NMP) project. Soilmarks form a small proportion of the records, and are not separately identified from cropmarks in the database; both represent sub-surface features. Soilmarks appear in bare soils after ploughing, particularly in those soils with a lighter-coloured sub-soil material, for example chalk, limestone and also silt fen, which provides a tonal contrast with the fill of archaeological deposits. Certain archaeological features may have been photographed, at different times, as soilmarks and as cropmarks.

A proportion of the archaeological features recorded by this aerial survey of Lincolnshire have been recovered from vertical, non-specialist photography held by RCHME in the NMR. (The historical perspective given by the 1946 RAF coverage proved particularly useful in recording the earthwork remains of medieval settlement.) Even so, the overall distribution of recorded features remains strongly influenced by the pattern of flying for specialist, oblique photography. The pattern of this photography reflects those areas where cropmarks are most often produced, which is itself influenced by the solid and drift geology which forms the basis of the different soil types. Detailed soil survey maps are only available for selected areas of the country at present, but a comparison between the more general 1:250,000 map produced by the Soil Survey of England and Wales, and the British Geological Survey's 1:50,000 maps, showing solid and drift geology, will help to understand the distribution of cropmark features. Modern drainage has often improved those soils which were affected by groundwater in the past, so that there is less difference now between some soil groups such as brown sands and sandy gley soils. The sub-soil material and lack of soil depth appear to have a greater influence on the development of cropmarks. Figure 1 also shows those areas where the combination of soil and geology is considered most likely to produce favourable conditions for the appearance of cropmarks.

The Trent Valley.

In the west of the county the majority of cropmark sites have been recorded on soils of the BLACKWOOD ASSOCIATION (821b), deep, permeable, sandy and coarse loamy soils which are formed over glaciofluvial sand and gravel. Together with the heavier soils of the WICKHAM 2 ASSOCIATION (711f) they are the most predominant soils of this region. The numbers of cropmark sites found on the BLACKWOOD ASSOCIATION soils in this part of the county are not exceptional at the moment, but it is noticeable that the photographic coverage in this area is also relatively sparse. These soils are found in an area which lies immediately west of the airfields of Waddington and Cranwell and the approach to Scampton, and consequently their full potential may yet be recorded. In the north of the region, cropmarks were also found on the sandy, acid soils of the Crannymoor association (631f) and the HOLME MOOR ASSOCIATION (641c), but to a lesser extent. Large areas of the Crannymoor soils, which are generally rather poor in nutrients, support coniferous plantations. In the southern half of this region, between the rivers Witham and Brant (Fig.2) and near Stubton and Brandon, cropmark sites were recorded on RUSKINGTON ASSOCIATION soils (512c) in fairly high numbers in comparison to the relatively small area of this soil type. The RUSKINGTON ASSOCIATION are loamy soils overlying river sand and gravel. Other soils in this region are formed over glacial sand and gravel: the ESCRICK 2 ASSOCIATION (571q) are well drained, coarse loamy soils; a small area of these soils occurs to the south of Grantham and cropmark sites were recorded here also. In the south of this region, several cropmark sites have been found on small areas of BANBURY ASSOCIATION soils (544), well-drained,

brashy, loamy soils which are formed here over the Marlstone Rock Bed, an outcrop of ferruginous oolitic limestone, ironstone and calcareous sandstone. Throughout this region, a few cropmark sites were also recorded on the FLADBURY 2 ASSOCIATION soils (813c) which are generally clayey soils overlying river alluvium. When cropmarks were recorded on these soils, their location was almost always found to coincide with deposits of river sand and gravel, within the alluvium.

Cropmark sites were sometimes also found on some of the heavier soils, those of the WICKHAM 2 ASSOCIATION (711f), and in the south, the EVESHAM 2 ASSOCIATION (411b) and the DENCHWORTH ASSOCIATION (712b). These are all slowly permeable soils, which are formed over Jurassic deposits. The EVESHAM 2 ASSOCIATION soils lie over Lower Lias shales and thin limestones, and the WICKHAM 2 and DENCHWORTH ASSOCIATION soils each lie over both Middle Lias sandy clays and Lower Lias clay with calcareous siltstones and thin sandstones. A few cropmark sites appear to coincide with a band of ferruginous limestone which outcrops between the Lower Lias shales and clays. In comparison to the large extent of these heavier soils, the number of cropmark sites which have been recorded on them is quite low at present, but more recent reconnaissance has recorded several new cropmark sites on the WICKHAM 2 ASSOCIATION soils. Earthworks, mostly remnants of medieval ridge-and-furrow surviving in pasture, are far more prevalent on the WICKHAM 2 ASSOCIATION soils, but are not unknown on some of the lighter soils also, such as the BANBURY and BLACKWOOD ASSOCIATIONS. The existence of these earthworks may mask pre-medieval features which could become visible if the areas were to revert to arable. However, as the great majority of these remains are found on the heavier soils, this possibility is not likely to have a very significant effect on the potential for future cropmark recording here. Figure 3a shows cropmark sites on the BLACKWOOD ASSOCIATION soils in an area to the east of Dry Doddington; Figure 3b shows the underlying solid and drift geology of the same area.

Lincoln Edge and the Limestone Heath.

Further to the east, on the limestone uplands the most predominant soil types are formed over the Lincolnshire Limestone. Soils of the ELMTON 1 ASSOCIATION (343a) occur throughout this region. The MARCHAM ASSOCIATION (343e) occur largely between Navenby and Sleaford. The Elmton 3 association (343c), which are formed over Jurassic limestone and clay, occur along the eastern edge of the limestone to the north of the Lincoln Gap, and together with the ELMTON 1 ASSOCIATION soils in the area north of Stamford. All are shallow, well-drained soils. To the north of the Lincoln Gap, cropmark sites have been recorded on the ELMTON 1 ASSOCIATION soils. Further north, in an area which lay in south Humberside at the time of the project, cropmark sites were recorded on the ABERFORD ASSOCIATION (511a) and Milton association (512f) soils, particularly to the east of Ermine Street. The ABERFORD ASSOCIATION soils are shallow, well-drained and are formed over the Lincolnshire Limestone, which here includes beds of Kirton Cementstones on the west. The Milton association soils are permeable but deeper, and here are formed largely over glacial sand and gravel deposits to the south of Hibaldstow. Although the numbers of cropmark sites recorded in the north of this region are not particularly large, they appear to be more numerous than on any part of the limestone further to the south. However, this contrast in numbers may result, not so much from a difference in soils and drift deposits, but from the influence of restricted airspace in the south. In this region also, cropmark sites were recorded on the BANBURY ASSOCIATION soils (544), although these soils are more limited in extent here than in the previous region. They occur along the Lincoln Edge north

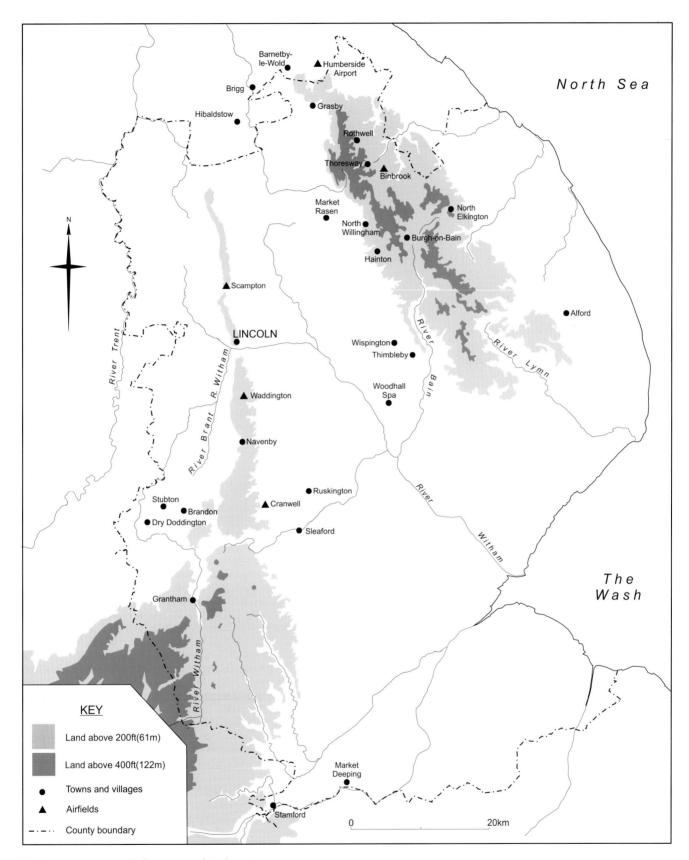

Fig.2. Location map of places named in the text.

of the Lincoln Gap, over intermittent outcrops of the Marlstone Rock Beds. Proportionately much greater numbers of cropmark sites were recorded in this region on soils of the ASWARBY ASSOCIATION (512a) and the RUSKINGTON ASSOCIATION (512c), which are found on the east side of the limestone, towards the foot of the dip slope. The ASWARBY ASSOCIATION soils are shallow, permeable and fine loamy soils. In the north of the region they overlie the Snitterby Limestone, the Cornbrash, and small bands of Blisworth Clay and shelly sandstones; in the south they overlie limestone and larger outcrops of the Cornbrash. The RUSKINGTON ASSOCIATION soils are deep, permeable, loamy and sandy soils which overlie pockets of alluvium, and sand and gravel in the north of the region, and the fen sand and gravel in the south. Both soil associations are more extensive in the south of the region where the greater numbers of cropmark sites appearing on these two soil types is particularly noticeable, especially near the village of Ruskington itself, and further south beside Mareham Lane. Here, the cropmarks of complex roadside settlements were recorded where these soils appear as 'islands' within the surrounding areas of heavier soils which overlie Oxford Clay (Fig.4a). By far the greatest concentration of cropmark sites in this region was found in the extreme south on BADSEY 2 ASSOCIATION soils (511i) between Stamford and Market Deeping. These well-drained, fine loamy soils overlie fen gravel. Crops also produced a response on the very much smaller areas of SUTTON 1 ASSOCIATION soils (571u) overlying river terrace gravel to the east of Stamford, and WICK 1 ASSOCIATION soils (541r) further to the north, which overlie glacial sand and gravel. As in the Trent Valley region, cropmark sites were recorded on BLACKWOOD and FLADBURY 2 ASSOCIATION soils (821b and 813c) although both soils are limited in extent in this region.

Some cropmark sites were also recorded on the heavier soils, those of the WICKHAM 2 ASSOCIATION (711f), and in the south of the region on the RAGDALE ASSOCIATION soils (712g). The RAGDALE ASSOCIATION soils are clayey and fine loamy soils which are formed over till, and which in this region overlie both Lincolnshire Limestone and Oxford Clay. The numbers of cropmark sites on both these heavier soils were low in comparison with the extent of area which these soils cover.

The Clay Vale.

Despite its name, the Clay Vale which lies between the limestone and chalk uplands is not devoid of cropmark sites although naturally the heavier soils predominate here. The BECCLES 1 ASSOCIATION soils (711r) are the most extensive, but there are smaller areas of WICKHAM 2 ASSOCIATION (711f) and RAGDALE ASSOCIATION soils (712g) which are all slowly permeable, seasonally waterlogged, fine loamy and clayey soils which overlie deposits of till and the Upper Jurassic clays. The recorded survival of earthwork sites in the vale is greater on all these soils, which used to be considered more suited to permanent pasture. However, in recent years, many areas have been rapidly reverting to arable or improved pasture (Everson 1983). This may have some implications for future reconnaissance where there is a conversion to arable, because there is the possibility that earlier features, which may have been covered by medieval ridge-and-furrow, could start to be revealed as cropmarks. At present, records show only a scattering of cropmark sites on the BECCLES 1 ASSOCIATION soils, a few on those of the WICKHAM 2 ASSOCIATION, and in the river valleys on the FLADBURY 2 ASSOCIATION soils. There is no detailed geological information currently available for the central part of the vale, but elsewhere it seems that small pockets of sand and gravel underlie the BECCLES 1 soils.

There is a slightly higher proportion of records relating to cropmark sites on the eastern side of the vale. In the north-east of the vale and to the east of Brigg, glacial sand and gravel deposits lie against the foot of the western scarp of the Wolds; together with pockets of clay silts and alluvium, these deposits are overlain by soils of the LANDBEACH ASSOCIATION (512b). Although these are permeable, coarse, loamy soils only a few cropmark sites have been recorded here so far; the proximity of Humberside airport and the difficulty of access for reconnaissance, may explain the low numbers. Further down the eastern side of the vale there are blown sand deposits between Grasby and North Willingham which underlie both soils of the BLACKWOOD ASSOCIATION (821b) and smaller areas of the HOLME MOOR ASSOCIATION (641c). Here and in the south of the vale, to the south of Woodhall Spa, a number of cropmark sites have been recorded on the BLACKWOOD ASSOCIATION soils; fewer have been seen on the HOLME MOOR soils although these acid, sandy soils support some large areas of coniferous plantation, particularly around Market Rasen. Further down the eastern side of the vale from Hainton as far as Thimbleby, on the west bank of the River Bain, soils of SWAFFHAM PRIOR and CANNAMORE ASSOCIATIONS (511e and 513) overlie deep drift deposits of till over the Kimmeridge Clay Formation, which is composed of grey, shelly limestones and shale. Few cropmark sites have been recorded in this area so far, although a number were recorded in a relatively small area between Wispington and Thimbleby, particularly on the fine, loamy and clayey soils of the CANNAMORE ASSOCIATION. The underlying geology appears to be the same throughout this area; however, the cross-section depicted on the geology map (British Geological Survey 1995) suggests that the drift cover of till could be less deep at this approximate location, which might provide an opportunity for favourable conditions for the development of cropmarks.

The Lincolnshire Chalk Wolds.

At the northern end of the Wolds in Lincolnshire, an extensive area of SWAFFHAM PRIOR ASSOCIATION soils (511e), which are well-drained and loamy, overlies the chalk. This might be expected to be an area where conditions would allow the development of cropmarks if archaeological features were present, but so far, only a few small and generally discrete cropmark sites have been recorded here. The predominant soils throughout the rest of the Wolds belong to the ANDOVER 1 ASSOCIATION (343h) which are shallow, well-drained and silty soils. Smaller areas of similar soils on the hill tops at the northern end of the Wolds belong to the PANHOLES ASSOCIATION (511c); both soils have proved to provide conditions for the formation of cropmarks. Both these soil types are also the predominant soils on the chalk Wolds of East Yorkshire, but in comparison with that area (Stoertz 1997) few cropmarks have been recorded on this northern half of the Lincolnshire Wolds. This may be the result of restricted airspace and a lack of reconnaissance. However, earthworks of deserted villages have survived on these two soils and on those of the NEWMARKET 1 ASSOCIATION (343f) along the valley bottoms, where they have been photographed by RCHME. The survival of earthworks may be masking earlier features.

Approximately halfway down the length of the Lincolnshire Wolds, extensive till deposits overlie the whole breadth of the chalk outcrop between Burgh-on-Bain to the west, and North Elkington on the east. Soils of the CARSTENS ASSOCIATION (581d) which are well-drained, fine, silty soils are formed in this area. Along the eastern side of the Wolds till deposits are overlain by soils of the TATHWELL ASSOCIATION (571n) which are well-drained and loamy. In both these areas cropmark sites are absent, except in a few instances on the CARSTENS soils, noticeably where these soils lie directly over the chalk or near the limits of the till deposits, where these deposits are possibly less deep. At the extreme south-western end of the Wolds, outcrops of Spilsby Sandstone

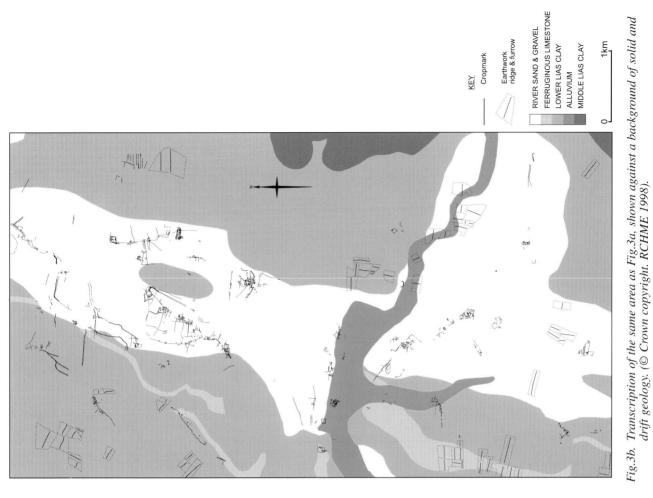

Fig.3b. Transcription of the same area as Fig.3a, shown against a background of solid and drift geology. (© Crown copyright. RCHME 1998).

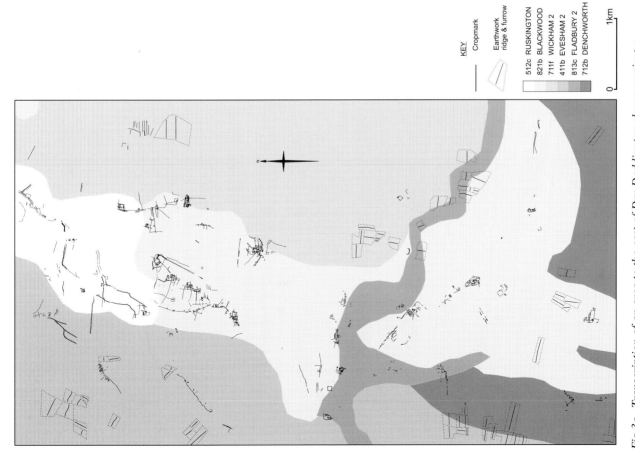

Fig.3a. Transcription of an area to the east of Dry Doddington shown against a background of soil types. (© Crown copyright. RCHME 1998).

and Claxby Ironstone underlie soils of the CUCKNEY 2 ASSOCIATION (551c) which are well drained, sandy and ferruginous, fine loamy soils. Also formed over these outcrops, at a point mid-way down the western side of the Wolds, are soils of the ARROW ASSOCIATION (543) which are deep, permeable, coarse loamy soils. Some drift deposits of till and glacial sand and gravel also underlie these latter soils on the west side of the upper reaches of the River Bain. Cropmarks have been recorded on both soils, but most noticeably on the CUCKNEY 2 ASSOCIATION soils, with some large concentrations to the north of the River Lymn. On the east of the River Bain the situation mirrors that on the west bank which was previously noted on the edge of the Clay Vale. SWAFFHAM PRIOR and CANNAMORE ASSOCIATION soils and small areas of CARSTENS ASSOCIATION soils are formed over deep deposits of till, which overlie the western edge of the sandstone and ironstone outcrop and the Kimmeridge Clay; very few cropmark sites have been recorded here. They might have been expected over the sandstone and ironstone outcrops, but the depth of drift deposits is a probable reason for their absence.

The Lincolnshire Marshland.

The majority of soils in the Lincolnshire Marshland are slowly permeable, seasonally waterlogged, loamy soils which overlie till deposits and chalk. By far the most extensive are the HOLDERNESS ASSOCIATION soils (711u), which are found throughout the region, whilst the SALOP ASSOCIATION soils (711m) are found at the foot of the Wolds, where some small areas of these soils overlie the chalk directly. The number of cropmark sites recorded on these soils is sparse and well scattered. Soilmarks and earthwork sites are much more numerous, particularly those representing settlement remains which are found along the spring line. Recent conversion to arable is just as typical in the Marshland as in the Clay Vale (Everson 1983) and may provide further opportunities for reconnaissance. More permeable soils are to be found at the northern end of the Marshland, against the eastern slope of the Wolds. Here, coarse loamy soils of the LANDBEACH ASSOCIATION (512b) are formed over both fluvioglacial sand and gravel and some smaller till deposits, which overlie the Burnham Chalk. Small areas of deep, fine loamy soils of the BURLINGHAM 2 (572o) and Bishampton 1 Associations (572s) also overlie till, small pockets of sand and gravel and the chalk; although cropmark sites have been recorded on these soils, they are few in number at present. Towards the southern end of the Marshland and to the south-east of Alford, a small and narrow area of WICK 1 ASSOCIATION soils (541r) is formed over a band of glaciofluvial drift. These soils are deep, well-drained and coarse, loamy and sandy soils. A small cluster of cropmark sites has been recorded here. Down the extreme eastern side of this region, the soils are all formed over marine alluvium; they are deep, stoneless, calcareous clayey or silty soils which are unlikely to provide the conditions suitable for the development of cropmarks.

Discussion.

Figure 1 shows the distribution of records of cropmark and soilmark sites which result from the Lincolnshire NMP project, shown against those areas where the combination of geology and soil is likely to provide favourable conditions for the appearance of cropmarks. This is not to suggest that it is impossible for cropmarks to be found outside these areas, but that there is less likelihood. The evidence from other methods of archaeological survey proves that the lighter soils were not the only areas to be settled, but the evidence which results from aerial photography and survey will inevitably be biased towards them. It seems improbable, for instance, that the complex linear settlement recorded at the foot of the dip slope near Sleaford

(Fig.4a) should not continue over the heavier soils but, in some areas, aerial survey may never be able to contribute information.

The quantities of cropmark and earthwork features recorded by the Lincolnshire NMP project are not too dissimilar: 7,483 cropmark sites and 6,560 earthwork sites. As mentioned previously, the rate at which photographs continue to be taken in Lincolnshire shows no signs of decreasing, which implies that plenty of new discoveries continue to be made, although there are no hard figures for their percentage. The rate at which earthwork sites continue to be discovered is likely to decrease sooner than that of cropmark sites. The opportunities for recording cropmarks are less frequent because of the ephemeral nature of cropmarks and their unpredictable visibility. Climatic conditions can vary so much from one year to the next, and there are so many variable factors interacting with one another that it is not possible to predict their appearance; some cropmarks may appear year after year; others may show only occasionally, some perhaps only once in a decade or more. However, it has been suggested that whether a year is considered exceptional or poor for the development of cropmarks, the ratio of photographs of new sites in relation to repeat photographs of known sites, does not appear to differ significantly (Whimster 1983). This appears to be the case, in spite of the fact that the quantity of photographs will be much greater in exceptional years. The discovery of entirely new cropmark sites and additional information on known sites is likely to continue for several decades.

Although it has proved possible to record cropmark sites in most parts of Lincolnshire, they are obviously more abundant in some areas than others, and it has become apparent that there are certain areas, where although suitable conditions appear to exist, very few cropmark sites have been noted. Consequently, these areas are recommended as a priority for aerial survey in order to examine whether the current lack of sites results from a lack of reconnaissance, or whether there may be other explanations.

The first obvious example is the eastern side of the Trent Valley, where suitable conditions appear to exist, but numbers of cropmark sites are relatively low. The soil and geology combination here of BLACKWOOD ASSOCIATION soils and river sand and gravel has proved to provide suitable conditions for the formation of cropmarks, in all parts of the county. The low numbers of cropmark sites in this area is particularly noticeable in comparison with the area immediately west of the Trent where cropmark sites are known to be fairly abundant (Whimster 1989, Deegan, forthcoming), the majority being found on ARROW ASSOCIATION soils (543). However, it has also been noted that there is little specialist photographic coverage for the eastern side of the river, most probably as a result of the restricted airspace to the east, around Scampton, Waddington and Cranwell military airfields. Only a conscious attempt at reconnaissance in this area will determine whether the River Trent may have formed some kind of cultural divide in the prehistoric and Romano-British periods, or whether it is simply the case that pilots tend to steer clear of the MATZ areas and follow the river along the west bank.

The limestone area of the Heath is the second example where few cropmark sites have been recorded even though the conditions, which the Lincolnshire Limestone and the shallow, well-drained ELMTON 1 ASSOCIATION soils (343a) create, ought to be favourable. Again the proximity of those same MATZ areas probably exerts a powerful influence on reconnaissance with a resulting lack of photographs of cropmark sites. It is uncertain at present whether the limestone Heath is indeed a blank area, as has been suggested in the past, or whether the few features recorded here might suggest a particular function for the area. Those cropmark features which have been recorded on the limestone plateau tend to represent ditched boundaries or fragments of linear systems, while settlement appears to be focused on the foot of the dip slope. This may prove to be a situation comparable to that found in

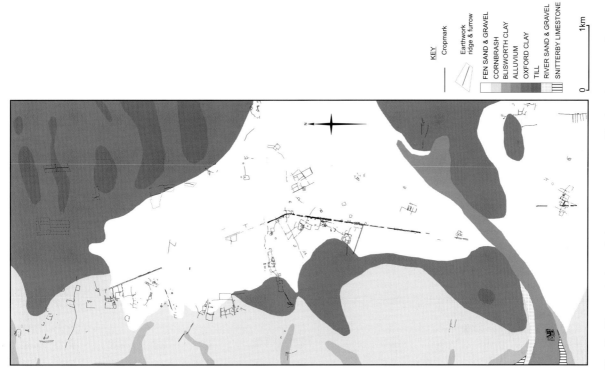

Fig.4b. Transcription of the same area as Fig.4a, shown against a background of solid and drift geology. (© Crown copyright. RCHME 1998).

KEY

Cropmark

Earthwork
ridge & furrow

FEN SAND & GRAVEL
CORNBRASH
BLISWORTH CLAY
ALLUVIUM
OXFORD CLAY
TILL
RIVER SAND & GRAVEL
SNITTERBY LIMESTONE

0   1km

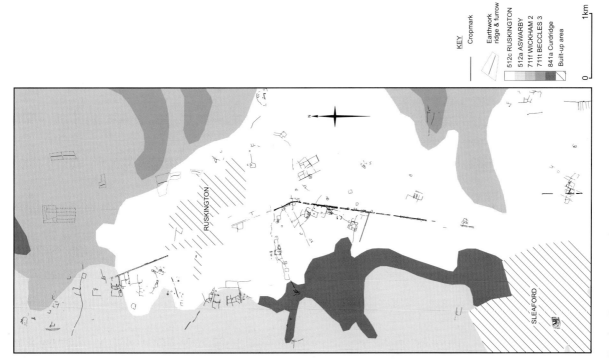

Fig.4a. Transcription of roadside settlement seen as cropmarks, shown against a background of soil types. (© Crown copyright. RCHME 1998).

KEY

Cropmark

Earthwork
ridge & furrow

512c RUSKINGTON
512a ASWARBY
711f WICKHAM 2
711t BECCLES 3
841a Curdridge
Built-up area

0   1km

RUSKINGTON

SLEAFORD

other parts of the country, for example, that which has been shown to exist on the northern part of the Yorkshire Wolds (Stoertz 1997, maps 1-2), where areas of large-scale land division do not include any enclosures or settlement. The cropmarks of ditch fragments tend to attract less attention than settlement complexes, so that a concerted effort in reconnaissance may be needed to begin to establish the real nature of this region. Also, the unpredictable response of crops growing on limestone, although frequently overflown, was noted by Riley (1983) who concluded that a greater number of years of reconnaissance would be required, in comparison to gravel areas, to reach a comparable level of information.

A third area which ought to have potential lies towards the northern end of the chalk Wolds. It is a sizeable area, stretching from Barnetby-le-Wold in the north to Binbrook in the south. The soils here belong to the SWAFFHAM PRIOR ASSOCIATION, and against the eastern edge of the Wolds, the LANDBEACH ASSOCIATION. Further south the PANHOLES and ANDOVER 1 ASSOCIATIONS predominate. Although surviving earthwork sites have been recorded in the valleys, only a scatter of small and discrete cropmark sites are known throughout the area. There are prehistoric and Roman period find-spots recorded for this area, particularly to the east of the High Street between Rothwell and Thoresway, but few cropmark sites on this higher ground. There are some large areas of woodland at the northern end of the Wolds, and once again restricted airspace may be another explanation for this lack of recorded cropmarks. Humberside Airport lies to the north of this area; in the south lies Binbrook airfield, until quite recently, an active military airbase.

These three areas are the most obvious areas where cropmark sites are clearly lacking so far, but where favourable conditions ought to exist which should have the potential to reveal archaeological remains. The problems caused by restricted airspace will necessitate future reconnaissance in these areas to be focused and pre-planned if it is to make any real impact on our knowledge.

There are still many things about the appearance of cropmark sites which are not fully understood because excavation invariably reveals many more features than are revealed by cropmark evidence. The appearance of archaeological features as cropmarks could depend on the size and nature of the fill of those deposits, and alternatively, it may be that there are subtle differences in the conditions prevailing between different localised soil types where those features are found. One example of this possibility may be seen in the cropmarks of the roadside settlement shown in figure 4a, which largely appear on soils of the RUSKINGTON ASSOCIATION (512c). The cropmarks have not been recorded as continuing on the heavier soils which overlie the Oxford Clay, but to the west and north of Ruskington village there is some continuity on the closely related soils of the ASWARBY ASSOCIATION (512a), although the cropmarks might be considered less detailed here. The visibility of one feature in particular is worth noting; the cropmarks which reveal a Roman road appear to end at the junction between these two soils types. The two soil types are related but the underlying geology is different (Fig.4b), and this may have an effect on the water regimes of the two soils. The RUSKINGTON ASSOCIATION soils overlie fen sand and gravel, which suggests rapid permeability. The ASWARBY ASSOCIATION soils overlie the Cornbrash, composed of limestone debris with thin bands of marls and sands, which while permeable, may provide less predictable conditions. The cropmark evidence recorded here may be a true record of the

lack of continuity of the archaeological features, but equally it may reflect a subtle difference in the response of crops growing over two different soil/geology combinations. Perhaps there is a difference in the timing of the response. Only careful monitoring of selected areas such as this would help our understanding of some of the factors involved. Where regular monitoring of small areas is necessary, it would particularly benefit from local involvement to take advantage of local conditions and familiarity with the area. The current commitments and resources of RCHME as a national survey body means that their involvement in such investigations would be unlikely; detailed monitoring of specific areas might be more appropriate for local initiatives.

The completion of this NMP project will add considerably to the volume of archaeological information available for Lincolnshire. As expected, that information shows an inevitable bias towards the distribution of lighter soils with permeable sub-soil material. Information has been gained from other areas, but with much less regularity. In Lincolnshire, another influence on the contribution of this particular survey method has certainly been the existence of restricted airspace. Providing that such limitations are recognised, and this information is not used in isolation, but in conjunction with that recovered by other survey methods, then the results of this project can provide a very useful contribution to Lincolnshire's archaeology. None of the different regions of Lincolnshire has yet reached a stage where we can feel that the survey has been exhaustive; there is still plenty of potential for increasing our knowledge from aerial survey, with opportunities to highlight further areas or topics that would benefit from investigation.

Bibliography.

British Geological Survey. 1995. *Horncastle, England and Wales Sheet 115, Solid and Drift Geology 1:50,000 Provisional Series*, Keyworth, Nottingham.

Deegan, A., forthcoming. *Nottinghamshire NMP project*. RCHME internal report.

Everson, P. 1983. Aerial photography and fieldwork in north Lincolnshire. In Maxwell, ed. 1983, pp.14-26.

Jones, R. J. A. and Evans, R. 1975. Soil and crop marks in the recognition of archaeological sites by air photography. In *Aerial Reconnaissance for Archaeology*, edited by D. Wilson, Council for British Archaeology, Research Report 12, pp.1-11.

Maxwell, G. S., ed. 1983. *The Impact of Aerial Reconnaissance on Archaeology*. Council for British Archaeology, Research Report 49.

Riley, D. N. 1979. Factors in the development of crop marks. *Aerial Archaeology*, vol.4, pp.28-32.

Riley, D. N. 1983. The frequency of occurrence of cropmarks in relation to soils. In Maxwell ed. 1983, pp.59-73.

Soil Survey of England and Wales 1983. *Legend for the 1:250,000 Soil Map of England and Wales.*

Stoertz, C. 1997. *Ancient Landscapes of the Yorkshire Wolds: Aerial Photographic Transcription and Analysis*. Swindon.

Whimster, R. P. 1983. Aerial reconnaissance from Cambridge: a retrospective view 1945-80. In Maxwell ed. 1983, pp.92-105.

Whimster, R. P. 1989. *The Emerging Past, Air Photography and the Buried Landscape.*

Wilson, D. R. 1978. Light soils and heavy soils: a question of priorities. *Aerial Archaeology*, vol.2, pp.46-49.

Wilson, D. R. 1979. Factors affecting the distribution of crop marks in the Anglian region. *Aerial Archaeology*, vol.4, pp.32-36.

Index of Place Names

Page numbers that are in bold type refer to the page numbers of figures.